THE MASTER CHEF

THE MASTER CHEF

by
Jean Conil

JG PRESS

This edition produced 1995 by the Promotional Reprint Company Ltd
Deacon House, 65 Old Church Street
Chelsea, London SW3 5BS

Published in the USA 1995 by JG Press
Distributed by World Publications, Inc.

The JG Press imprint is a trademark of
JG Press, Inc.
455 Somerset Avenue
North Dighton, MA 02764

Publishing Manager: Casey Horton
Design Manager: Ming Cheung
Cookery Consultant: Maggie Pannell
Assistant Editor: Jennifer Spaeth
Designed by: Clearest Communications Ltd

ISBN 1 57215 136 6

Printed and bound in Malaysia

Illustration page 1: *Steaks Capsicum* (see page 36); page 3: *Beef Bourguignon* (see page 57).

Contents

INTRODUCTION

World Prime Cuisine

Diet has been subjected to many fads and fashions in this century; however, dieticians throughout the world are now returning to the notion of a well-balanced diet. Three parts vegetable and cereal to one part meat, poultry or fish is the combination considered to be the most beneficial. In my opinion, this balance produces delicious dishes where interesting permutations of flavors and textures can be fully appreciated.

In *The Master Chef* I have created and collected for you a large selection of dishes from many different countries and from many different traditions and styles of cooking. I have chosen elaborate dishes suitable for lavish entertaining as well as simple, inexpensive, but nourishing family meals.

In each chapter I have suggested suitable garnishes and additional side dishes of vegetables or salads for each recipe. Where appropriate, long or short sauces, or gravies have been incorporated into the main recipe to avoid tedious cross-referencing. Most of the recipes, therefore, are completely self-contained. Success on a plate depends very much on the attractive presentation of the ingredients as much as the taste of the ingredients. Harmony in all good things makes for perfect enjoyment.

Most people can broil a steak or chop, but it takes a little more skill and care to produce a good *Pot au Feu*, Veal Blanquette or Steak and Kidney Pie. This book aims to encourage you to try a wide variety of dishes. Whether you prefer the meat rare or well-done, the texture and taste should be your main concern. Make it simple but good, always.

A few points worth remembering are: always use fresh meat, avoid leftovers by preparing the correct amount for each meal and always use first-class ingredients. By all means use cheaper cuts of meat for certain dishes, but never compromise on the quality.

To follow a balanced diet you should aim to eat at least five portions of fruit and vegetables daily, plenty of bread, cereals (preferably wholegrain) and potatoes and moderate amounts of dairy products, meat, fish and poultry (choosing lower fat versions whenever possible). Fatty and sugary foods should be taken in small amounts only.

In this meat guide, most of the recipes combine ingredients from different food groups – i.e. milk, cream or eggs with white meats or poultry; cheeses with pasta meat dishes; root vegetables with beans, peas or lentils and nuts and fruit with meat or seafood. Accompany your meat dishes with plenty of vegetables and salads. Drink wine or beer in moderation to improve your appetite and aid your digestion. Sip fresh fruit juice before each meal and eat crusty bread, preferably wholewheat, as your cereal intake. I am very positive that a balanced diet can be fun and healthy too. What more could you ask?

NUTRITIONAL MEAT VALUES
Meat is a valuable source of protein, B vitamins and minerals. It is best eaten with cereals or potatoes and with plenty of green or root vegetables in order to provide all the essential nutrients for a balanced diet.

In general, animal proteins – i.e. those provided by meat, milk, cheese, eggs and fish are of better quality than proteins from vegetable sources, like pulses and cereals. There are, however, some notable exceptions, like soya protein, which is an excellent source. Generally vegetable proteins are able to complement each other when they are served together at a meal, such as rice with a lentil curry.

The quality of protein is of particular importance when the diet is very low in protein or when it is lacking in variety, with animal protein in short supply. Low protein diets are, in fact, sometimes prescribed for some liver and kidney diseases.

In Western countries, however, we have plenty of food variety, and enough to satisfy our energy needs, so it is unusual for there to be any shortage of protein in the average diet.

Meat, especially red meat, liver and other offal, is also rich in iron and vitamin B12, both important in helping to prevent anemia. Pork is richer in thiamin and vitamin B1 than any other meat. Meat juices produced during cooking should be used to make the gravy if the minerals and vitamins are not to be lost.

Today, healthy eating guidelines recommend reducing fat, particularly saturated fat, in the diet. Meat does provide a significant amount of saturated fat, but this can be substanially reduced by choosing leaner cuts, trimming excess fat and by employing low-fat cooking methods. Poultry should also be skinned.

Historically, meat has formed a staple part of our diet. Even the hunter-gatherers of prehistoric times knew that to survive they needed animal flesh as well as vegetable matter.

As man developed, he sought to control his supply of food by domesticating the animals that were most fit to eat. His success in these early farming endeavours depended very much upon the climate in which he lived. For instance, farmed animals thrived best in temperate climates with moderate rainfall. The incidence of disease among cattle is inevitably greater in tropical countries where flies and bacteria infect herds of animals and where they are prey to attacks by carnivorous animals.

Today most of our meat is farmed, but wild animals and birds still provide interesting alternative types of meat. In recent years we have seen the domestication of an increasing number of birds – pheasants, quails, guinea fowls, turkeys, mallards and a trend towards wild ducks being available throughout the year.

LIVESTOCK FEEDING

Today there is, rightly, a growing demand from the public that animals should be looked after humanely and, whenever possible, fed organically grown crops. The difficulty here comes in balancing these demands with the economies of scale in animal production, which farmers have historically argued, keep down the cost of meat to the consumers. Increasingly, however, attempts are being made to reconcile the two considerations. The important factor is that animals must be fed adequately on feed containing the correct nutrients if they are to produce quality meat.

Meat is an important part of a balanced diet and to produce good meat you need healthy animals fed on high quality grain and grass that can be grown only on well-fertilized soil. Butchers have become skilled in better methods of dissection, and the customer is now fortunate in having a huge range of attractive cuts to choose from. It is with great confidence that I present you *The Master Chef* as a book for daily reference. It is the product of a lifetime of culinary and butchery experience acquired in many parts of the world working as a chef.

Jean Conil, London, 1995

COOKERY TERMS

AMERICAN   **ENGLISH**

Equipment

AMERICAN	ENGLISH
Cookie cutter	Biscuit cutter
Cookie sheet	Baking tray
Pastry bag	Piping bag
Roasting pan	Roasting tin
Strainer	Sieve
Tip	Nozzle

Ingredients

AMERICAN	ENGLISH
Almonds, shredded	Almonds, flaked
Bell peppers	Peppers
Biscuits	Scones
Broil (ing; er)	Grill (ing; er)
Butter, sweet	Butter, unsalted
Catsup	Ketchup
Celery root	Celeriac
Cheese, Swiss	Gruyère or Emmenthal cheese
Cherries, candied	Cherries, glacé
Coconut, unsweetened shredded	Coconut, Desiccated
Corn syrup	Golden syrup
Eggplant	Aubergine
Fava beans	Broad beans
Golden raisins	Sultanas
Green beans	French beans
Ground	Minced
Heavy cream	Double cream
Light cream	Single cream
Lima beans	Butter beans
Navy beans	Haricot beans
Pie dough	Shortcrust pastry
Rutabaga	Swede
Scallions	Spring onions
Snow peas	Mangetout
Sugar, superfine	Sugar, caster
Zucchini	Courgette(s)

Meat and Game

AMERICAN	ENGLISH
Bison	Buffalo
Beef foreshank	Shin
Beef, bottom round	Beef, silverside
Beef, top round	Beef, topside
Beef, round steak	Beef, rump steak
Ham steaks	Gammon steaks
Lamb rib roast	Rack of lamb
Lamb, sirloin chops	Chump chops
Rib chops	Cutlets
Shanks	Knuckles
Scallops	Escalopes
Veal, round roast	Veal topside

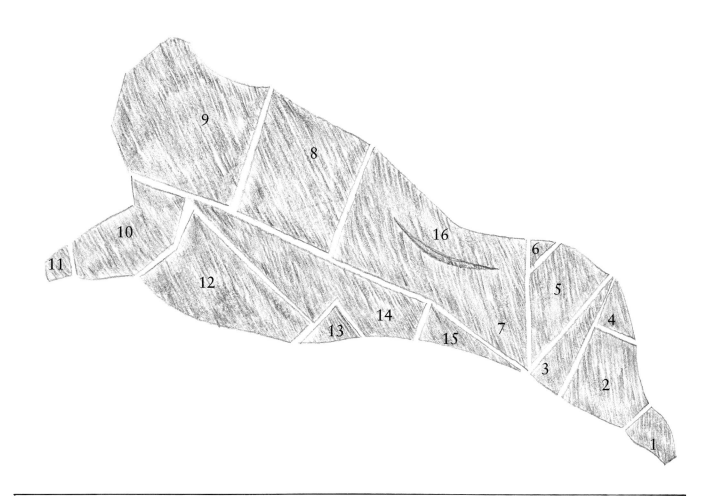

AMERICAN BEEF CUTS

1. Butt end or Knuckle bone

2. Top round; round steak

3. Aitchbone

4. Bottom round

5. Rump roast

6. Sirloin tip

7. Sirloin steak (tail end section); rib or club steak (head end of section)

8. Rib roast

9. Chuck roast; stewing beef

10. Shank

11. Knuckle

12. Brisket

13. Rattleran

14. Shortribs; plate (tail end of section)

15. Flank

16. Tenderloin and Porterhouse (T-bone)

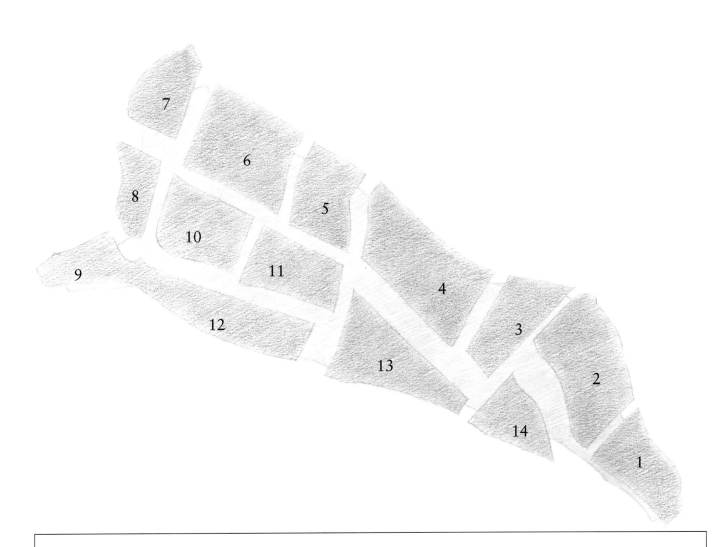

BRITISH BEEF CUTS

1. Leg

2. Topside and Silverside

3. Rump

4. Fillet (right side) and Sirloin (left side)

5. Fore rib

6. Chuck and Blade

7. Neck

8. Clod

9. Shin

10. Thick rib

11. Thin rib

12. Brisket

13. Thin flank

14. Thick flank

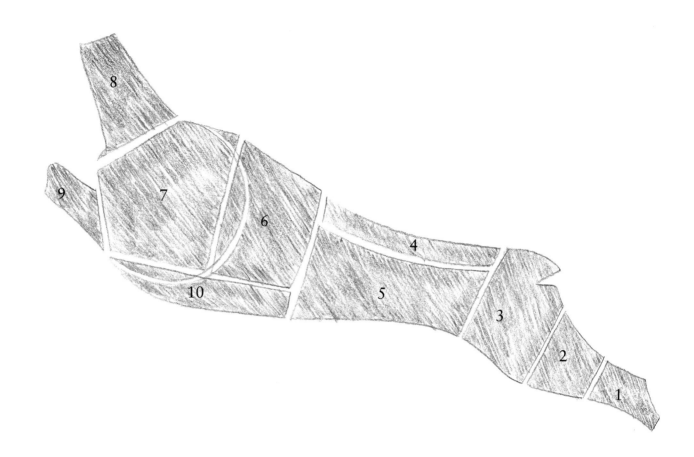

AMERICAN LAMB CUTS

1. Shank end of leg

2. Leg steaks

2. & 3. French leg or gigot

4. & 5. Saddle, only when cut takes in both sides
   of back; centerloin chops

6. Whole cut is called a 'rack'; if cut, rib chops; crown roast

7. Shoulder; if boned, rolled shoulder

8. Neck

9. Shank

10. Breast

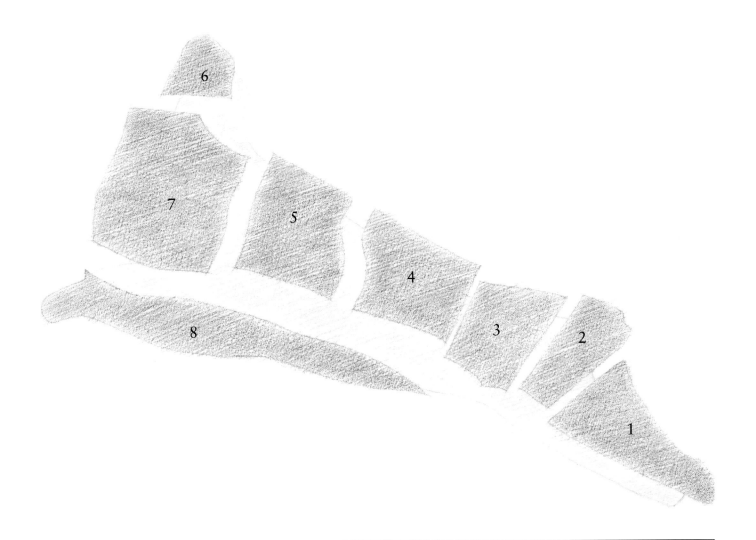

BRITISH LAMB CUTS

1. Shank end of leg

2. Fillet end of leg

3. Chump

4. Loin

5. Best end of neck

6. Scrag

7. Shoulder/Middle neck

8. Breast

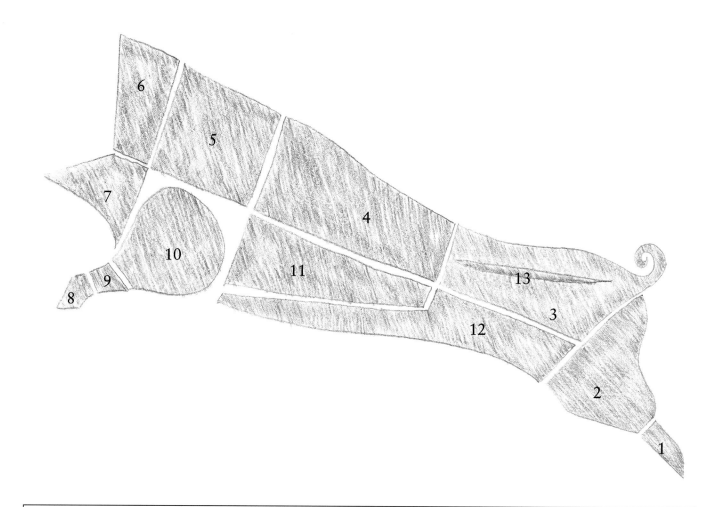

AMERICAN PORK CUTS

1. Shank

2. Ham or ham slices

3. Loin roast; butterfly chops if both sides of back

   are used

4. Loin chops; loin roast (in one piece)

5. & 6. Shoulder butt or shoulder slices

7. Jowl butt

8. Foot

9. Hock

10. Picnic shoulder

11. Spareribs

12. Bacon piece

13. Tenderloin

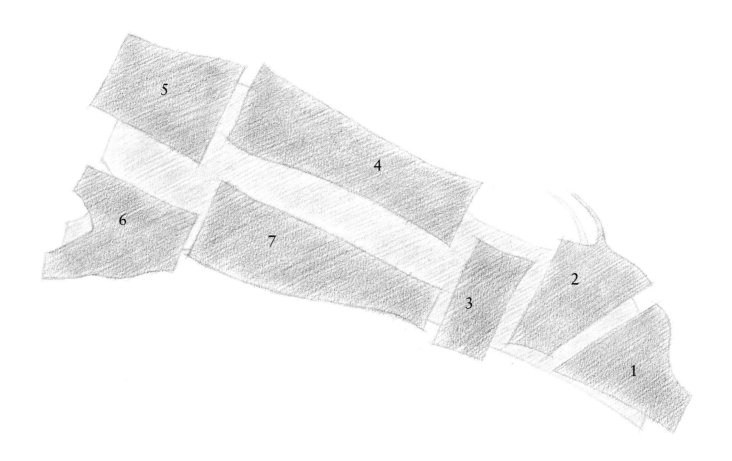

BRITISH PORK CUTS

1. Knuckle or Shank end of leg

2. Fillet of leg

3. Chump

4. Loin

5. Neck end

6. Shoulder (hand and spring)

7. Belly

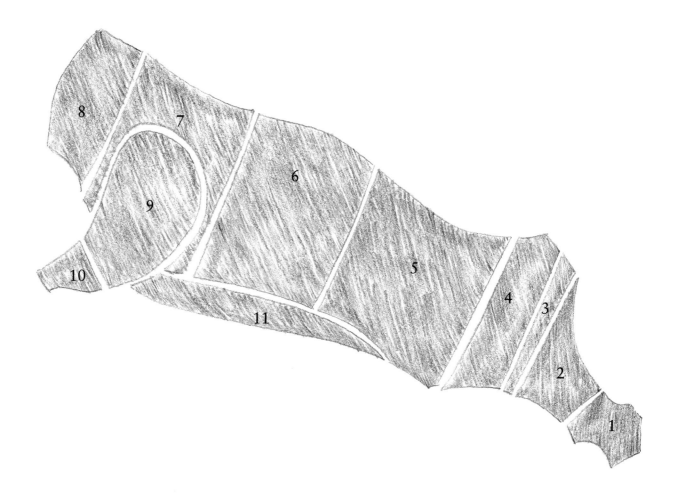

AMERICAN VEAL CUTS

1. Knuckle

2. Leg from which veal birds are made; if boned,

   round roast

3. Round steaks (scallops)

4. Rump roast

5. Loin roast: loin chops; loin steaks (nearest to tail end)

6. Center rib chops or roast

7. Shoulder chops

8. City chicken, when cut into cubes

9. Shoulder

10. Shank

11. Breast

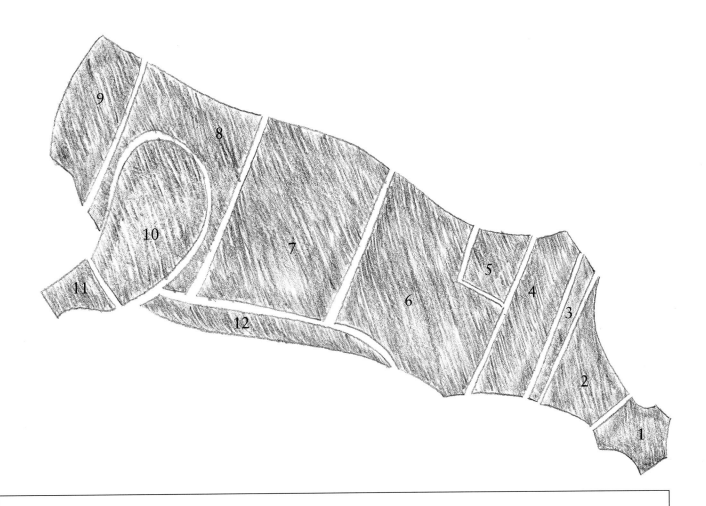

BRITISH VEAL CUTS

1. Knuckle or shin

2. Leg

3. Escallops or scallops

4. Fillet roast; escallops in slices

5. Rump end of loin

6. Saddle, if both sides of back are used; loin roast or loin cutlets

7. Best end of neck cutlets, or roasted if boned

8. Middle neck cutlets, or roast if boned

9. Scrag end of neck

10. Shoulder

11. Knuckle and foot

12. Breast

SAUCES AND GLAZES

Introduction

Sauces are served to complement meats and poultry, by moistening them and enhancing their flavor. Therefore, they are an essential part to any dish. It is true what many people say – the secret is in the sauce. I have also included in this section aspic stock jelly, which, as you will see, is used in some of the recipes.

Always remember that the basis of any good sauce is a meaty stock. Add vegetables and herbs to give a rich flavor. Also note that the sauce can be thickened with a roux – fat and flour – or with cornstarch mixed with cold water.

ASPIC STOCK JELLY

Preparation time: 15 minutes
Cooking time: 3 1/2 hours, plus cooling time

Aspic jelly is used to glaze cold meat, poultry and vegetables or to fill the gap in meat pies between the pastry and the filling that is left after baking. A good jelly should be clear with a light amber hue and a meaty taste similar to beef or chicken consommé. Beef foreshank and calves' trotters boiled in water will produce a jelly on cooling. Leaf or powdered gelatin can be added to the aspic stock when a firmer texture is required.

INGREDIENTS
1 lb (450 g) beef foreshank, cut into pieces (for brown stock only)
2 calves' or sheeps' trotters, blanched and boned
1 lb (450 g) bones, cut into small pieces
8 chicken winglets
1 large carrot, roughly chopped
1 large leek, roughly chopped
1 medium onion, roughly chopped
1 celery stick, roughly chopped
1 sprig of thyme
1 sprig of fennel

METHOD
1. For a brown stock, start by putting the beef, trotters, bones and winglets in a roasting pan and cook in a hot oven at 400°F (200°C/Gas mark 6) for 30 minutes. For a white stock, omit this stage and go straight to boiling the bones.
2. Drain off the fat and place the bones in a stock pot with 8 cups (2 liters/3 1/2 pints) water, the vegetables and herbs. Boil gently for 3 hours. Remove the scum and fat as it floats to the surface.
3. Any meat that is left should be allowed to cool, then, when cold, diced and used with a dressing for a beef salad with chopped dill pickles or cucumbers. Alternatively, the meat could be ground with chopped carrots and cooked potatoes and made into small pies.
4. Cool to produce a jelly.

CHEF'S TIPS:

The broth can be used to make a good meat aspic jelly or to make brown or white chaudfroid sauces.

When aspic jelly is to be used to glaze cold dishes, it must be clear and firm enough to stand the heat of the room in which it is to be served.

WHITE CHAUDFROID SAUCE

Preparation Time: 15 minutes, plus 3 1/2 hours for stock
Cooking Time: 15 minutes

INGREDIENTS

1 1/4 cups (300 ml/1/2 pint) white aspic stock*
3 tsp gelatin
1 1/4 cups (300ml/1/2 pint) light cream
2 tbsp (25 g/1 oz) butter
4 tbsp (25 g/1 oz) plain flour
salt and white pepper
grated nutmeg

METHOD

1. Sprinkle the gelatin over the aspic stock, standing the pot in a pan of hot water, being careful not to overheat the mixture. Stir until dissolved.
2. Melt the butter in a saucepan and stir in the flour. Stir in the cream and heat gently until thickened. Then stir in the gelatin/aspic stock and season to taste. Allow to cool stirring frequently. Use when at the consistency of thick cream for coating cold poultry, fish or eggs.

BROWN CHAUDFROID SAUCE

Preparation time: 15 minutes, plus 3 1/2 hours for stock
Cooking Time: 15 minutes

Make as above, but use a brown stock rather than a white stock – i.e. brown the bones in a hot oven and use some foreshank of beef to add extra color and flavor to the stock. Add the gelatine in the same way as before but then add to a classic brown Espagnole sauce (see page 29), rather than to a white béchamel sauce. A brown chaudfroid sauce should be used to coat game, duck or rib chops.

*The aspic stock can either be made as above or more simply by dissolving an envelope of aspic jelly powder in 1 1/4 cups (300 ml/ 1/2 pint) hot water.

DEVIL SAUCE

Preparation time: 15 minutes, plus 3 1/2 hours for stock
Cooking time: 15 minutes

This recipe is a simple variation of your basic brown sauce (see page 29).

To every 2 1/2 cups (600 ml/1 pint) of brown sauce, add 4 crushed peppercorns, 2 slices of chopped chili and 1 teaspoon of vinegar.

BARBECUE SAUCE

All cuts of beef can gain flavor by being marinated in a spicy barbecue-type sauce for at least 2 hours prior to cooking.

Preparation Time: 5 minutes, plus 2 hours if marinating
Cooking Time: 15 minutes

INGREDIENTS
6 tbsp tomato paste
4 tbsp clear honey or corn syrup
2 tbsp wine, sherry, malt or cider vinegar
2 tbsp soy sauce or yeast extract
1 garlic clove, crushed
1 tsp Chinese five spice powder
1 green chili, thinly sliced
2 tbsp oil
a little cornflour, to thicken

METHOD
1. Combine all the ingredients in a blender and liquidize. Coat the meat with this sauce and leave to marinate for at least 2 hours. Grill, fry or braise the meat until tender.
2. Boil the marinade and thicken with a little cornflour. Serve as a sauce.

CHEF'S TIPS

On the following three pages I give some helpful 'Chef's Tips' which, consequently, you will also find at the end of the recipes that follow. I hope that these suggestions will help you not only with the wonderful recipes included in this book but also in your day-to-day cooking.

CHEF'S TIPS ON COLORING STOCKS

1. To give the stock a golden color, cut an unpeeled onion in half and brown the two halves, cut side down, in a non-stick frying pan until golden, but not burnt.
2. Peeled raw beets also give the stock a golden color.
3. For a reddish color: pickle boiled beets in red wine. After 20 minutes add the wine and chopped beets to the liquid.
4. For an amber color stock: use the green parts of leeks and whole carrots.
5. For a pink color: add tomato paste to the stock.
6. For an orange color: use a package of saffron or a pinch of turmeric powder.
7. For a green color: use spinach juice.
8. Always avoid using artificial colors.

CHEF'S TIPS ON SEASONING

Seasoning is an important part of any dish, but it need not be a problem or a matter of guesswork.

1. For every 2 1/2 cups (600ml/1pint) of liquid, add 1 tsp of salt. This is equivalent to one percent.
2. For every 1 1/4 lb (500g) of stuffing you need 2 tsp of pepper. This is equivalent to two percent.
3. Onion flavor will increase if you leave the chopped onions exposed to air for 1 hour. However, remember that the color of the onions will darken.
4. Garlic cloves soaked in lemon juice are less pungent. Garlic which is toasted or fried in butter for 10 seconds over a low heat will have a better flavor.
5. Keep any surplus sauce from stews. If cornflour and not wheatflour has been used, the sauce can be frozen and used elsewhere later. A sauce thickened with wheatflour may separate on freezing.

CHEF'S TIPS ON STUFFING TO STRETCH JOINTS

1. Stuffed marrow, tomatoes or mushrooms can be served with joints of meat to make the meat go further. The vegetables can be stuffed with any of the following fillings:

   a) With raw pork sausage meat or fresh, raw ground pork: for every 1 1/4 lb (500 g) of sausage meat, add 1 cup (50g/2oz) of fresh white breadcrumbs, 2/3 cup (100 g/4 oz) of dried apricots, apples or golden raisins, 2 tbsp of chopped fresh parsley, 1 tsp salt and 1/2 tsp black pepper.

   b) With ground beef: for every 1 1/4 lb (500 g) beef, add 1 tbsp horseradish cream, 1 cup (50 g/2 oz) cooked mashed potato, 1 beaten egg, 1 tsp salt and 1/2 tsp black pepper.

2. Stuff poultry or veal with 1 1/4 lb (500 g) of raw pork sausage meat, with 1 tsp dry sage, 2 cups (50 g/2 oz) chopped chives, 1/2 cup (50 g/2 oz) skinned almonds, 1 tsp grated lemon rind, 1 tsp salt, 1/2 tsp white ground pepper and coriander.

3. Stuff ham with 1 1/4 lb (500 g) raw ground chicken, 1/4 cup (50 g/2 oz) roasted chicken skin, ground thoroughly, 1/2 cup (50 g/2 oz) toasted peanuts, 1 tsp salt, 1/2 tsp white ground pepper and a good pinch of ground mace.

4. Stuff liver with 1 1/4 lb (500 g) ground meat, (50 g/2 oz) ground raw liver, 1 tsp salt, 1/2 tsp black pepper and 2 cups (100 g/4 oz) fresh white breadcrumbs.

5. Stuffed peppers, pumpkins or cabbage leaves can also be served to stretch the meat. Stuff these vegetables with 1 cup (100 g/4 oz) boiled long grain rice, 1/3 cup (50 g/2 oz) golden raisins, 1/2 cup (50 g/2 oz) chopped nuts, 1 cup (50 g/2 oz) cooked peas, 1 cup (225 g/8 oz) raw ground pork, lamb or turkey meat, 1 tsp salt and 1/2 tsp coarsely crushed black peppercorns.

NOTE: Dishes stuffed with raw meat need to be cooked thoroughly.

CHEF'S TIPS ON VEGETABLES AS PART OF A BALANCED DIET

Vegetables are an important source of carbohydrates, minerals and vitamins.

1. Fresh raw salads with tomatoes, oranges, grapefruit and salad leaves are rich in Vitamin C.
2. Raw tomato and peppers, eaten with the skin left on, provide fiber as well as Vitamin C.
3. Lentils, beans, peas and nuts are good sources of protein and can be used to supplement a diet where little or no meat is being consumed.
4. Most cereals, in the form of pasta, bread, stuffing and pancakes or in the form of a garnish like rice, maize polentas, cracked wheat, dumplings or pearl barley in soups and stews can help stretch the meat content of a meal.
5. Vegetables come in the form of leaves, stems, roots, flowers or fruits of various plants. Dark green leaves tend to be the superior sources of nutrients.
6. Green and yellow vegetables provide Vitamin A as carotene. Carrots, kale, cress and broccoli are the richest sources.
7. Most vegetables have a better flavor and higher nutritional value when blanched or scalded for only a few minutes.

CHEF'S TIPS ON GARNISHING

Garnish should be light and elegant and used to display the food to its best advantage. An artistic eye helps but, with a little patience and practice, success will be guaranteed.

Examples of garnishes are as follows.
1. Carrot, lightly cooked so it is still firm and bright in color.
2. The green of a leek, tarragon leaf or the peelings of a cucumber that have been placed in a pan of boiling salted water until soft, then refreshed in cold water to preserve the color.
3. Radishes, turnips, ham, truffles, black olives and tomatoes can all be used.

Many varieties of fruit are used to accompany meat and poultry in the form of sauces, purées or garnishes.

The following are just a few of the ways in which fruit can complement cooked meat.
1. Fried bananas with fried chicken.
2. Glazed pears with ham.
3. Pineapple or apple purée and fritters with pork dishes.
4. Melon, pawpaw, grapes and fresh figs with smoked ham.
5. Gooseberries with broiled pork chops.
6. Plums with Asiatic stir-fried chicken or pork.
7. Dried prunes with stewed rabbits.
8. Raisins in poultry stuffings.
9. Apricots, peaches, oranges and cherries with duck.

Fruit sauces can be made with vinegar and flavored with many different berries such as raspberries, redcurrants or strawberries.

Chutneys and pickles made from guava, mangoes, dates and other fruits are all used to garnish cold meats or curries. Thanksgiving turkey would not be the same without the cranberry sauce.

Fruits also make a tempting ornamental garnish. Who can resist a slice of chicken decorated with a couple of strawberries and mint leaves?

ALL ABOUT BEEF

Introduction

I was born in the small country town of Fontenay Le Comte in France and spent many happy holidays on our family farm in the village of Auzais, in the Vendée.

This lovely farm was located at the foot of a hill crowned by a 12th century, crenellated castle. To reach the farm, you had to follow a lane that wound through marshes and fields, beside the river, up the hill, past the old church and through the village. I made this journey daily with the cowherd in charge of 24 cows and a bull named Toro.

This was my earliest introduction to the world of cattle. Here I learned about milking, making butter and cheeses and I soon became interested in the physiology of meat and the terminology of butchery. The elderly 'vacher' was my first mentor who taught me much about the breeding of animals.

The term 'cattle' is applied to different breeds in different countries: buffalo in Africa, Canada and India; bison in Europe and North America; the yak in Tibet and China; gayal and batin cattle in India; the zebu in Africa and domesticated cattle, which are bred all over the Western world. Cattle are sold as males or bulls, if sterilised they become steers. Young females are called heifers, once they have produced a calf they become cows. A sterilized cow is called a 'spayed heifer'. Emasculation is practiced on animals to improve the fattening process. Some cattle are bred for their meat (beef breeds) others for their milk (dairy breeds) and some for both (dual-purpose breeds). Over the years, breeders have developed various types of domestic cattle to suit different climates and depending on the pasture available. Jersey, Guernsey, Ayrshire and Holstein are some of the best known dairy breeds and Hereford, Angus, Charolais and Brahman are some of the finest beef breeds.

Crossbreeding over the years has produced France's finest regional cattle from Brittany, Flanders, Normandy and the Vendée. It was as a child in the Vendée that I first learned the names and origins of the various breeds. Aberdeen Angus with its black markings from Scotland; the Shorthorn from Durham with its red and white markings; the Sussex, South Down and Simmental are champion breeds; and the beautiful small Jersey and Guernsey breeds with their fawn colouring and rich milk.

I well remember the few gentle Jersey cows we had on our farm and the wonderful butter and cheeses they produced. Good beef can only come from healthy, well-reared livestock.

It is interesting to note that animal feeds constitute 85 percent of the cost of producing cattle. Pastures, which provide a mixture of grasses and legumes, are best for all cattle, sheep and goats. In winter, root crops, hay and straw are needed to supplement the diet.

Prime meat is the result of careful breeding and quality feeding. Toughness in beef is due to the thickness and density of muscle fibers and connective tissues. Thickening occurs with use and activity so the meat from older animals tends to be tougher than the meat from the younger ones. The front half (forequarter) of a carcass has more muscle and more connective tissue than the hindquarter because it is the front half of the animal that has to work the hardest. Therefore, cuts from the neck and shoulder are far tougher than cuts from the loin and rump, which have come from muscles performing the least work.

BEEF

The method of cooking suitable for a particular cut naturally depends on the type of muscle fiber it is made up of and the amount of connective tissue it contains. Cuts from the forequarter therefore need longer, slower cooking than hindquarter cuts which can be cooked much more quickly.

Grading is done on the basis of conformation, age and finish. The criteria of tenderness, juiciness and palatability are considered when designating quality. Conformation deals with the form or shape of an animal – those having broad, large full muscles with a relatively smaller proportion of bone are graded the highest. The finish is a term referring to the amount, quality and color of the fat within and around the muscles. Beef fat becomes more yellow with age, so whiter fat is graded higher than creamy or more yellow fat. In animals of the same age, yellow fat may also indicate that carotene – in the form of sugar beets, rutabagas or carrots – was used in the feed. Grass fed animals may be graded lower.

FILLET: The fillet is located under the loin, from the rump to the first wing rib along the lumbar vertebra and the ventral surface of the ileum.

SIRLOIN: The strip loin called *contre filet* is the part of the boned sirloin without the fillet attached to it.

RIB LOIN (*Faux filet*): This is the boned part of the rib muscle between the caudel and the fourth rib, including the 13th rib.

SHORT LOIN (including wing rib joint): The short loin is separated from the rump at the level of the lumbar vertebra and sacral bones and the ileum leg bone. The fillet remains attached in part and, with the bone, consists of the T-bone steak piece.

RIB JOINTS: The rib joints start at the fourth ribs from the shoulder bone and include the wing rib; the whole side rib is called in French 'Train de Côtes'.

RUMP: The whole rump is called in French, *surlonge*. It is part of the rump (called *culotte*) from which rump steaks are cut.

ROUND: The round is the inside rump part of the leg, detached along the main bone by the seaming operation of separating the part in segments including the eyeround (*gîte*) and the hampe, used for cheap steaks.

SHOULDER BLADE (joint known as '*palette*'): The tendons are removed and the two parts surrounding the shoulder blade are also removed. This can be rolled and tied for *Pot au Feu* (boiled beef) or cut in cubes for Beef Bourguignon.

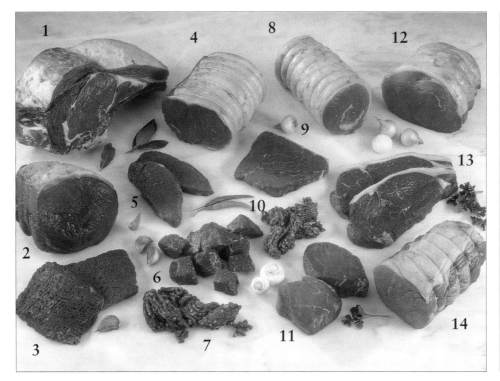

British Beef Retail Cuts

1. Forerib
2. Topside
3. Flash fry steak
4. Sirloin
5. Braising steak
6. Stewing beef (cubes)
7. Mince (coarse)
8. Brisket
9. Rump steak
10. Mince (fine)
11. Fillet steaks
12. Thick flank
13. Sirloin steak
14. Silverside

American Beef Retail Cuts

1 Chuck eye roast	7 Boneless shoulder pot roast	12 Flank steak	18 Round steak	24 Beef for stew	29 Cubed steak	36 Rib roast, small end	41 Rib roast, large end
2 Arm pot roast	8 Mock tender	13 Top round roast	19 Top round steak	25 Boneless top loin steak	30 Cubes for kebabs	37 Rib eye roast	42 Rib steak, small end
3 Cross rib pot roast	9 Under blade pot roast	14 Boneless rump roast	20 Bottom round roast	26 Porterhouse steak	31 T-bone steak	38 Back ribs	43 Rib eye steak
4 Blade roast	10 Short ribs	15 Tip roast cap off	21 Eye round roast	27 Shank cross cut	32 Tenderloin roast	39 Sirloin steak, flat bone	44 Top sirloin steak
5 7-Bone pot roast	11 Flanken-style ribs	16 Flank steak rolls	22 Tip steak	28 Corned brisket, point half	33 Tenderloin steak	40 Top sirloin steak	
6 Boneless top blade steak		17 Skirt steak	23 Ground beef		34 Brisket, whole		
					35 Brisket, flat half		

Beef and Bacon Hot Pot with Peanuts

Serves: 4
Preparation time: 20 minutes
Cooking time: 1 1/2 hours

INGREDIENTS

2 tbsp oil
1 lb (450 g) stewing beef, cubed
1 red onion, chopped
2/3 cup (150 ml/1/4 pint) fresh pineapple juice
1 tbsp tomato paste
salt
1/2-1 tsp ground cumin
1 green chili pepper, deseeded and finely chopped
1 1/3 cups (225 g/8 oz) canned flageolet beans, drained
1 1/4 cups (150 g/5 oz) peanuts, slightly toasted
4 slices rindless bacon
4 dried prunes, pitted

METHOD

1. Heat the oil and brown the beef for 5 minutes. Add the onion and cook for a further 5 minutes, then stir in the pineapple juice, tomato paste and 2 1/2 cups (600 ml/1 pint) water. Season with the salt, cumin and chili pepper.
2. Cover and cook gently for 1 1/2 hours on a low heat or braise in the oven at 350°F (180°C/Gas mark 4).
3. When the meat is done, add the beans and peanuts.
4. Wrap a bacon slice around each prune and insert a skewer to hold them in position. Broil until crisp. Remove the skewers and place the bacon-wrapped prunes on top of the stew before serving.

CHEF'S TIPS:

Stews and casseroles provide the best methods of cooking the tougher cuts of beef. They all involve slow cooking at a low heat with a measured volume of liquid (that is, one measure of meat to one measure of liquid). Although you can use a pressure cooker or a covered pan on top of the stove, for best results, cook in a casserole in a moderate oven at 350°F (180°C/Gas mark 4).

The cooking liquor should be slightly acidic, to help tenderize the meat. Include a little wine, cider, beer, tomato paste or fruit juice. The meat can be marinated first, and the marinade included in the cooking liquor. For a better flavor, fry the meat quickly in fat to brown it and to seal in the juices. Root vegetables and onions, which are added for flavor, should be lightly fried before you add stock and any aromatic herbs. To thicken the sauce, flour can be added when the meat is browned, or a roux (flour and butter mixed) stirred into the cooking liquor when the stew is nearly done.

Serve with boiled potatoes.

Beef and Eggplant Bake

Serves: 4
Preparation time: 20 minutes
Cooking time: 45 minutes-1 hour

INGREDIENTS

1 1/2 lb (675 g) ground beef
1 medium onion, finely chopped
salt and pepper
1 cup (225 g/8 oz) clarified butter*
4 medium-sized eggplants
1 green bell pepper, deseeded and sliced.
2 1/2 cups (600 ml/1 pint) tomato juice
1 1/4 cups (300 ml/1/2 pint) stock

GARNISH:
3 large tomatoes, thickly sliced

METHOD

1. Mix the meat and onions and season to taste.
2. Melt 1/2 cup (100 g/1 oz) of the butter in a frying pan and brown the meat lightly. Drain on paper towels.
3. With a sharp knife, lightly peel away the stems of the eggplants, leaving 1 1/2-inch (4 cm) in length.
4. Melt the remaining butter in a pan and fry the eggplants over a high heat until lightly colored. Slit each eggplant in the middle and make a pocket with a teaspoon.
5. Fill the pocket with the meat and arrange the stuffed eggplants in a baking dish.
6. Insert the slices of bell pepper between the eggplants and garnish with the tomatoes.
7. Mix together the tomato juice and stock. Pour over the stuffed eggplants.
8. Cover with foil and bake for 45 minutes-1 hour at 350°F (180°C/Gas mark 4).

CHEF'S TIPS:
Serve with rice or fried potatoes.

---

* To clarify butter: heat the butter gently until it melts, then continue to heat slowly, without burning, until all bubbling ceases (this shows the water has been driven off). Remove from the heat and let it stand for a few minutes for the salt and sediment to settle, then gently pour off the fat. Store in the fridge.

Individual Beef Wellingtons

Serves: 4
Preparation time: 45 minutes, plus 2 hours for the puff pastry
Cooking time: 45 minutes

INGREDIENTS

4 fillet steaks
salt and pepper
oil, for frying
1 1/4 cups (300 ml/1/2 pint) pouring batter for pancakes
   (see page 150)
1 1/2 lb (675 g) puff paste
flour, for dusting
egg wash, for glazing
1 1/4 cups (300 ml/1/2 pint) Madeira sauce (see recipe below)

LIVER FORCEMEAT:
2 tbsp oil, for frying
4 oz (100 g) calves' liver
2 shallots, chopped
4 large mushrooms, chopped
2 cups (50 g/2 oz) chopped fresh parsley
2 tbsp heavy cream
1 cup (50 g/2 oz) fresh breadcrumbs

GARNISH:
4 cups (225 g/8 oz) wild oyster mushrooms
1/4 cup (50 g/2 oz) butter

PUFF PASTRY:
Puff pastry can be frozen for a very long time, providing it is
well wrapped.

1 lb (450 g) strong white bread flour
1 tsp salt
1/3 cup (75 g/3 oz) butter
1 3/4 cup (400 g/14 oz) butter
1 tsp lemon juice

BASIC BROWN SAUCE (ESPAGNOLE SAUCE)
1/4 cup (50 ml/2 fl oz) oil or beef fat
4 slices bacon with rind, diced
1 onion, finely chopped
1/2 cup (50 g/2 oz) all-purpose flour
1 tbsp tomato paste
1 sprig of thyme
1 cup (50 g/2 oz) mushroom peels and stalks
2 1/2 cups (600 ml/1 pint) beef stock (see page 46)
salt and pepper

METHOD

1. Season the steaks. Heat the oil and fry in a shallow pan for 2 minutes only on each side. When cooked, remove from the heat and cool quickly.
2. To make the liver forcemeat: heat the oil in a frying pan and quickly fry the liver, shallots and mushrooms for 3 minutes. Remove from heat. Cool the mixture and grind to a fine paste. Season and add the parsley, cream and breadcrumbs. Spread some of this mixture on top of the steaks.
3. Cook four 6-inch (15 cm) pancakes, as thin as possible.
4. Roll the pastry out to 1/4-inch (5 mm) thick and cut four rounds of the same diameter as the pancakes. Place a steak on each pancake (this is to absorb the juices and prevent the pastry becoming soggy) and cover completely with a round of puff pastry. Brush with egg wash, to glaze.
5. Let rest for 30 minutes, then bake at 400°F (200°C/Gas mark 6) for 10-12 minutes until golden.
6. Heat the butter and sauté the wild oyster mushrooms.
7. Warm Madeira sauce (see recipe below).
8. To serve, cut each Wellington steak in half and place the two pieces on a plate with a pool of sauce and the cooked mushrooms.

PUFF PASTRY

1. Cut 1/3 cup (75 g/3 oz) butter into the flour and salt to a crumble texture. Add 1 1/4 cups (300 ml/1/2 pint) cold water and lemon juice to produce an elastic dough. Let rest for 10 minutes.
2. Roll the dough out into a rectangle. Cut the 1 3/4 cups (400 g/ 14 oz) of butter into small pieces. Cover three-quarters of the dough rectangle with the butter pieces. Fold the uncovered part of the rectangle into the center, over half the butter-covered portion. Fold the remaining butter-covered portion over the top. There should be three layers of dough enclosing the butter. Turn so the fold is at the side and repeat this process several times, resting the dough after every turn for 10 minutes in the fridge. Let the dough rest for 2 hours before using.

BASIC BROWN SAUCE (ESPAGNOLE SAUCE)/MADEIRA SAUCE

1. Heat the oil or fat and fry the bacon and onion until light brown. Sprinkle over the flour and stir to form a paste. Cook for 1 minute, then mix in the tomato paste. Add the thyme, mushroom peels and stalks and stock. Bring to a boil and simmer for 45 minutes. Season and strain. To make the Madeira sauce add (75 ml/ 3 fl oz) of Madeira wine to every 2 1/2 cups (600 ml/1 pint) of brown sauce.

Beef with Cashew Nuts and Spinach

Serves: 4
Preparation time: 15 minutes
Cooking time: 10 minutes

INGREDIENTS

1 lb (450 g) fillet of beef
1 lb (450 g) fresh spinach
2 tbsp butter
2-inch (5 cm) piece of fresh ginger root, peeled and finely
    chopped
1 cup (100 g/4 oz) cashew nuts, toasted
2 sticks celery, diced
2 tbsp oil
salt and black pepper

SAUCE:
2/3 cup (150 ml/1/4 pint) beef stock
2/3 cup (150 ml/1/4 pint) medium sherry or sake
1 tsp tomato paste
1 tsp cornstarch mixed with 3 tbsp cold stock or water

METHOD

1. Cut the beef into 8 slices and, with a meat mallet, beat them down to make thin scallops.
2. Wash the spinach well and drain well. Pat dry with a dish towel. Heat the butter and cook the spinach without any liquid. Add the ginger and seasoning. Strain the juice of the spinach through a colander and keep as a stock for the sauce. Press the spinach to extract as much moisture as possible. Add the nuts and celery to the spinach.
3. Heat the oil in a shallow pan and quickly fry the steaks for 2 minutes on each side, or less if rare steaks are preferred.
4. Mix the sauce ingredients, including the reserved spinach juice, in a pan and boil for 5 minutes. Season to taste. Pour over the steaks and heat through.
5. To serve, place the spinach mixture on a dish and top with the steaks. Guests should help themselves from the dish in Chinese fashion.

CHEF'S TIPS:
The popularity of this very interesting Asian type of beef is richly deserved. This dish can be cooked with or without spinach, using more celery and cashew nuts.

Beef Fillet Scallops with Onion Rings

Serves: 4
Preparation time: 15 minutes, plus 30 minutes marinating
Cooking time: 8 minutes

INGREDIENTS

1 lb (450 g) beef fillet, trimmed
3 tbsp oil

MARINADE:
1/2 tsp baking soda
2 tbsp soy sauce
4 tbsp sake or medium sherry
1 pinch Chinese five spice powder
salt and pepper

GARNISH:
1 lb (450 g) Spanish onions, cut into thin rings
2 tbsp (25 g/1 oz) butter
1 tbsp oil
1 tbsp honey
juice and grated rind of 1/2 lemon

METHOD

1. Slice the meat 1/4-inch (5 mm) thick. Gently flatten these slices to scallops with a rolling pin or a meat mallet.
2. Combine the marinade ingredients in a deep dish and soak the beef for 30 minutes.
3. Heat the butter and oil for the garnish in a frying pan and gently fry the onions for 8 minutes without browning. Toss and turn all the time. Add the honey, lemon juice, grated rind and seasoning.
4. Heat the oil and quickly cook the beef scallops for 1 minute on each side for rare meat, or longer if the meat is to be medium or well-done.
5. To serve, pile the onions onto a dish and arrange the beef scallops on top.

CHEF'S TIPS:

The universal popularity of steaks and onions must be in part due to the mouth-watering flavor and aroma of fried onions. Steaks can be cut from many parts of beef including the rump, flank and boneless sirloin. The fillet is the most tender and also the most expensive cut, but sirloin steaks are also firm favorites.

For this recipe, the steaks should be cut thin and small. Use large Spanish onions and make sure to fry them slowly in butter over a low heat. The Chinese use baking soda in their marinades to counteract the acidity of their sweet-and-sour sauces.

Chili Steak

Serves: 4
Preparation time: 20 minutes, plus marinating overnight
Cooking time: 10-15 minutes

INGREDIENTS

4 sirloin steaks
1 bay leaf
1 tsp peppercorns, crushed

MARINADE:
2 beef bouillon cubes
1 stalk celery, chopped
1 medium carrot, chopped
2 medium onions, chopped
3 tbsp tomato paste
2 tbsp red wine vinegar
1 tbsp brown sugar
1/2 tsp chili powder or 1 green chili pepper, split and deseeded
2 tsp Worcestershire sauce

SERVE WITH:
baked potatoes
salad

METHOD

1. To make the marinade: crumble the bouillon cubes into 2 cups (450 ml/3/4 pint) water in a saucepan over a medium heat. Add the celery, carrot, onions, tomato paste, vinegar, brown sugar, chili powder or chili pepper and Worcestershire sauce. Bring the mixture to a boil. Reduce the heat and simmer, uncovered, for 20 minutes. Let cool.
2. Mix to a purée in a blender and then press through a strainer.
3. Place the steaks, bay leaf and peppercorns in a shallow dish and pour over the marinade. Cover the dish with plastic wrap and chill overnight.
4. Drain the steaks and reserve the marinade. Barbecue or broil the steaks until done.
5. Bring the marinade to a boil and serve as sauce.
6. Serve with baked potatoes and a mixed salad.

CHEF'S TIPS:
These steaks can either be cooked on a barbecue or under the broiler. Cook some extra vegetables on the barbecue, such as bell peppers, eggplants, tomatoes and onions wrapped in foil.

Beware of fresh chili peppers – always split chili peppers and remove the seeds in order to reduce the pungency. Wash hands well after preparing.

Beef Kebabs

Serves: 4
Preparation time: 15 minutes, plus 1 hour marinating
Cooking time: 10-20 minutes

INGREDIENTS

1 1/2 lb (675 g) beef fillet, cut into 1-inch (2.5 cm) cubes
2 small eggplants, cut into thick slices
8 small tomatoes, halved
4 medium onions, quartered
red and green bell peppers, deseeded and cut into squares
olive oil, for broiling

MARINADE:
2 tbsp soy sauce
1 garlic clove, crushed
2/3 cup (150 ml/1/4 pint) tomato juice
1 small green chili pepper, deseeded and finely chopped
2 tbsp oil

METHOD

1. Blend together the marinade ingredients and soak the meat cubes for 1 hour.
2. Remove the meat and thread onto long kebab skewers, alternating the meat with eggplants, tomatoes, onions and bell peppers. Brush with the olive oil. Broil for 10-12 minutes according to taste.
3. Boil the marinade sauce and serve it separately in a sauce boat.

CHEF'S TIPS:
Kebabs are usually served with rice, although they are equally delicious served with baked or fried potatoes. Broiled bell peppers, eggplants, tomatoes, mushrooms, onions, salads and spicy sauces are all good accompaniments for kebabs. Kebabs can be made with cubes of meat or with ground meat shaped into small balls.

Beef with Almonds Valencia

Serves: 4
Preparation time: 15 minutes, plus 30 minutes freezing
Cooking time: 15 minutes

INGREDIENTS

4 x 6-oz (175 g) sirloin steaks, trimmed
oil, for frying
black pepper

ALMOND PASTE:
5 oz (150 g) marrow bone (optional)
1 cup (100 g/4 oz) ground almonds
2 tsp chopped chervil or parsley
1/2 cup (50 g/2 oz) grated Parmesan cheese
salt and pepper

SAUCE:
1 slice bacon, chopped
1 small onion, chopped
1 fennel bulb, chopped
1 tsp yeast extract
1 1/4 cups (300 ml/1/2 pint) orange juice
1 tsp wine vinegar
1/2 cup (100 ml/4 fl oz) beef stock or water
1 tsp sugar
2 tsp cornstarch mixed with 2 tbsp water
salt and pepper.

METHOD

1. Wrap the marrow bone, if used, in cheesecloth and poach for 6 minutes. Remove the marrow and let set in a bowl, over ice cubes, for 12 minutes to harden. Mix together all the paste ingredients, including the poached marrow, if used. Roll the mixture into the shape of a sausage. Wrap in plastic wrap and freeze for 30 minutes.
2. Brush the steaks with oil and season with black pepper. Fry in a pan as required, then remove, reserving the juices. Make the sauce in the same pan. Reduce the meat juices and fry the bacon, onion and fennel for a few minutes. Stir in the yeast extract, orange juice, vinegar, stock or water and sugar and boil for 5 minutes. Thicken with the cornstarch paste and boil for a further 4 minutes until clear. Season to taste.
3. Cover each steak with the almond paste, cut in pats. Brown the steaks under the broiler for 3 minutes.
4. Serve steaks with the sauce.

CHEF'S TIPS:

In this recipe the steaks are coated with a paste made from beef marrow bone (optional), cheese, herbs and almonds. This mixture is spread on top of the steak as a coating before broiling. The meat is served with a sweet-and-sour sauce enriched with the meat juices.

Serve with mixed seasonal vegetables.

Rib Steak with Béarnaise Sauce

Serves: 4
Preparation time: 45 minutes
Cooking time: 15-20 minutes

INGREDIENTS

2 short rib steaks, trimmed to 1-inch (2.5 cm) thick
1 tbsp olive oil

BEARNAISE SAUCE:
2 shallots, chopped
1 tbsp tarragon and chervil, chopped
4 tbsp white wine
4 tbsp tarragon vinegar
1/2 tsp coarsely ground black pepper
3 egg yolks
2/3 cup (150 g/5 oz) butter

SERVE WITH:
potatoes, sautéed

GARNISH:
watercress

METHOD

1. To make the sauce: put the shallots and half of the herbs in a small saucepan with the wine, vinegar and pepper. Boil until reduced to one tablespoon. Remove from the heat.
2. Place the saucepan in a shallow metal baking dish half-filled with hot water. Keep on a low heat but do not allow the water to go above simmering point. Add the egg yolks, whisking the mixture until it becomes frothy and thick like a custard. Gradually stir the butter into the sauce while whisking continually, until the sauce is thick like mayonnaise. When the sauce is ready, add the remaining herbs.
3. Heat the oil in a shallow pan to cook the steaks or broil them as required. Remember to season the steaks only after they are cooked if they are required rare. You may season before cooking if well-done steaks are requested.
4. Serve the steaks with sautéed potatoes and garnish with watercress. The sauce should be served separately.

CHEF'S TIPS:
Steak served with the famous Béarnaise sauce is a popular classic. Although the sauce needs to be prepared carefully, it is both satisfying for the cook and a real treat for the guests.

Steaks Capsicum

Serves: 4
Preparation time: 15 minutes
Cooking time: 15 minutes

INGREDIENTS

4 x 5-oz (150 g) fillet or sirloin steaks
2 tbsp oil
salt and pepper

SAUCE:
1/4 cup (50 ml/2 fl oz) sweet sherry
1/4 cup (50 ml/2 fl oz) soy sauce
1/2 cup (100 ml/4 fl oz) beef stock

SERVE WITH:
3 bell peppers of different colors, deseeded and cut into thin strips
2 zucchini, cut into julienne strips
1 small onion, cut into julienne strips
2 tbsp oil or butter

GARNISH:
bunch of chives

METHOD

1. Heat the oil and fry the steaks as required. Season. Remove the steaks from the pan.
2. In the same pan make the sauce. Stir in the sherry, soy sauce and stock and boil to reduce by half. Season to taste.
3. In a clean pan, heat the oil or butter and stir-fry the bell peppers, zucchini and onion for 4 minutes. Season to taste.
4. Serve the steaks with the vegetables and a little sauce poured by the side of the meat. Garnish with chives.

CHEF'S TIPS:
The colorful sweet bell peppers make an attractive garnish to these steaks.

Serve with a bean sprout or alfalfa salad tossed in a lemon dressing for a highly nutritious accompaniment.

Beef Fillet with Strudel

> **Serves:** 4
> **Preparation time:** 20 minutes, plus 30 minutes resting time for the strudel dough
> **Cooking time:** 25 minutes

INGREDIENTS

4 x 5-oz (150 g) fillet steaks, trimmed
2 tbsp oil
freshly ground black pepper

MARROW AND SPINACH STRUDEL:
4 phyllo leaves or 8 oz (225 g) strudel dough (see opposite)
4 marrow bones
ice, to harden marrow bones
2 lb (1 kg) fresh spinach, washed
a little butter, melted

STRUDEL DOUGH:
2 cups (225 g/8 oz) strong bread flour
pinch of salt
1 egg, beaten
1 tsp olive oil

SAUCE:
2 egg yolks
2/3 cup (150 ml/1/4 pint) melted butter
1/3 cup (75 ml/3 fl oz) natural yoghurt
juice of 1/2 lemon

METHOD

1. Brush the steaks with oil and season with pepper only.
2. To make the strudel dough: combine the flour, salt, egg, oil and 2 tbsp lukewarm water to form a dough. Knead well and rest for 30 minutes. Roll out on a floured board until very thin. Place the dough on a cloth and stretch it until paper thin. Leave until required.
3. Wrap the marrow bones in cheesecloth and poach for 4 minutes. Remove the marrow and cut it into slices. Chill on ice to harden.
4. Blanch 12 spinach leaves in boiling water for 30 seconds. Keep the rest for garnish. Remove from the water and pat dry.
5. Wrap each marrow with three spinach leaves, then wrap again in either strudel or a phyllo leaf. Make into small packages like Chinese rolls, and brush with melted butter. Bake at 400°F (200°C/Gas mark 6) for 4 minutes.
6. To make the sauce: place the egg yolks in a small saucepan in a deep roasting pan half-filled with hot water. Add 2 tablespoons of warm water to the eggs and whisk until the mixture begins to thicken. Gradually stir in the butter a little at a time and when the mixture has thickened stir in the yoghurt and lemon juice. Do not let the sauce boil.
7. Cook the remaining spinach in a little butter for 3 minutes. Season and drain well.
8. Broil the steaks as required.
9. To serve, place a little spinach on each plate, top with a steak and garnish with a small marrow and spinach strudel. Pour a little of the sauce beside each steak.

CHEF'S TIPS:

In this recipe, the steaks are served with a marrow and spinach 'strudel' or pastry packages. You can either make your own strudel dough or use ready-made phyllo leaves. Marrow bone is considered by many to be a great delicacy when served on its own or as a savory on toast. Marrow bone is often used to enrich sauces and can be used as a stuffing for strudel (as here), ravioli, or other savory pastries.

Beef Medallions with Cauliflower Timbale

Serves: 4
Preparation time: 40 minutes
Cooking time: 30 minutes

INGREDIENTS

4 x 5-oz (150 g) fillet steaks, trimmed and cut 1-inch
    (2.5 cm) thick
2 tbsp oil

BECHAMEL SAUCE:
2 tbsp (25 g/1 oz) butter
4 tbsp (25 g/1 oz) flour
1 1/4 cups (300 ml/1/2 pint) milk
salt, pepper and grated nutmeg, to taste

BASIL SAUCE:
1/2 cup (100 ml/4 fl oz) white wine
8 basil leaves, roughly chopped
8 spinach leaves, roughly chopped
1 shallot, chopped

CAULIFLOWER TIMBALES:
2 cups (225 g/8 oz) cauliflower florets
3 tbsp heavy cream
2 eggs, beaten
1 tsp grated Parmesan cheese
Fresh basil leaves, to garnish

METHOD

1. To make the Béchamel sauce: heat the butter and mix in the flour to form a paste, cook for 1 minute. Gradually stir in the milk and heat, stirring, until the mixture is smooth and thick. Season to taste.
2. To make the basil sauce: boil all the ingredients together for 6 minutes. Add half the Béchamel sauce, stir together or process to a thin purée.
3. To make the timbales; cook the cauliflower for 15 minutes until soft. Drain and pass through a strainer. Add cream and remaining Béchamel sauce. Beat in the eggs and grated cheese and season to taste.
4. Fill eight x 4-fl oz (100 ml) ramekin dishes with this mixture. Place them in roasting pan, half-filled with hot water and bake for 25 minutes at 350°F (180°C/ Gas mark 4). Remove from the oven and let rest for 10 minutes before turning them out onto the plates.
5. Meanwhile, brush the steaks with the oil, season and broil or fry as required. Reheat the basil sauce just before serving.
6. To serve, place a steak with two cauliflower timbales on each plate. Pour a little basil sauce over one of the timbales. Garnish with basil leaves.

CHEF'S TIPS:

In this recipe, steaks are served with cauliflower, made into a sort of egg timbale served with a basil sauce. The timbales are prepared by cooking the cauliflower mixture in individual dishes in a *bain-marie*, a roasting pan half-filled with water, to allow gentle cooking.

Serve with small potatoes.

Tournedos with Wild Mushrooms

Serves: 4
Preparation time: 15 minutes
Cooking time: 15 minutes

INGREDIENTS

4 x 5-oz (150 g) fillet steaks
1 tbsp (15 g/1/2 oz) butter
2 tbsp oil
1 1/2 cups (150 g/5 oz) oyster and chanterelle mushrooms,
    trimmed

SAUCE:
2/3 cup (150 ml/1/4 pint) port wine
1 tsp yeast extract
1/2 cup (100 ml/4 fl oz) beef stock
1 small pinch of fresh or dried thyme
1 garlic clove, crushed
salt and black pepper, to taste

GARNISH (optional):
6 canned artichoke hearts, drained
6 asparagus tips, cooked and chopped
12 trimmed baby carrots, cooked and chopped

METHOD

1. Heat the butter and oil in a shallow pan and fry the steaks as required. Remove from the heat and keep warm.
2. In the same pan fry the mushrooms for 4 minutes. Remove and keep warm.
3. Deglaze the juices in the pan with the port wine, yeast extract and stock. Add the thyme and garlic and boil for 6 minutes to reduce. Season to taste.
4. Serve the steaks with the mushrooms and a little sauce. If serving the garnish, arrange cooked, chopped asparagus tips and carrots in the artichoke hearts and heat through.

CHEF'S TIPS:
A tournedos is a cut from the middle fillet, 1-inch (2.5 cm) thick and tied with string. A wide range of wild mushrooms are now available, so take your pick from morels, chanterelles, oyster or ceps. To accentuate the flavor of the mushrooms, fry in butter with a little thyme and garlic.

Serve with green beans, stuffed tomatoes and potato cakes (see page 105).

Pot Roast of Fillet of Beef Stuffed with Pesto

Serves: 4
Preparation time: 20 minutes
Cooking time: 25-30 minutes

INGREDIENTS

1 x 4-inch (10 cm) long beef fillet, middle cut, skinned and trimmed
4 garlic sausages, 1-inch (2.5 cm) in diameter, skinned
2-3 tbsp oil, for frying
salt and pepper

PESTO FILLING:
1/2 cup (50 g/2 oz) finely chopped pine nuts
2 tbsp chopped fresh basil leaves
1 garlic clove, crushed
2 tbsp chopped fresh parsley
1/2 cup (50 g/2 oz) soft cream cheese
good pinch of ground black pepper

SAUCE:
2/3 cup (150 ml/1/4 pint) beef stock
2/3 cup (150 ml/1/4 pint) Chianti or other Italian red wine
1 garlic clove, crushed
2 tsp cornstarch mixed with 2 tbsp cold water
1 tsp yeast extract
1 tsp tomato paste
salt and pepper

GARNISH:
1 red and 1 yellow bell pepper, deseeded and cut into strips
1-2 tbsp olive oil
1 cup (100 g/4 oz) pitted green olives
1 cup (100 g/4 oz) pitted black olives
8 oz (225 g) canned baby artichokes

METHOD

1. Cut a tunnel 3/4-inch (2 cm) in diameter through the length of the beef fillet, using an apple corer on both ends to ease the operation. Insert a small knife to remove the strip of beef inside. The removed meat can be ground and added to the pesto.
2. In a bowl, mix the pesto ingredients to a paste.
3. Roll the garlic sausages in the pesto mixture, then push them into the beef cavity, using your thumb or the handle of a wooden spoon.
4. Season the beef all over and tie up with string.
5. Heat the oil in a shallow pan and brown the fillet all over for 7 minutes. Remove the fillet and place in a metal baking dish. Roast the beef for 20 minutes for underdone, more for well-done, at 400°F (200°C/Gas Mark 6).
6. Meanwhile, make the sauce. Boil the stock, wine and garlic for 8 minutes. Mix in the cornstarch paste, and stir until thickened.
7. Remove the fillet, discard the strings and rest for 8 minutes. Pour the meat juice into the wine gravy and add the yeast extract and tomato paste. Season to taste.
8. Stir-fry the bell peppers in the oil for 4 minutes. Add the olives and artichokes and heat them through.
9. To serve, cut the fillet in four pieces 1-inch (2.5 cm) thick. Pour a little sauce onto each plate and arrange the steak and the vegetable garnish attractively.

CHEF'S TIPS:

This Italian dish is a specialty of Tuscany. The filling is a pesto mixture with pine nuts, parsley, cheese and a little garlic. The special garnish of this dish consists of pitted green and black olives, canned baby artichokes and strips of fried red and yellow bell peppers.

Asian Beef Casserole

Serves: 5
Preparation time: 15 minutes
Cooking time: 1 1/2 hours

INGREDIENTS

2 lb (1 kg) stewing steak, cubed
5 tbsp sunflower oil
2 shallots, diced
2 garlic cloves, crushed
1 star anise or pinch of Chinese five spice powder
1 small piece fresh ginger root, peeled and chopped
2 tbsp soy sauce
4 1/2 cups (1 liter/1 3/4 pints) beer
1 tbsp sugar or honey
salt and pepper
2 tsp cornstarch mixed with 3 tbsp of cold beer
2 1/2 cups (150 g/5 oz) dried mushrooms, soaked in water

SERVE WITH:
1 cup (150 g/5 oz) parsnips and turnips, peeled and sliced

GARNISH:
chives

METHOD

1. Heat the oil in a casserole dish and stir-fry the meat until brown. Add the shallots, garlic and spices and cook for 3 minutes. Stir in the soy sauce, beer, sugar or honey and seasoning. Simmer gently for 1 1/2 hours, or until the meat is tender. Add the soaked mushrooms 15 minutes before the meat is cooked.
2. Meanwhile, cook the parsnips and turnips in boiling, salted water for 20-30 minutes until tender.
3. Stir the cornstarch paste into the sauce, bring to a boil, stirring, until thickened. Check seasoning.
4. Serve the stew with the parsnips and turnips and garnish with chives.

CHEF'S TIPS:
Seal the meat and vegetables by shallow frying in oil or fat to brown the outside. This will keep the juice in the meat and help develop the flavor. Cook at a low temperature with the same amount of liquid as meat and vegetables combined and season at the last minute when ready to serve. Always cook at the lowest possible temperature and remove all surplus fat during cooking. Remember that the tougher the meat the longer it will take to cook. Marinating meats in fresh pineapple juice will help to tenderize tougher meats.

The best temperature for hot pot cookery is 325°F (170°C/ Gas mark 3). Cooking time varies from 1-3 hours depending on the cut and thickness of the meat. Chops cooked on the bone have more flavor than boneless cuts.

Vegetable garnishes look better when freshly cooked separately. Finally, flavoring root and tuber vegetables should be cooked whole for easier removal.

Steak with Blue Cheese Sauce

Serves: 4
Preparation time: 10 minutes
Cooking time: 30 minutes

INGREDIENTS

4 x 8-oz (225 g) sirloin steaks
1 tbsp oil
1 medium onion, chopped
1 garlic clove, crushed
2 tbsp white port wine
1/2 cup (100 ml/4 fl oz) beef stock
salt and freshly ground black pepper
1/2 cup (100 ml/4 fl oz) heavy cream
1/3 cup (50 g/2 oz) blue cheese, mashed and pushed
    through a strainer

SERVE WITH:

tagliatelle, cooked (a mixture of plain, spinach and tomato
    varieties looks attractive)
a little butter

METHOD

1. Heat the oil in a pan and fry the steaks for 6-8 minutes. Remove the steaks and keep warm.
2. Drain away some of the oil and stir-fry the onion for 1 minute, then add the garlic and continue to stir-fry for 30 seconds. Pour in the port wine and boil for 30 seconds to reduce the sauce. This is a standard procedure known as *déglacéagé* (deglazing). Stir in the stock. Boil for a further 5 minutes and season to taste. Finally, add the cream and the cheese and simmer for 3 minutes.
3. Slice the steaks across in 4-5 pieces. Pour a pool of sauce onto each plate and arrange the pieces of steak on the diagonal, fanning them for better effect.
4. Serve with the cooked tossed tagliatelle with a little butter and seasoned to taste.

CHEF'S TIPS:
Use a mild blue cheese or a strong one according to your taste. The flavor of the sauce is enhanced by the addition of white port wine.

Steak Stroganoff

Serves: 4
Preparation time: 10 minutes
Cooking time: 15 minutes

INGREDIENTS

1 lb (450 g) fillet steak (cut from the thin end), trimmed
1/4 cup (50 ml/2 fl oz) oil
1 tbsp vodka or brandy
1 medium onion or 3 shallots, chopped
1 cup (50 g/2 oz) sliced wild mushrooms
1 tbsp paprika
1 1/2 tbsp (25 g/1 oz) tomato paste
2/3 cup (150 ml/1/4 pint) heavy cream, sour cream or
    Sauce Smitane (see below)
salt and pepper

GARNISH:
scallions, trimmed

SERVE WITH:
boiled rice and okra

SAUCE SMITANE:
1 small onion, chopped
2 tbsp (25 g/1 oz) butter
1/3 cup (75 ml/3 fl oz) dry white wine
2/3 cup (150 ml/1/4 pint) sour cream

METHOD

1. Cut the steak into cubes 3/4-inch (2 cm) thick.
2. Heat the oil in a frying pan. Brown the meat for 4 minutes, stirring constantly. Add the vodka or brandy and set alight. Remove from the pan.
3. In the same pan, fry the onion or shallots gently for 2 minutes without coloring. Add mushrooms. Cook for 1 minute.
4. Sprinkle on the paprika, add the tomato paste and cook for 2 minutes, stirring continually.
5. Add 2/3 cup (150 ml/1/4 pint) water and heavy cream, sour cream or sauce smitane and boil for a further 5 minutes.
6. Reheat the meat in the sauce for 3 minutes. Remove from the heat.
7. Just before serving, check the seasoning. Garnish with scallions.

SAUCE SMITANE
1. Gently fry the onion in the butter. Add the wine and boil to reduce.
2. Pour in the sour cream and simmer gently for a few minutes. Pour through a strainer, then use as required.

CHEF'S TIPS:
Another Russian variation is to use caraway seeds instead of paprika and to add a little kummel. Kummel is a liqueur flavored with caraway seeds.

For a more impressive garnish, shape the cooked rice in small ring molds, then turn out and garnish with slices of okra.

Minute Steak Stilton with Stuffed Onions

Serves: 2
Preparation time: 15 minutes
Cooking time: 30 minutes

INGREDIENTS

2 sirloin steaks, trimmed
pepper
4 medium onions, peeled
melted butter, for brushing
2 tbsp oil

ONION STUFFING:
3 oz (75 g) Stilton or other blue cheese
1 tbsp heavy cream
1 hard-cooked egg, pressed through a strainer
1/4 cup (25 g/1 oz) finely chopped walnuts
coarsely ground black pepper

MUSTARD SAUCE:
1 small shallot, chopped
2/3 cup (150 ml/1/4 pint) port wine
1/4 cup (50 ml/2 fl oz) heavy cream
1 tsp mustard
salt and pepper, to taste

SERVE WITH:
1 lb (450 g) Swiss chard or spinach, washed
salt, pepper and grated nutmeg

GARNISH:
1 1/4 cups (150 g/5 oz) pickles, sliced

METHOD

1. Beat the steaks with a meat mallet to produce thin scallops. Sprinkle with pepper.
2. In a bowl combine the stilton or other blue cheese, cream, egg and walnuts for the onion stuffing.
3. Boil the onions for 15 minutes, then press the onions to remove the core leaving a cavity for the cheese filling. Chop the removed part of the onions and mix it into the cheese paste. Fill the onions with this mixture. Place the stuffed onions in a small gratin dish, brush with butter and reheat for 8 minutes.
4. Wash the Swiss chard or spinach, keeping the stems. Boil for 8 minutes in salted water. Drain well and squeeze away surplus moisture. Season with salt, pepper and nutmeg.
5. Heat the oil and pan-fry the steaks for 1 minute on each side. Remove the steaks from pan and deglaze the meat juices with the shallot and the port wine. Boil for 5 minutes, then stir in the cream. Boil 1 more minute, stir in the mustard and season to taste.
6. Pour a pool of the mustard sauce onto each plate. Place the Swiss chard or spinach in the center. Cut each steak in two halves and arrange them on top of the chard leaves or spinach. Cut the stuffed onions in two halves and place them around the steaks, cut sides up. Garnish with sliced pickles.

CHEF'S TIPS:
There are numerous recipes for steaks with savory cheese. This one is a favorite of Anne, the Princess Royal, who attended a banquet I organised at Claridge's hotel, London, for Save the Children. The simple garnish of boiled onions stuffed with a blue cheese mixture has a distinction of its own.

Beef Carpaccio Salad with Salsa Verde

Serves: 2
Preparation time: 10 minutes, plus 1 hour marinating
Cooking time: 5 minutes

INGREDIENTS

6 x 4-oz (100 g) beef fillets, trimmed
assorted salad leaves – rocket, radicchio, oak leaves, chicory,
    chives and cress, roughly shredded
1 eggplant, peeled and sliced
2 tbsp olive oil
4 x 4-oz (100 g) slices of fresh parmesan or similar cheese
1/2 cup (100 ml/4 fl oz) salsa verde dressing (see below)
1 red bell pepper, grilled, peeled and cut, to garnish
1 tbsp small pickled capers, to garnish

SALSA VERDE:
6 tbsp olive oil
2 tbsp wine or balsamic vinegar
1 small shallot, chopped
1 garlic clove, crushed
2 tbsp freshly chopped mixed herbs (i.e. tarragon, basil, mint,
    parsley or lemon grass)
juice of 1/2 lemon
1 tsp good mustard
1 tsp small pickled capers
1 tsp grated Parmesan cheese
ground black pepper and salt

METHOD

1. Thin down each beef fillet with a wooden mallet, between two polythene sheets, to produce scallops.
2. To make the salsa verde dressing: combine all the ingredients in a bowl and whisk gently to produce a slight emulsion.
3. Pour the salsa verde dressing over the beef and marinate for 1 hour to sterilize the meat and improve the flavor.
4. Roll each beef fillet into a cornet and fill the cornets with the mixed salad leaves. Reserve the marinade.
5. Heat the oil and fry the eggplants for 3 minutes. Season and drain or absorb with paper towels. Roll the parmesan cheese or other similar type of cheese into cornets and fill them with the cooked eggplant slices. If liked, mark the cheese with a hot skewer for flavor and decorative effect.
6. Place three small beef cornets and two Parmesan cornets on each plate. Garnish with the strips of red bell peppers and capers and pour over the reserved marinade.

CHEF'S TIPS:

Beef eaters will always rave about the merit of eating raw or underdone beef of the best quality, such beef having been bred in pasture and not confined indoors. Bacteriologists tell us, however, that raw meat is not free from bacteria, but coating a raw steak with a dressing, such as salsa verde, acts as a bacteria inhibitor due to the action of the acetic acid in vinegar, mustard, garlic, onions and shallots.

The Carpaccio is a more refined Italian form of the famous Russian steak featured and popularized in Harry's Bar in Venice. The Carpaccio is usually served as an appetizer in many of the best Italian restaurants. The meat should be from the tail end of the fillet of beef, thinly sliced and battered like an scallop and chilled for 1 hour.

This same dressing can be used for tartare steaks, and for any kind of tartare fish. It is also suitable for boiled beef, veal, lamb, bacon and poultry and can be used for any kind of green or tomato salads or cooked vegetables, such as artichokes, asparagus and small potatoes.

Beef Consommé

Serves: 8
Preparation time: 40 minutes
Cooking time: 2 hours

INGREDIENTS

2 1/2 quarts (2 liters/3 1/2 pints) beef stock

FOR CLARIFICATION:
1 cup (225 g/8 oz) ground beef foreshank
2 egg whites
1 1/2 cups (225 g/8 oz) mixture of chopped raw celery, onion, leek, carrot and beets
1 tsp salt
1/4 tsp ground pepper
1/2 tsp brown sugar

METHOD

1. Combine the clarification ingredients in a bowl.
2. Place the cold stock in, if possible, a large pot fitted with a tap, or a large saucepan. Stir all the clarification ingredients into the stock. Bring gently to a boil. The solids will gradually solidify on top and form a crust. On no account disturb this crust. Let simmer for 1 hour.
3. If you have a pot with a tap the liquid can be removed without disturbing the crust. If you are using a saucepan gently make a hole in the crust and ladle the liquid through it into another pan over which is placed a conical strainer. The strainer should be lined with a double-thickness cheesecloth to strain the consommé and to keep it clear. The consommé should remain clear and golden in color and will gel on cooling.

BASIC METHOD FOR WHITE STOCK
1. Remove the fat and marrow from the bones and break them into small pieces for easier extraction.
2. Place the bones and meat in cold water and let them soak for 1 hour before bringing the liquid to a boil. Simmer for two hours before adding vegetables. Remove the scum as it rises and do not add vegetables until the liquid is clear. For most people it is more economical to boil a roast of meat, which can be served as a main dish, the cooking liquor will form the stock.

BASIC METHOD FOR BROWN STOCK
1. Roast bones and meat for 30 minutes to bring out the flavor and color. Then place in hot water and simmer for two hours.
2. Stir-fry the vegetables until golden brown. Drain well and add to the liquid, continue simmering for a further hour.

CHEF'S TIPS:

This consommé can be flavored with 1/4 cup (50 ml/2 fl oz) of fortified wine per 4 1/2 cups (1 liter/1 3/4 pints) – Madeira, white and red port wine or medium sherry may be used. The consommé can be garnished with diced or julienne vegetables, or with cooked vermicelli, rice or other cereals – tapioca, semolina, barley, corn kernels etc. All garnishes should be lightly cooked in separate saucepans.

Boiled Beef

Serves: 8-10
Preparation time: 30 minutes
Cooking time: 2 1/2 hours

INGREDIENTS

1 lb (450 g) brisket on the bone, salted
1 lb (450 g) thin flank
1 lb (450 g) shin beef or knuckle of veal
(All meat should be tied with string)

5 quarts (4.5 liters/8 pints) beef stock
1 carrot, peeled
1 leek
1 onion, studded with cloves
1 celery stick and one sprig of thyme, tied with a bay leaf
4 garlic cloves
1 tsp anise seeds (optional)
2 tsp salt
6 peppercorns, crushed
1 tsp brown sugar

GARNISH VEGETABLES:
1 lb (450 g) small carrots, peeled
1 lb (450 g) small turnips, peeled
1 lb (450 g) leeks, cleaned
1 lb (450 g) small potatoes, scrubbed
1 lb (450 g) celery

METHOD

1. Place meat and bones in a large stock pot or heavy-bottomed pan and cover with stock or water. Add all the vegetable flavorings and seasonings. Bring to a boil, cover and simmer for 2 1/2 hours. (For a more pronounced color you can include a peeled beet with the vegetables, or shallow fry and caramelize an onion and include this in the pot).
2. Skim frequently and remove any surplus fat floating on top. At the end of the cooking time, the meat should be a rich amber color.
3. Prepare the garnish vegetables. All the vegetables should be a uniform size, neatly trimmed and cut, if too large. Remember that smaller root vegetables are usually more attractive.
4. Cook the garnish vegetables separately in lightly salted boiling water until just tender.
5. Strain the stock and discard the vegetable flavorings.
6. Return the meat to the clear stock, add the garnish vegetables and heat through.

CHEF'S TIPS:

This is a delicious one pot meal. All the garnish vegetables are added to the gently simmered meat and the flavors combine to produce a wonderfully aromatic dish. It is the basis of all good stocks, soups and sauces. Try to use meat on the bone as it will produce a better flavor stock.

Herb and onion dumplings made from whole wheat flour and poached in some beef stock could be served or, more simply, potatoes.

Poached Beef Fondue

Serves: 4
Preparation time: 15 minutes
Cooking time: 5-10 minutes

INGREDIENTS

4 x 4-oz (100 g) fillet steaks, trimmed and cut into 1-inch (2.5 cm) cubes
4 1/2 cups (1 liter/1 3/4 pint) good beef stock

PICKLED PLUM CHUTNEY: (make in advance)
1 1/2 lb (675 g) large plums, pitted
1/2 cup (100 ml/4 fl oz) red wine
1/2 cup (100 ml/4 fl oz) wine vinegar
generous 1 cup (225 g/8 oz) sugar
1/2 tsp ground mixed spice
1/2 tsp ground black pepper
pinch of chili pepper

HORSERADISH SAUCE:
2/3 cup (150 ml/1/4 pint) strong stock
1/3 cup (100 g/4 oz) freshly grated horseradish or horseradish cream
1 tsp cornstarch
3 tbsp cream
salt and pepper
1 tsp mustard

METHOD

1. To make the plum chutney: bring all the ingredients to a boil and simmer like jam for 8 minutes. Cool and serve cold.
2. To make the horseradish sauce: boil the stock and mix in the horseradish or horseradish cream. Mix the cornstarch and cream and stir into the stock to thicken it. Cook for 4 minutes. Season to taste and remove from the heat. Add the mustard and 2 tablespoons of the strained plum chutney. Serve hot.
3. Bring the stock for the fondue to a boil and poach the meat for 8-10 minutes. Keep the temperature of the stock below boiling point as actual boiling will toughen the meat. Serve with the chutney and sauce.

CHEF'S TIPS:
Fondues are always popular and are an excellent way of cooking beef fillet. Guests poach the meat for themselves at the table on long-handled forks or skewers in a strong stock and help themselves to a variety of garnishes, pickles, chutney and sauces. Two recipes are included here but you can add your own additional dips.

Boiled Pickled Ox Tongue

Serves: 6
Preparation time: 20 minutes, plus 4-8 days for pickling and 3 hours for desalting
Cooking time: 2-3 hours

INGREDIENTS

1 ox tongue

PICKLING MIXTURE:
2 1/2 quarts (2 liters/3 1/2 pints) water
2 lb (900 g) salt
1/3 cup (25 g/1 oz) saltpeter (sodium nitrate) or curing salt
scant 1/2 cup (100 g/4 oz) brown sugar
8 peppercorns, crushed
6 juniper berries
1 sprig of thyme

PIQUANT SAUCE:
2 tbsp oil
1 medium onion, chopped
2 tbsp vinegar
2 tsp sugar
1 tbsp tomato paste
1 tbsp yeast extract
2 1/2 cups (600 ml/1 pint) beef stock or water
2 tsp cornstarch mixed with 3 tbsp cold water
1 small dill pickle, diced
1 tsp mustard
2-3 tbsp chopped parsley
salt and pepper, to taste

METHOD

1. To make the pickling mixture: place all the ingredients in a large pan and boil for 20 minutes. Let cool completely.
2. Prick the meat all over with a needle as this will allow the salt to penetrate quicker. Completely immerse the tongue (or other meat) in the pickling mixture. Put a plate and a weight, such as a large food can, on top of the meat to ensure that it sinks.
3. Chill in the fridge for 4 days in the summer and 8 days in the winter. When ready to cook, first soak the meat in cold water for 3 hours to desalt it.
4. Place the desalted meat in cold water, bring to a boil and simmer for 2-3 hours.
5. Meanwhile make the piquant sauce. Heat the oil in a saucepan and stir-fry the onion, without coloring, for 2 minutes. Add the vinegar and boil, to reduce by half. Add the sugar and let it cook until it begins to brown. Stir in the tomato paste, yeast extract and stock or water. Boil for 15 minutes and then stir in the cornstarch and water mixture to thicken. Boil for 4 more minutes, stirring, until clear. Add the dill pickle, mustard, chopped parsley and season to taste.
6. Remove the skin from the tongue and cut it into thick slices. Serve the sauce separately.

CHEF'S TIPS:
Boiled ox tongue is a very nutritious meat. It can be eaten hot or cold with vegetables or salad. The recipe for the brine in which the tongue is pickled is the same for other cuts of beef, i.e. brisket or veal and also for lamb and pork. Curing salt is available from drug stores and butchers.

This dish is delicious served with assorted vegetables and sautéed potatoes.

Beef Olives

Serves: 6
Preparation time: 25 minutes
Cooking time: 1 1/2 hours

INGREDIENTS

6 x 5-oz (150 g) sirloin or round steaks

STUFFING:
2/3 cup (150 g/5 oz) ground beef
2 1/2 cups (150 g/5 oz) fresh breadcrumbs
2 tbsp sour cream
1 egg
1 small onion, chopped
salt and black pepper
1 cup (100 g/4 oz) chopped, pitted green olives
flour, for dusting
oil, for frying

SAUCE:
2 tbsp oil
1 small onion, chopped
1 garlic clove, crushed
2 tbsp tomato paste
1 tsp yeast extract

GARNISH:
green and black olives
sprigs of parsley

METHOD

1. Flatten the steaks with a meat mallet or rolling pin so that they look like thin scallops.
2. Combine all the ingredients for the stuffing in a bowl. Divide into six balls and spread them on each scallop. Roll up tightly and tie with strings in two places to hold together securely. Dust with flour.
3. Heat a little oil in a pan, and fry the beef 'olives' for 8 minutes, until brown. Place in an earthenware dish.
4. To make the sauce: heat the oil in a saucepan and stir-fry the onion for 3 minutes. Add the garlic, tomato paste, yeast extract and 2 1/2 cups (600 ml/1 pint) water and bring to a boil. Pour the sauce over the beef olives and cover with a lid. Braise at 350°F (180°C/Gas mark 4) for 1 1/2 hours.
5. Discard the string from the beef olives. Strain the sauce and check the seasoning.
6. To serve, pour some of the strained sauce over the 'olives' and hand round the remaining sauce in a serving jug. Garnish with green and black olives and sprigs of parsley.

CHEF'S TIPS:

This dish was originally devised to make the beef go further. The beef was filled with a stuffing made with ground meat, breadcrumbs and chopped olives. For some reason the olives have been omitted from many British recipes, but in this Middle Eastern version they remain an important ingredient.

Serve with mashed potatoes enriched with egg yolks and butter. This looks attractive piped in a scroll around the serving dish, as shown in the photograph.

Roast Beef

Serves: 4-8
Cooking time: Weigh the joint in order to calculate cooking time. Allow: For rare – 15-20 minutes per 1 lb (450 g), plus 20 minutes; For medium – 25 minutes per 1 lb (450 g), plus 25 minutes; For well-done – 30 minutes per 1 lb (450 g), plus 30 minutes.

INGREDIENTS

3 lb (1.5 kg) joint of beef
1 sprig of thyme
1/4 cup (50 ml/2 fl oz) beef drippings

GRAVY:
See point 2 of Method

POPOVERS (to serve 4):
1 cup (100 g/4 oz) strong white bread flour
1/2 tsp salt
2 eggs
1 1/4 cups (300 ml/1/2 pint) milk and water mixed

METHOD

1. Place the joint, uncovered, on a trivet in a roasting pan so that the largest cut surfaces are exposed and any fat is on top. Baste occasionally, and cook at 400°F (200°C/Gas Mark 6), reducing to 350°F (180°C/Gas Mark 4) after the first 20 minutes of the calculated time. For fan ovens, refer to the manufacturer's instructions regarding lowering the cooking temperature and preheating the oven.
2. To make the gravy: collect the juices from the rested cooked joint and with the meat residues and bits of cooked bones reduce to a glaze. Add water and then boil it to reduce by a quarter. Season to taste.
3. To serve, place two slices of beef on each plate with some gravy and a popover.

POPOVERS
1. To make the batter: mix the flour and salt in a bowl and make a well in the center. Break in the eggs, add half of the milk and water mixture and beat until smooth. Stir in the remaining liquid and beat until well mixed.
2. Pour 1 teaspoon of the beef drippings into each section of the muffin pan and heat in the oven for 5 minutes.
3. Pour 1/4 cup (50 ml/2 fl oz) of the batter into each section of the pan and bake for 20 minutes at 400°F (200°C/Gas Mark 6) until they rise and are golden brown.

CHEF'S TIPS:
Serve with roast potatoes and accompanying vegetables.

The cooking times listed above are for open-roasted bone-in joints. When roasting a stuffed joint, weigh the joint after it is stuffed and calculate the cooking time.

You can use a meat thermometer to check whether the meat is cooked as required by taking the temperature towards the end of the cooking time. Insert the thermometer into the center of the joint, at the thickest point, and allow a few seconds for the temperature to stabilize. The internal temperature readings should be: Rare – about 140°F (60°C); Medium – about 160°F (70°C); Well-done – about 175°F (80°C) although, without a thermometer, you can tell the meat is cooked if the juices run out clear.

Braised Beef Colcannon

Serves: 4
Preparation time: 15 minutes
Cooking time: 1 1/2 hours

INGREDIENTS

1/4 cup (50 ml/2 fl oz) oil
1 1/2 lb (675 g) piece thick flank or chuck steak
1 celery stick, roughly chopped
1 onion, chopped
1 carrot, peeled and roughly chopped
2/3 cup (150 ml/1/4 pint) Guinness
1 sprig of thyme
1 tbsp tomato paste
1 tsp yeast extract
salt and pepper,
pinch of ground mace or nutmeg
2 tsp cornstarch mixed with 3 tbsp cold Guinness, to thicken gravy

COLCANNON CAKE:

8 oz (225 g) shredded cabbage or spinach
5 cups (150 g/5 oz) lovage leaves or 1 cup shredded celery leaves
8 oz (225 g) small potatoes, boiled, skinned and cooled
1 egg beaten
salt and freshly ground black pepper
flour, for dusting
1/4 cup (50 g/2 oz) melted butter

ROOT VEGETABLES:

2 carrots, cut in batons
2 celery sticks, cut in batons
1/2 rutabaga, cut in batons
12 button or small onions, peeled

GARNISH:

lovage leaves

METHOD

1. Heat the oil in a pan and brown the joint, all over, for 8 minutes. Transfer the meat to an ovenproof casserole dish.
2. In the same frying pan, sweat the celery, onion and carrot for 5 minutes.
3. Braise the meat in a moderate oven for 1 1/2 hours at 350°F (180°C/Gas mark 4). Turn the meat over twice during cooking. Cover the casserole with a lid after the first 20 minutes of the cooking time. After the first hour, add the vegetables to the meat with the Guinness, 2/3 cup (150 ml/1/4 pint) water, thyme, tomato paste, yeast extract, salt, pepper and the mace or nutmeg.
4. To make the sauce: strain the liquid into a saucepan and reduce it by half by boiling it quickly. Simmer for 4 minutes and stir in the cornstarch mixture to thicken.
5. For the Colcannon cake: wash the spinach three times. Drain well and cook with the lovage leaves for 4 minutes. Squeeze the mixture and chop it finely. Mash the boiled potatoes and pass through a strainer. Mix the greens and potato together. Add the egg to bind the mixture and season to taste. Divide the mixture into eight balls. Dust with flour to make handling easier and shape into small cakes, 2-inches (5 cm) in diameter and 1-inch (2.5 cm) thick. Place on a buttered cookie sheet and when ready to serve, brush with the melted butter and bake in a hot oven for 12 minutes at 400°F (200°C/Gas mark 6). Alternatively, they can be fried in shallow oil or butter on both sides until crisp and golden.
6. To perpare the root vegetables: blanch the carrots, celery, rutabaga and onions in boiling water until just tender. Arrange one thick or two thin slices of beef and two colcannon cakes on each plate. Serve with the root vegetables and garnish with a small lovage leaf.

CHEF'S TIPS:

Braising is a long, slow cooking process by which meat is cooked in liquid in a sealed dish in a moderate oven. The meat can be marinated in wine, beer or cider for extra flavor. Before braising, shallow fry the meat to brown it and to accentuate the taste. A mixture of root vegetables called a 'mirepoix' and herbs are added to the meat.

Colcannon, originally spelt 'Kol', means cabbage in German. The garnish for this braised beef consists of a mixture of equal weights of Savoy cabbage, or spinach, and potatoes. The vegetables should be boiled separately, left to cool, mixed together and reheated in a pan with butter. In this recipe, I have used the herb lovage. Lovage has a distinctive celery flavor and has always grown well in my garden.

Steamed Beef and Kidney Puddings

Serves: 8
Preparation time: 30 minutes, plus 30 minutes chilling time
Cooking time: 2 1/2-3 hours

INGREDIENTS

MEAT FILLING:
1 lb (450 g) stewing steak, diced into 1/2-inch (2.5 cm) cubes
5 oz (150 g) ox kidneys, defatted, cored and cubed
1 medium onion, chopped
1/2 cup (125 ml/4 fl oz) stock, port wine or water
2 tsp Worcestershire sauce
1 tbsp chopped fresh parsley
2 tbsp all-purpose flour
salt and black pepper

SUET CRUST PIE DOUGH:
2 cups (225 g/8 oz) self-rising flour
1 tsp salt
1 tsp baking powder (treble the amount if all-purpose flour is used)
3/4 cup (100 g/4 oz) shredded beef suet or vegetable margarine
1/2 cup (25 g/1 oz) fresh white breadcrumbs
margarine, to grease

SERVE WITH:
fresh seasonal green vegetables

METHOD

1. Put all the filling ingredients into a large bowl and stir well. The flour will help the ingredients to cohere during steaming. Chill the mixture for 30 minutes while preparing the pie dough. This standing time will allow the full flavor to develop.
2. To make the pie dough: sift the flour, salt and baking powder together in a bowl. Cut in the suet or margarine and add the breadcrumbs. Mix in about 1/2 cup (100 ml/4 fl oz) water to make a firm dough.
3. Grease eight individual heatproof bowls, each with a capacity of 2/3 cup (150 ml/1/4 pint), with margarine. Take two-thirds of the pie dough and roll it out on a floured pastry board to 1/4-inch (5 mm) thick.
4. Cut rounds of pie dough and line each dish smoothly. Use the remaining third of the pie dough to produce lids for the puddings.
5. Fill each lined dish with the meat mixture (reserve some to serve as sauce). Brush water around the rim of the dough and cover with the lids. Crimp the edges to make the lids stick firmly to the edges. Cover the puddings with waxed paper and foil to protect them against condensation.
6. Steam for 2 1/2-3 hours and serve with the reserved meat mixture and blanched green vegetables.

CHEF'S TIPS:

For best results use a steamer to prepare this dish. Food which does not come into contact with water does not lose its flavor. The steaming process, which is one of the principle methods used in Chinese cookery, has become very popular with modern cooks.

The meat mixture can be placed inside a round of suet crust pie dough folded over like a turnover and steamed without a mold in the Asian way as an alternative to the pudding bowl English version.

Stuffed Pancakes with Avocado

Serves: 4
Preparation time: 20 minutes
Cooking time: 45 minutes

INGREDIENTS

One quantity pancake batter (see page 150)

STUFFING:
2 tbsp oil
1 small onion, chopped
1 cup (225 g/8 oz) lean ground beef
1/2 green chili, deseeded and chopped
salt and pepper
1 egg

SAUCE:
1 tbsp oil
4 tomatoes, skinned, deseeded and chopped
1 tbsp tomato paste
salt and pepper
1/2 tsp sugar

GARNISH:
2 avocados, peeled and sliced
1 bunch corn salad

METHOD

1. Prepare the pancake batter, then cook eight pancakes in a 6-inch (15 cm) pancake pan, using about 3 tablespoons of batter for each pancake.
2. To make the stuffing: heat the oil in a frying pan and stir-fry the onion for 2 minutes. Add the meat and brown it for 4 minutes. Stir in 2/3 cup (150 ml/1/4 pint) water, add the chili pepper and cook the mixture for 30 minutes. Season to taste, then cool. When cold, mix in the egg.
3. Fill each pancake with a spoonful of this mixture. Place on a greased cookie sheet and warm in a moderate oven at 350°F (180°C/Gas mark 4) for 10 minutes.
4. To make the sauce: heat the oil in a saucepan and cook the tomatoes and tomato paste gently. Season to taste.
5. To serve, pour a little of the tomato sauce onto each plate and arrange two pancakes on each. Garnish with sliced avocado and corn salad.

CHEF'S TIPS:
Stuffed pancakes are a popular and economical snack dish, which can use the cheaper cuts of meat.

Steak and Kidney Pies (individual)

Serves: 4
Preparation time: 30 minutes, plus 20 minutes resting
Cooking time: 2 hours, plus 30-40 minutes baking

INGREDIENTS

FILLING:
8 oz (225 g) stewing beef, cut into 1-inch (2.5 cm) cubes
5 oz (150 g) ox kidney, defatted, cored and cubed
2 tsp all-purpose flour
1/2 tsp dried mixed herbs
pinch of mustard powder
3 tbsp oil
1 tbsp Worcestershire sauce
1 cup (225 ml/8 fl oz) Guinness
1 cup (225 ml/8 fl oz) stock or water
salt and black pepper, to taste
6 small onions, peeled and blanched in boiling water
1 cup (50 g/2 oz) sliced field or wild mushrooms

PIE DOUGH:
2 cups (225 g/8 oz) all-purpose flour
pinch of salt
pinch of dried mixed herbs
1 tsp mustard powder
1/2 cup (100 g/4 oz) margarine
beaten egg or milk, to glaze

METHOD

1. To make the filling: place the meat, kidney, flour, herbs and mustard powder in a plastic bag. Shake well to coat the meat well.
2. Heat half the oil in a heavy-bottomed saucepan or casserole. Add the meat and cook until brown on all sides. Add the Worcestershire sauce, Guinness and stock or water. Bring to a boil slowly, stirring. Season with salt and pepper to taste. Cover and cook gently on top of the stove or in a preheated oven at 350°F (180°C/Gas mark 4) for about 2 hours or until the meat is tender.
3. To make the pie dough: sift the flour into a bowl with the salt, herbs and mustard powder. Cut in the margarine and mix with 1/3-1/2 cup (75-100 ml/3-4 fl oz) water to make a soft dough. Knead until smooth on a lightly floured surface. Let stand.
4. Heat the remaining oil in a frying pan and fry the onions and mushrooms. Cook until lightly browned and remove from the pan. Stir the onions and mushrooms into the meat mixture.
5. Place in four individual 1 1/4 cup (300 ml/1/2 pint) pie pans, piling the mixture higher than the rim of the dish to prevent the pie dough shrinking during cooking.
6. Roll out the pie dough on a floured surface and cut out four lids to fit each dish and a strip the size of the edge. Moisten the rim of the dish with water and make the strips into a border on each dish. Brush with water and place the dough lids over the filling. Brush all over with egg or milk. Decorate with a few pie dough leaves and again brush with the egg glaze. Let rest for 20 minutes before baking.
7. Bake at 375°F (190°C/Gas mark 5) for 30 to 40 minutes, until the pastry is crisp and golden.

CHEF'S TIPS:

Steak and kidney pie remains a popular lunchtime dish. This classic recipe was given to me by a naval cook when I served in the Royal Navy during the Second World War. The pie can be baked in one operation if you use tender meat, but it is not as good, in my opinion, as cooking the meat like a stew before covering the pie with a pie dough lid. Individual pies look more attractive. Fresh, field or wild mushrooms provide the best flavor although, if unavailable, use small cup mushrooms. Either pie crust dough or puff pastry may be used for this dish.

Serve with green vegetables, boiled potatoes and carrots or, in winter, a purée of peas or mashed potato. If liked, garnish with some extra onions and mushrooms cooked separately.

Spanish Onions Stuffed with Saffron Beef

Serves: 6
Preparation time: 25 minutes
Cooking time: 35 minutes

INGREDIENTS

6 large onions (about 5 oz (150 g) each), peeled

STUFFING:
3 tbsp oil
1 cup (225 g/8 oz) ground lean beef
1 garlic clove, crushed
1 small green chili pepper, deseeded and chopped
2 tbsp flour
2/3 cup (150 ml/1/4 pint) Spanish red wine
1 small package of saffron
1 tsp tomato paste
3 tbsp yoghurt
1 egg, beaten
salt and pepper, to taste

SAUCE:
4 tomatoes, skinned, deseeded and chopped
salt and pepper and a little sugar

cooked rice, to serve
fresh cilantro or chervil leaves, to garnish

METHOD

1. Cut a slice off the top of each onion near the stem. Boil the onions in salted water for 15 minutes. Remove from the water, drain and cool. Squeeze each onion to remove most of the center and leave a cavity for the beef stuffing.
2. Chop the scooped-out centers of the onions.
3. Heat 2 tablespoons of the oil in a frying pan and stir-fry the chopped onion for 1 minute. Add the meat, garlic and chili pepper. When the meat is brown, after about 4 minutes, add the flour. Cook for 8 minutes then pour in the wine and add the saffron. Cook for a further 10 minutes. Stir in the tomato paste, yoghurt and egg and season to taste. Remove from the heat.
4. Fill the onions with this mixture. Place them in a braising dish. Bake for 10-15 minutes at 400°F (200°C/Gas Mark 6).
5. Heat the remaining tablespoon of oil in a saucepan and cook the tomatoes until reduced to a purée. Season to taste with salt, pepper and sugar.
6. To serve, pour the tomato sauce into a large dish. Arrange the stuffed onions in the center and surround them with a border of rice. Garnish with cilantro or chervil leaves.

CHEF'S TIPS:
The quickest way to prepare stuffed onions is to boil them for 15 minutes before stuffing them. When boiled, squeeze the onions to remove the centers and fill the onions with pre-cooked ground meat.

Beef Bourguignon

Serves: 6
Preparation time: 25 minutes
Cooking time: 1 1/2 hours

INGREDIENTS

2 lb (1 kg) stewing steak, cut into 1-inch (2.5 cm) cubes
1/2 cup (50 g/2 oz) all-purpose flour
50 ml (2 fl oz) oil
1 medium onion, diced
1 celery stick, diced
1 tbsp tomato paste
1 1/4 cups (300 ml/1/2 pint) red Burgundy wine
1 1/4 cups (300 ml/1/2 pint) beef stock or water
1 tsp yeast extract
1 sprig of thyme
2 garlic cloves, crushed
salt and black pepper
1 tsp ground mixed spice

GARNISH:
12 small onions, peeled
1 tbsp oil
1 tbsp (15 g/1/2 oz) butter
5 slices rindless bacon, diced
12 small ceps or similar mushrooms
1 tbsp chopped fresh parsley

METHOD

1. Coat the meat with the flour, shaking off any surplus.
2. Heat the oil in a flameproof casserole and brown the meat for 6 minutes. Add the onion and celery and cook for a further 5 minutes. Stir in the tomato paste, wine, stock, yeast extract, thyme and garlic. Bring to a boil, cover with a lid and simmer, over a low heat, for 1 1/2 hours, or braise in an oven at 325°F (170°C/Gas mark 3). Remove the thyme when the meat is cooked. Season the dish with salt, pepper and the mixed spice.
3. Boil the onions for 4 minutes and then drain.
4. Heat the oil and butter in a frying pan and stir-fry the bacon for 4 minutes or until cooked. Remove from the pan. In the same fat, stir-fry the mushrooms for 1 minute only.
5. Add the onions and mushrooms to the meat and heat through for 5-10 minutes. Sprinkle with the parsley.

CHEF'S TIPS:
By soaking the meat in wine for two hours prior to cooking a better flavor is produced.

Beef Bourguignon was featured daily on the menu of my father's restaurant Le Ducastaing, in Paris. Made with a good, potent red Burgundy wine, such as a Macon or a Beaune, the sauce was as delicious as the meat, judging by the number of regular customers who mopped their bread in it. For this recipe use small field mushrooms, rather than the cultivated white mushrooms, since they have a stronger flavor. As a variation you can add carrots 20 minutes prior to end of cooking time and peas with the onions and mushrooms

Serve with boiled potatoes or pasta shells.

Mexican Beef Hot Pot

Serves: 4
Preparation time: 15 minutes
Cooking time: 1 1/2 hours

INGREDIENTS

1 lb (450 g) stewing steak, diced
2 tbsp oil
1-2 tsp mild chili powder
1 tsp ground cumin
4 tbsp (25 g/1 oz) flour
4 tomatoes, skinned, deseeded and chopped
1 1/2 tsp salt
1 tbsp chopped onion
2 1/2 cups (600 ml/1 pint) beef stock or water
1 green bell pepper, chopped
8 oz (225 g) canned red kidney beans, drained
1 1/3 cups (225 g/8 oz) frozen or canned corn kernels, drained

METHOD

1. Heat the oil and brown the meat for 10 minutes. Drain off any surplus fat. Stir in the chili powder and cumin and cook over a low heat for 1 minute.
2. Stir in the flour, tomatoes, salt, onion and stock or water. Bring to a boil.
3. Transfer to a Dutch oven, cover and cook for 1 3/4 hours at 350°F (180°C/Gas mark 4).
4. Add the green bell pepper, kidney beans and corn and return to the oven for a further 15 minutes.

CHEF'S TIPS:

The French *cassoulet* consists of meat and beans cooked together in an earthenware casserole using pork, beans, sausages, duck or goose depending on the season of the year. The Spanish introduced their versions in all Latin American countries, using more spices. In this recipe red kidney beans and chili peppers are used.

Serve with boiled long grain rice.

Spicy Nut Crust for Corned Beef

Serves: 4
Preparation time: 15 minutes
Cooking time: 12-15 minutes

INGREDIENTS

1 brisket roast, cooked
1 tbsp flour

MUSTARD PASTE:
2 tbsp wholegrain mustard
1 egg, beaten

SPICY CRUST:
1 tsp Chinese five spice powder
1 tsp crushed black peppercorns
1 tsp coriander seeds
1 tbsp chopped mixed nuts

GARNISH:
2 carrots, peeled and finely grated

METHOD

1. Dust the top of the cooked meat with the flour.
2. Combine the paste ingredients in a bowl and spread over the top of the meat.
3. Combine all the crust ingredients and sprinkle over the mustard paste.
4. Bake at 400°F (200°C/Gas mark 6) for 12-15 minutes to form a crust.
5. Place the meat on a serving dish and sprinkle the grated carrots over the crust. To serve, carve the meat in thick slices.

CHEF'S TIPS:
Any kind of boiled corned meat such as brisket can be flavored with a spicy coating made up of mustard and coriander seeds, peppercorns and nuts. Any mixture of nuts can be used, such as peanuts, hazelnuts, cashews, etc. This coating is spread over the meat after it has been boiled. The meat can be served hot or cold.

Oxtail Soup or Stew

Serves: 6
Preparation time: 20 minutes
Cooking time: 2 1/2 hours

INGREDIENTS

2 lb (1 kg) oxtail, cut into small pieces with fat removed
2 carrots, peeled and thickly sliced
1 large onion, cut into quarters
1 leek, trimmed, washed and sliced crosswise
2/3 cup (150 ml/1/4 pint) red wine
1 sprig of thyme
2 garlic cloves, crushed
2 tbsp tomato paste
1 tsp yeast extract
salt and pepper
1 tbsp cornstarch mixed with 1/2 cup (100 ml/4 fl oz) water

METHOD

1. Brown the oxtail pieces in a baking dish in a hot oven at 425°F (220°C/Gas mark 7) for 20 minutes. Remove and drain the pieces well.
2. Place the oxtail pieces in a large, heavy-bottomed saucepan, cover with 2 quarts (1.7 liters/3 pints) cold water and bring to a boil. Remove the scum as it rises and after 1 hour, when the broth is clear, add the vegetables, wine, thyme, garlic, tomato paste and yeast extract. Simmer for another hour until the meat falls away from the bones.
3. Drain all the ingredients in a colander placed over a bowl. Strain the liquor for a second time, and return to the pan.
4. Separate the meat from the bones and grind it. Add to the liquor (stock).
5. Process the vegetables to a purée in a blender and add to the pan with the rest of the soup. Season to taste. Bring to a boil and stir in the cornstarch mixed with water. Stir until thickened, then continue cooking for a further 10 minutes.

CHEF'S TIPS:

Boiling an oxtail will produce a very rich stock which can be used to make soups and sauces. The soup can either be clear, like broth, or it can be thickened with oxtail meat and vegetable purée. For an even richer soup, add Madeira, port wine or medium sherry.

If a clear soup is required, use the oxtail meat for another dish, i.e. brawn. To prepare brawn, place the meat in an earthenware container with the same volume of reduced oxtail stock. Cool and chill until well set. When cold, cut into thick slices and serve with a salad.

For Oxtail Stew, simply serve the oxtail pieces on the bones with a thickened sauce made from the stock. Serve with a garnish of small onions, baby carrots, turnips and boiled potatoes that have been cooked separately.

Peppercorn Fillet Steaks

Serves: 4
Preparation time: 15 minutes
Cooking time: 15 minutes

INGREDIENTS

8 x 4-oz (100 g) fillet steaks
1 tbsp black, white or pink peppercorns, crushed
1 tbsp oil
1 tbsp (15 g/1/2 oz) butter
2 tbsp brandy
1/2 cup (100 ml/4 fl oz) white port wine
1/2 cup (100 ml/4 fl oz) beef stock
2 tbsp green peppercorns
2 tbsp brine (optional)
salt and pepper
1/2 cup (100 ml/4 fl oz) heavy cream

SERVE WITH:
4 slices of any type of rustic bread, toasted

GARNISH:
string beans, thinly sliced

METHOD

1. Coat the steaks with the crushed peppercorns.
2. Heat the oil and butter and fry the steaks as required – rare, medium or well-done.
3. When the steaks are cooked, add the brandy and set alight. Remove the steaks and keep warm.
4. In the same pan, add the port wine, stock, green peppercorns and brine, if using the bottled kind, and boil for 8 minutes to concentrate the sauce. Season to taste and stir in the heavy cream.
5. To serve, pour some sauce onto the serving plates and place a slice of the toasted rustic bread on each plate also. Place the steaks on top of the bread and sauce.

CHEF'S TIPS:
Make your choice from black, white and pink peppercorns for this recipe. For green peppercorns, either use fresh or those in bottles preserved in brine.

Serve with snow peas.

ALL ABOUT PORK

Introduction

When I was young, my main meal often consisted of pork in some form or other, simply because it was the cheapest food available. Lard, called saindoux in French, spread on thick slices of country bread was a snack we children relished. Black and white pudding with mashed potatoes or pig's trotters, in a sharp vinaigrette, were popular tea-time dishes.

The 'cottage pig' sustained much of rural Britain and Europe until the Industrial Revolution. It was common for a pig to be kept in the cottage garden, fed on kitchen scraps and fattened on windfall apples from the nearby orchards. The pig was cheap to keep and ready for slaughter at Christmas. All parts of the pig can be used for food – head, trotters, flesh, variety meats and fat for lard – a truly economic investment.

In Britain, roast pork with crackling is a popular Sunday roast, in France, we prefer to remove the rind, using it to make a stock. The French prefer their roasts to be completely defatted and pot-roasted with vegetables and served with a sauce made from a wine or vinegar base. Various parts of the pig feature as appetizers in France – rillettes, rillons, chitterlings, known as andouille or andouilette, black pudding flavoured with rum, and herby sausages made from a mixture of pork, chicken and venison – and they are all considered to be gourmet foods. Chinese pork dishes have become very popular in the West – spare ribs in sweet and sour sauce and pork dumplings are in great demand. The Chinese venerate the pig, as the Indians do the cow, the Chinese; however, are more than happy to eat pork.

Pigs thrive best in temperate climates and are bred in huge numbers in the United States, Canada and Russia, as well as in most European countries. Muslims and Jews are forbidden from eating pork, or products derived from the pig, on religious grounds. The majority of pigs are still marketed in the winter and, although pork is now available all year round, pork dishes tend to feature on menus in the winter, to be replaced by ham and bacon dishes in the summer months.

QUALITY SIGNS
The carcass should be compact, straight-sided with a thickly fleshed loin. The shanks should be short and the legs plump and smooth, the shoulder should blend harmoniously with the rest of the body. The fat should be less than 1/2-inch (1 cm) thick, depending upon age and race. The flesh should be bright pink and fine textured.

The most popular cuts are the tenderloin, loin, chops and leg. The belly is best used for bacon slices or spare ribs. Pig's trotters are considered gourmet food. Blood sausages, known as black puddings, and German salami are much prized by lovers of big breakfasts.

Pork can be stored for three days under refrigeration and can be frozen for up to a year. When preserved in salt or brine, i.e. for bacon or ham production, it can be kept for a year providing that it has also been smoked.

Quality ham is pickled using herbs, spices, sugar, honey, molasses and other sweeteners. Sodium nitrate is used as a preservative. The curing process can take as long as one month, with repeated doses of salt being added until the ham becomes saturated. Sodium nitrate is responsible for giving and maintaining the characteristic dark or bright pink color of ham.

In Britain, the Yorkshire or Suffolk smoked cured ham has the sweetest flavor and is of the highest quality. American Virginia hams are cured in hickory smoke. The Italian ham from Parma is often served as an appetizer with melon or fresh figs. The Jambon des Ardennes from France and Belgium and the Prague hams from the Czech Republic are also famous for their distinctive taste. The pigs from which Italian Bologna ham is produced, are fed on chestnuts and it is this that accounts for the high quality of the ham. The quality of pork and bacon depends, as does the quality of all meat, upon the way in which the animals are bred and fed and the ways in which the meat is processed.

RECOMMENDED PORK ROASTING AND COOKING TIMES

- When purchasing a pork roast allow 4-6 oz (100-175g) per person for a boneless rolled roast or 8-12 oz (225-350 g) per person on the bone.
- Ensure that the meat is thoroughly defrosted in the refrigerator before cooking. Roasting meat from frozen is not recommended.
- Position the shelves in the oven so that the meat is in the center.
- Preheat the oven to 350°F (180°C/Gas mark 4).
- Weigh the roast in order to calculate the cooking time. Allow:

FOR MEDIUM	– 30 minutes per 1 lb (450 g), plus 30 minutes
FOR WELL-DONE	– 35 minutes per 1 lb (450 g), plus 35 minutes

Timings are for bone in and boneless joints open roasted. When roasting a stuffed joint, weigh the roast with the stuffing to calculate the appropriate cooking time.

Place the joint, uncovered, on a trivet in a roasting pan. Position the meat so that the largest cut surfaces are exposed and any fat is on the top, in this way the roast will be basted automatically. Cook in a preheated oven for the calculated time.

An alternative or additional method of checking whether or not the meat is cooked is to insert a meat thermometer into the center of the roast at the thickest part. Take the temperature towards the end of the cooking time. The temperature should read approximately 170-175°F (75-80°C) for Medium and approximately 175-185°F (80-85°C) for Well-done. Once cooked, let roast to stand for 10 minutes before carving.

For good pork crackling, score the rind well (many supermarket joints are already prepared in this way). Alternatively have your butcher do it for you. Dry the surfaces and then brush them with oil and rub in a little salt. Do not baste the roast while roasting.

The shape of the roast and the design of your oven can affect cooking, therefore, slight adjustments may be needed to achieve the degree of cooking preferred.

PORK BUTCHERY

Modern dissection methods of butchery are ideal for producing leaner cuts of meats to satisfy customers demand for less fat in pork. The techniques involve the production of boneless cuts from whole sides of pork and provide a number of options for cutting a combination of steaks and roasts. Seaming out individual muscles from the shoulder and the leg enables a smaller diameter to be achieved. Excess rind is trimmed so that none is included within the joint.

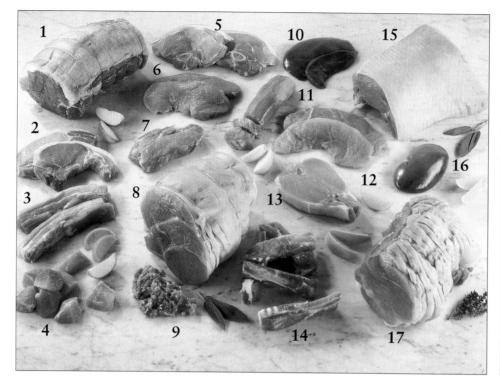

British Pork Retail Cuts

1. Neck end
2. Loin chop
3. Belly slice
4. Cubes
5. Chump chop
6. Leg steak
7. Shoulder steak
8. Leg
9. Mince
10. Liver
11. Fillet
12. Escalope
13. Double loin steak
14. Spare rib
15. Loin
16. Kidney
17. Shoulder

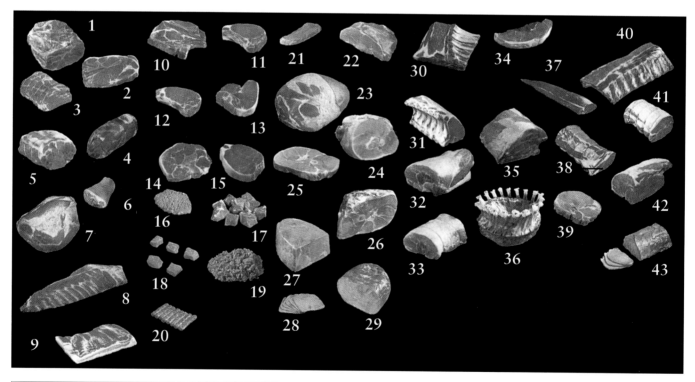

American Pork Retail Cuts

1 Blade roast	6 Smoked hocks	13 Loin chop	20 Sausage links	25 Smoked ham, center slice	29 Boneless smoked ham	34 Sirloin cutlet	39 Smoked loin chop
2 Blade steak	7 Smoked picnic	14 Sirloin chop	21 Leg cutlet	26 Smoked ham, rump portion	30 Country-style ribs	35 Blade roast	40 Back ribs
3 Boneless blade roast	8 Spareribs	15 Butterfly chop	22 Top leg	27 Canned ham	31 Center rib roast	36 Crown roast	41 Top loin roast
4 Smoked shoulder roll	9 Sliced bacon	16 Cubed steak	23 Smoked ham	28 Sliced ham	32 Sirloin roast	37 Tenderloin	42 Center loin roast
5 Boneless arm picnic roast	10 Blade chop	17 Pork pieces	24 Smoked ham, shank portion		33 Boneless sirloin roast	38 Boneless blade roast	43 Canadian-style bacon
	11 Rib chop	18 Cubes for kebabs					
	12 Top loin chop	19 Ground pork					

Roast Loin of Pork with Grapefruit and Cointreau Sauce

Serves: 4
Preparation time: 15 minutes
Cooking time: 45 minutes

INGREDIENTS

1 1/2 lb (675 g) pork loin roast boned and defatted
1 tsp ground ginger
salt and pepper
2 tbsp oil

SAUCE:
1 medium onion, roughly chopped
1 carrot, roughly chopped
1 celery stick, roughly chopped
1 1/4 cups (300 ml/1/2 pint) water or stock made
      from bones and defatted rind
juice of 1 grapefruit
1 tsp wine vinegar
3 mint leaves, chopped
1/4 cup (50 ml /2 fl oz) medium sherry
1 tsp honey
1 tbsp Cointreau or other orange liqueur
1 tsp cornstarch blended with 3 tbsp of water
1 tsp tomato paste

GARNISH:
8 oz (225 g) raw spinach leaves
2 grapefruit, in segments
julienne strips of 2 grapefuit peels, blanched

METHOD

1. Sprinkle salt, pepper and ground ginger over the roast. Heat the oil in a large shallow pan and fry the meat to seal it, until brown on all sides. Remove the pork from the pan and place in a roasting pan on a trivet of bones with the rind, carrot, onion and celery. Roast for 20 minutes at 400°F (200°C/ Gas mark 6).
2. Pour off some of the melted fat and add the stock or water. Cover with a lid, reduce the heat to 350°F (180°C/Gas mark 4) and cook for a further 20 minutes. During the cooking time baste the roast with the grapefruit juice, continue cooking, then turn it over and baste again.
3. Remove the roast from the pan and place the pan on the stove top to finish the sauce. Remove any surplus fat and add the vinegar and mint, sherry, Cointreau and honey. Stir the cornstarch and water together in a cup with the tomato paste. Pour this mixture into the gravy and boil for 4 minutes to clear the starch. Season to taste and strain.
4. Arrange slices of pork on plates over a pool of sauce. Garnish with the spinach leaves, grapefruit segments and strips of blanched grapefruit peels.

CHEF'S TIPS:

For this recipe the rind should be cut from the roast of pork and most of the fat removed. A thin covering of fat should be retained since this will prevent the roast from becoming too dry when roasted. The meat can be eaten hot with a light orange liqueur flavored gravy or cold with the same sauce that will become like jelly when it cools. The orange flavor of the sauce can be enhanced by the addition of a few mint leaves.

Roast Loin of Pork with Watercress Sauce

Serves: 6
Preparation time: 15 minutes
Cooking time: 45 minutes-1 hour

INGREDIENTS

2 1/2 lb (1.15 kg) loin of pork
2 tbsp melted butter

GRAVY SAUCE:
1 lb (450 g) broken bones
4 oz (100 g) piece of rind, defatted
1 carrot, roughly chopped
1 stick of celery, roughly chopped
salt and pepper, to season

WATERCRESS SAUCE:
2 large apples, peeled, cored and sliced
8 watercress leaves
1 tsp sugar
1 tsp cornstarch mixed with 2 tbsp water

GARNISH:
a little heavy cream
6 roses, made from tomato skins
sprigs of watercress

METHOD

1. Place the bones, rind and vegetables in a roasting pan to act as a trivet on which to place the roast. Brush the meat with the melted butter and roast for between 45 minutes and 1 hour, at 400°F (200°C/Gas mark 6). After 30 minutes, remove most of the melted fat. Baste with a cup of water occasionally for the rest of the cooking time.
2. Remove the roast from the oven and keep warm. To prepare the gravy: place the roasting pan on top of the stove and boil the liquid for 10 minutes. Strain and season the gravy.
3. Boil the apples and watercress leaves with 2 tablespoons of water until soft. Add the sugar and pass through a sieve or process in a blender. Reboil and thicken the purée with the cornstarch mixture. Cook for 4 minutes, stirring.
4. Place thin slices of pork on each plate with a pool of the watercress sauce. Serve the gravy separately. Garnish the sauce with piped cream that can be marbled with the point of a knife. For extra garnish, place a small bunch of watercress and a tomato rose on the side of each plate.

CHEF'S TIPS:

This roast may be cooked with or without the rind. If the rind is retained it should be well scored. If you prefer to remove the rind, use it with the bones as a trivet on which to cook the roast; cooked in this way it will form an excellent base for a strong gravy or sauce. Take care to remove the surplus fat from the roasting pan as it melts from the meat during cooking. Once the roast has been cooked most of the fat should be discarded, leaving the meat juices which can be reduced to make the gravy.

The watercress sauce is extremely simple to prepare and is a delicious accompaniment for the pork.

Serve with roast potatoes and seasonal vegetables.

Pork Tenderloin Balmoral

Serves: 4
Preparation time: 15 minutes,
plus 1 1/2 hours standing time
Cooking time: 15 minutes

INGREDIENTS

1 lb (450 g) pork tenderloin
1 tbsp oil
2 tbsp (25 g/1 oz) butter

BRIOCHE DOUGH:
2 1/4 cups (250 g/9 oz) strong plain flour
pinch of salt
1/4 cup (15 g/1/2 oz) yeast
1 tbsp (7 g/1/4 oz) superfine sugar
4 tbsp warm milk
2 eggs, beaten
1/2 cup (100 g/4 oz) softened butter

DUXELLE:
4 shallots, finely chopped
2 cups (100 g/4 oz) finely chopped mixed wild mushrooms
2 cups (225 g/8 oz) fine oatmeal
2 tbsp Scotch whisky
1 tsp chopped parsley
salt and pepper, to taste

PARSLEY CREPES:
1 egg
scant 1 cup (200 ml/7 fl oz) milk
1 cup (100 g/4 oz) all-purpose flour
1 tsp chopped parsley
pinch of salt
oil, for frying

SAUCE:
1/2 cup (100 ml/4 fl oz) medium-dry apple cider or apple juice
2 tbsp (25 g/1 oz) butter

GARNISH:
chanterelle mushrooms

METHOD

1. Fry the tenderloin in the hot oil and butter to seal (reserve the juices).
2. To make the brioche dough: add the salt to the flour. Let the yeast and sugar dissolve in the warm milk. Make a well in the center of the flour and pour the milk mixture and beaten eggs into it. Knead all the ingredients together for about 5 minutes. Then add the softened butter and knead again until the mixture forms a smooth paste. Set aside in a cool place for 1 hour.
3. To make the duxelle: lightly fry the shallots and mushrooms (reserve the trimmings). Remove from the heat and add the oatmeal. Mix well so that the juices are absorbed by the oatmeal. Add the whisky, parsley and seasoning. Make the mixture into a tight paste, adding a little water, if necessary.
4. To make the crêpes: mix the egg and milk together. Slowly fold in the flour and add the parsley. Make sure that the mixture remains thin and runny. Heat oil in a large frying pan, pour in a quarter of the crêpe mixture, cook for a few minutes until golden, turn and cook on the other side for a further 2 minutes. Remove from the pan and set aside on a plate to cool. Cook 3 further crêpes, using all the batter.
5. Spread the pork tenderloin with the duxelle paste. Wrap the coated tenderloin with the parsley crêpes, overlapping them to enclose the tenderloin completely. Let rest until the brioche is ready.
6. To make the sauce: fry the trimmings from the mushrooms and shallots in the juices left from sealing the tenderloin. Add the cider or apple juice and boil to reduce by half. Melt the butter in the sauce and mix together.
7. Roll out the brioche to 1/4-inch (5 mm) thick. Cover the prepared tenderloin and seal the ends. Let rest for 30 minutes.
8. Cook the pork in brioche dough at 400°F (200°C/Gas mark 6) for 15 minutes or until golden brown. Serve with the sauce and garnish with chanterelle mushrooms.

CHEF'S TIPS:
This dish could be served for a special dinner party. The pork is stuffed with mushrooms and herbs and is wrapped in brioche dough. It looks spectacular and tastes delicious. Serve with a simple garnish of seakale or spinach, baby leeks or, perhaps, a light purée of turnips and cream.

Dim Sum

Serves: 4
Preparation time: 30 minutes
Cooking time: 45 minutes

INGREDIENTS

1 cup (225 g/8 oz) lean pork, cut into small 1-inch (2.5 cm)
    cubes
2 tbsp oil
1/2 cup (100 g/4 oz) diced lean bacon
1 medium onion, chopped
1 tbsp flour
salt and pepper
1/2 cup (100 g/4 oz) beans in tomato sauce

PIE DOUGH:
4 cups (450 g/1 lb) self-rising flour
1 tsp salt
2/3 cup (150 g/5 oz) margarine
1 egg

METHOD

1. Heat the oil in a pan and stir-fry the pork, bacon and onion for 5 minutes. Sprinkle the flour and seasoning over the meat. Add 2/3 cup (150 ml/1/4 pint) water and simmer for 15 minutes. Stir in the beans in tomato sauce (canned beans are perfectly suitable for this dish). Drain away any surplus sauce and leave the mixture to cool completely.
2. To prepare the pie dough: place the flour and salt in a bowl and cut in the margarine until the mixture has the consistency of breadcrumbs. Bind the mixture with the egg and 3 tablespoons cold water to form a dough.
3. Roll the pie dough out on a floured board to a thickness of 1/4-inch (5 mm). Cut out rounds 3-inch (7.5 cm) in diameter.
4. Place a spoonful of meat mixture in the center of each round. Brush the edges with water and fold over. Crimp the edges. Put each half moon-shaped pie on a piece of foil and steam them for 45 minutes.

CHEF'S TIPS:
This dish is popular with children and the elderly because it is easy to eat and is as tasty cold as it is hot.

Serve with stir-fried or steamed vegetables.

Pork and Apple Fritters

Serves: 4
Preparation time: 15 minutes
Cooking time: 12 minutes

INGREDIENTS

1 lb (450 g) lean ground pork
1 egg, beaten
1 small onion, chopped
1 large crisp apple, peeled, cored and cut into rings
a little flour
oil, for frying

BATTER:
1 cup (100 g/4 oz) all-purpose flour
2 eggs, beaten
1 1/4 cups (300 ml/1/2 pint) water and milk, mixed
pinch of salt
oil, for deep frying

GRAVY:
1 1/4 cups (300 ml/1/2 pint) beef stock
1 tbsp tomato paste
salt and pepper
1 tsp sugar
1 tsp cornstarch mixed with 3 tbsp water

METHOD

1. Combine the ground pork, beaten egg and chopped onion in a bowl. Divide the mixture into four or eight small balls and shape them into 1/2-inch (1 cm) thick burgers.
2. To make the gravy: boil the stock with the tomato paste. Season to taste with the salt, pepper and sugar. Thicken with the cornstarch and water. Cook for a further 4 minutes.
3. To prepare the batter: combine the flour, eggs and milk in a bowl and lightly beat. Season with salt.
4. Coat the apple rings in flour and then batter and fry in oil for 4 minutes until golden. Drain well.
5. Heat a little oil in a pan and fry the pork burgers for 4 minutes on each side.
6. Serve the burgers, topped with the apple fritters, surrounded by a pool of gravy.

CHEF'S TIPS:
These pork burgers are just the thing to appeal to children who are fussy eaters. For a more exotic Chinese flavor, add a few drops of soy sauce, some grated ginger root and a clove of garlic.

Serve with French fries.

Pork Chops in Apple Juice

Serves: 4
Preparation time: 10 minutes
Cooking time: 1 1/2 hours

INGREDIENTS

4 pork chops, trimmed of excess fat
3 tbsp oil
1 medium onion, thinly sliced
6 tbsp (40g /1 1/2 oz) all-purpose flour
1 1/4 cups (300 ml/1/2 pint) chicken stock
scant 1 cup (200 ml/7 fl oz) pure apple juice
1 tsp sage
1/2 tsp salt
1/4 tsp citrus pepper
1/4 tsp ground ginger
2 apples, cored and sliced
2 tbsp Calvados (optional)
2 tbsp sour cream (optional)

METHOD

1. Heat the oil in a frying pan, brown the chops and transfer to a baking dish using a perforated spoon.
2. Add the onion to the oil remaining in the pan and fry until softened, but not brown. Stir in the flour and cook for 1 minute. Gradually stir in the stock and apple juice and bring to a boil, stirring continually. Add the herbs and seasoning to the sauce and pour it over the chops.
3. Cover the dish and cook in the oven at 350°F (180°C/Gas mark 4) for 1 1/2 hours, or until the meat is tender. For the last 20 minutes, add the apple slices and Calvados, if using. If sour cream is to be added, stir this into the sauce before serving. Reheat, but don't boil.

CHEF'S TIPS:

Pork and apple are a popular combination. This dish is very typical of Normandy cuisine utilizing all the best from that region. A little sour cream may be stirred into the sauce at the end, but this is optional.

The pork chops used in this recipe are cut from the loin still on the bone. The chops can be trimmed of rind and fat and the bone may be removed.

A number of herbs are used in this dish. It is rather ironic that when supermarkets have increased their ranges of dried herbs and have introduced many fresh ones, most people still only use a very few herbs in their day to day cooking. Herbs are divided into pot-herbs and sweet or aromatic herbs. These are described as follows:

Pot herbs: parsley, purslane, tarragon, fennel, borage, dill, chervil, horseradish, marigold and chives. Sweet herbs: thyme, sage, savory, mint, marjoram, basil, rosemary and lavender.

Modern usage has added all manner of vegetables to the list of herbs, including sorrel and chives. It has become increasingly popular to grow your own herbs and this is easily done in the garden or in pots on the kitchen window sill. It is best to pick herbs on a dry day just as they are about to flower. The roots should be cut off and the herbs washed before use.

Poached Pork Scallop Roulades

Serves: 4
Preparation time: 15 minutes
Cooking time: 40 minutes

INGREDIENTS

4 x 6-oz (175 g) pork scallops, flattened with a rolling pin
    or meat mallet
2 tbsp oil

STUFFING:
1 cup (225 g/8 oz) sausage meat
1 small onion, chopped
1 egg, beaten
2 tbsp heavy cream
2 tbsp fresh breadcrumbs
1 tsp sage
salt and pepper

SAUCE:
8 oz (225 g) mushrooms, sliced
sprig of thyme
1 1/4 cups (300 ml/1/2 pint) stock
1 pork bouillon cube
1 tsp tomato paste

SERVE WITH:
8 small carrots, turned
8 small potatoes, turned
2 sticks of celery, cut slantwise

METHOD

1. Make sure that the scallops have been flattened to an area as wide as your hand.
2. Combine the ingredients for the stuffing in a bowl and mix well. Divide it into four dumplings and place one in the center of each of the scallops. Roll the meat up and secure with strings or skewers.
3. Heat the oil in a shallow pan and cook the stuffed pork for 6 minutes until brown all round. Add the mushrooms and thyme and cook for a further minute. Transfer the meat and mushrooms to a baking dish.
4. Strengthen the stock with a bouillon cube and the tomato paste and pour over the meat. Put a lid on the dish and braise for 40 minutes at 350°F (180°C/Gas mark 4).
5. Cook the vegetables for 10 minutes until just tender.
6. Remove the baking dish from the oven, pour the sauce from the dish into a small saucepan. Season to taste and boil for 3 minutes.
7. Serve the scallops on a pool of the mushroom sauce. Serve with the vegetables.

CHEF'S TIPS:

Pork is a popular meat in Polish cuisine and it is used extensively in stews. This recipe is made in the same way as beef olives, but a scallop of pork is stuffed with sausage meat and onions flavored with fresh sage.

Alternatively you can serve the scallops with boiled white cabbage with caraway seeds or juniper berries. Celery leaves can be used to garnish and flavor the meat.

Pork Loin Steak with Calvados Sauce

Serves: 2
Preparation time: 15 minutes
Cooking time: 35 minutes

INGREDIENTS

2 x 6-oz (175 g) pork loin steaks
2 tbsp oil and butter, mixed

SAUCE:
2 tbsp Calvados or apple brandy
1 1/4 cups (300 ml/1/2 pint) stock
1 tsp yeast extract
3 tbsp heavy cream
salt and pepper

GARNISH:
2 Cox's apples, cored, peeled and quartered
2 tbsp butter

CROQUETTE POTATOES:
1 lb (450 g) potatoes
2 tbsp (25 g/1 oz) butter
salt and pepper
2 tbsp flour
1 egg, beaten, plus 1 egg yolk
6 tbsp bread crumbs
oil, for frying

METHOD

1. Heat the oil and butter in a frying pan and fry the pork steaks for 12 minutes. Remove the meat from the pan, pour away some of the fat. Boil the remaining juices for 2 minutes to reduce to a glaze. Add the brandy, stock, and yeast extract and boil to reduce to half its volume. Stir in the cream and season.
2. In a clean pan heat the butter and gently cook the apples for about 6 minutes, until soft.
3. Meanwhile, boil the potatoes, drain them well and mash them. Pass the mashed potato through a strainer or ricer to avoid lumps. Mix the potato purée with the egg yolk and butter in a bowl. Season and shape into balls. Roll the balls into cork shapes. Coat in flour, dip in the beaten egg and roll in the breadcrumbs.
4. Shallow fry in hot oil until golden brown. Drain well.
5. Serve the pork with a little pool of the sauce and some of the sautéed apples. Serve the croquette potatoes separately.

CHEF'S TIPS:

This is a typical Normandy dish using Calvados or apple brandy, cream and a garnish of apple segments cooked in butter, and it is very popular in France.

The croquette potatoes complement this rich pork dish very well.

Pork Casserole with Fennel and Rice

Serves: 4
Preparation time: 15 minutes
Cooking time: 45 minutes

INGREDIENTS

2 tbsp oil for cooking
1 1/2 lb (675 g) pork, cubed
1 red onion, chopped
1 fennel bulb, sliced
1 tbsp flour
1 tsp turmeric
2 1/2 cups (600 ml/1 pint) stock
1 tbsp tomato paste
2/3 cup (150 ml/1/4 pint) fresh pineapple juice
1 garlic clove, chopped
salt and pepper

GARNISH:
generous 1 cup (225 g /8 oz) long grain or mixed wild rice,
    boiled
2 tbsp (25 g/1 oz) butter, to flavor the cooked rice

METHOD

1. Heat the oil in a flameproof casserole dish and stir-fry the meat, onions and fennel for 5 minutes. Sprinkle over the flour and the turmeric, stir well and add the stock, tomato paste and pineapple juice. Mix in the garlic and seasoning. Simmer over a low heat for 45 minutes until the meat is tender.
2. Serve the pork on a bed of rice.

CHEF'S TIPS:

A plain flameproof casserole is a useful addition to any kitchen if you prefer to cook casseroles and stews in the oven. The advantage of a cast iron casserole, which my grandmother used in her farm kitchen, is that they can be used equally well on top of the stove to boil or stew, as they can be in the oven to bake. Earthenware casseroles were well able to stand the lower heat of ashes when dishes like Tagines, popular in Arab cuisine, were cooked in the embers of the fire. Today there are many different casserole dishes available, including glass ones which can resist extremely high temperatures, but they can be very expensive.

Accompany with side dishes of mango chutney, sliced banana, shredded coconut, natural yoghurt, golden raisins and popadums. A vegetable and potato curry could also be served.

Hungarian Pork Galuska

Serves: 4
Preparation time: 20 minutes
Cooking time: 30 minutes

INGREDIENTS

8 oz (225 g) smoked pork sausages, thinly sliced
1/4 cup (50g/2oz) butter, melted
2 tbsp oil
2 1/2 lb (1.15 kg) small even-sized potatoes, peeled
2/3 cup (150 ml/1/4 pint) heavy cream
4 eggs, hard-cooked and sliced
6 tomatoes, skinned, deseeded and sliced
1/4 tsp paprika pepper
1/4 tsp sage
1 garlic clove, crushed
salt and pepper
1 cup (50 g/2 oz) fresh breadcrumbs mixed with
    1 tsp ground sage

GARNISH:
tomatoes, peeled and sliced

METHOD

1. Brush a casserole dish with some of the butter and oil. Layer the potatoes, cream, eggs, sausages and half the tomatoes using the butter and oil mixture to brush
. each layer. Mix together the paprika, sage, garlic and salt and pepper, and sprinkle over.
2. Cover the dish with the breadcrumb mixture and pour over the remaining butter and oil. Bake, uncovered, at 350°F (180°C/Gas mark 4) for 30 minutes.
3. Garnish with peeled sliced tomatoes.

CHEF'S TIPS:

A goulash is a stew flavored with paprika, one of the sweet varieties of the capsicum family. Paprika has a characteristically sweet taste and smell and a rich dark red color. There are a number of different grades of paprika. The milder forms are used as colorants in sauces, while the more pungent varieties are used in curries and Hungarian meat and tomato stews.

Potatoes are usually served with a Hungarian stew, although fancy-shaped pasta would make an equally good accompaniment.

Pork Tenderloin with a Medley of Vegetables

Serves: 4
Preparation time: 12 minutes
Cooking time: 40 minutes

INGREDIENTS

1 lb (450 g) pork tenderloin, trimmed and cubed
2 tsp oil
1 garlic clove, crushed
8 small onions, peeled
1 lb (450 g) potatoes, peeled and cubed
2 1/4 cups (125 g /4 oz) button mushrooms
2 small zucchini, cut into julienne strips
1 medium green bell pepper, deseeded and cut into strips
1 x 14-oz (400 g) can chopped tomatoes
2/3 cup (150 ml/1/4 pint) beef stock
1 tsp dried sage
salt and black pepper

GARNISH:
2 plums, sliced
basil leaves

METHOD

1. Heat the oil in a large frying pan and gently fry the garlic and onions for 1 minute. Add the pork and cook until slightly browned.
2. Add the remaining ingredients and season well.
3. Bring to a boil, cover and simmer for 40-45 minutes until the meat is cooked and the vegetables are tender. Remove the lid for the last 5 minutes of the cooking time, if necessary, to let the sauce reduce and thicken slightly.
4. Garnish with the plum slices and basil leaves.

CHEF'S TIPS:

English Sage: leaves of *Salvia officinalis*. The flavor of fresh sage is best, but dried sage does keep well. The English sage is not as strong as Dalmatian sage, and for this reason it blends better with other herbs. Sage is used in many kinds of sausages and salami. It is also used to flavor the wood employed in various smoking processes. Fish sauces and salad dressings benefit from the addition of sage.

Dalmatian Sage: is a wild species of herb that contains thujone. It has a strong, pungent flavor with a peculiar sweetness and astringency. Like English sage, it is used in lamb, pork and veal dishes and with certain forcemeats and stuffings.

Serve with a fresh green vegetable.

Sweet and Sour Pork from Beijing

Serves: 4
Preparation time: 15 minutes,
plus 30 minutes marinating
Cooking time: 30 minutes

INGREDIENTS

1 lb (450 g) pork tenderloin, cubed

MARINADE:
2 tbsp sherry
1 tbsp soy sauce
1/4 tsp sugar
1/4-inch (5 mm) piece fresh ginger root, grated
salt and pepper

3 tbsp oil
4 celery sticks, sliced
1 red bell pepper, deseeded and diced
8 scallions, cut into 2-inch (5 cm) pieces
1/4 cucumber, cut into wedges
1 1/3 cups (225 g/8 oz) canned pineapple chunks with juice
1/4 cup (50 g /2 oz) cornstarch
1/4 cup (50 ml/2 fl oz) vinegar
1/2 cup (100 ml/4 fl oz) sweet white wine
1 tbsp brown sugar
oil, for deep frying

8 oz (225 g) fried noodles, to serve

METHOD

1. Mix the pork with the sherry, soy sauce, sugar and ginger. Add pepper to taste and mix well. Marinate for 30 minutes.
2. Heat the oil in a frying pan and fry the vegetables until soft, but not brown. Drain the pineapple chunks, reserving the juice, and add them to the pan. Stir-fry for 2 minutes.
3. Mix 2 tablespoons of the cornstarch with the vinegar and stir into the pan with the pineapple juice, wine and brown sugar. Season and simmer for 2 minutes, stirring continually.
4. Heat the oil for deep frying. Remove the pork from the marinade and add the marinade to the sauce.
5. Coat the pork in the remaining cornstarch and deep-fry it in the hot oil. Remove the meat and drain well. Serve the pork on a bed of fried noodles with the sauce poured over it.

CHEF'S TIPS:
The secret of successful fried noodles is simple: boil the noodles for 3 minutes, drain, pat dry and spread on a cloth, then deep fry the noodles a handful at a time. Rice noodles could also be used for this recipe, they only need to be soaked in water and drained before being fried. Both sorts of noodles (i.e. egg and rice) are ideal served with Chinese stir-fried dishes.

A side dish of bean sprouts and diced papaya or mango would go well with this dish.

Broiled Stuffed Pork Chops with Peppercorn Sauce

Serves: 2
Preparation time: 15 minutes
Cooking time: 15 minutes

INGREDIENTS
2 x 8-oz (225 g) pork rib chops
1 tbsp oil

STUFFING:
1/2 cup (100 g/4 oz) raw lean ground ham or lean bacon
1 egg, beaten
1 carrot, peeled and grated
1/4 cup (50 ml/2 fl oz) heavy cream
3 basil leaves, chopped
salt and pepper, to taste, with a pinch of grated nutmeg or mace

SAUCE:
2/3 cup (150 ml/1/4 pint) brown sauce or gravy (see page 29)
1 tbsp sherry
1 tbsp light cream
3 pink and 3 black peppercorns (in brine)

GARNISH:
carrots, turned
scallions

METHOD
1. To make the ham mousse: mix the stuffing ingredients together in a bowl. Check seasoning.
2. Make a slit pocket on the side of each pork rib chop and pipe the ham mousse into it. Press the chop lightly, to close the opening.
3. Brush the chops with the oil and broil them for 6 minutes on each side.
4. To make the sauce: pour the sherry and cream into the brown sauce and bring to a boil. Flavor with the peppercorns.
5. Cut each chop into three slices, vertically. Pour a pool of sauce onto each plate, place the chop slices in the center of the sauce in the shape of a fan and garnish with the turned carrots and scallions.

CHEF'S TIPS:
A pork chop stuffed with a ham mousse and served with a peppery sauce is an unusual, but delicious, dish. Remember that it is possible to buy green and pink peppercorns, as well as the more familiar black and white ones. Each type of peppercorn has its own distinctive flavor. If using those canned in brine when making a sauce, the liquid from the can should be added to the sauce.

Scallions look attractive if the ends are shredded, then left in iced cold water. The ends will curl, to look like brushes.

Stuffed Pork Tenderloin with Black Olive Sauce

Serves: 4
Preparation time: 15 minutes
Cooking time: 16-20 minutes

INGREDIENTS
1 1/2 lb (675 g) pork tenderloin, cut into 4 scallops
2 tbsp oil
string, to tie scallops

STUFFING:
1/2 cup (100 g /4 oz) lean ground pork
1/2 cup (50 g /2 oz) pitted and chopped black olives
1 tbsp pickled capers
2 anchovy tenderloins, chopped
1 small onion, chopped
salt and pepper
1 egg, beaten

SAUCE:
2 tbsp medium sweet vermouth
1 1/4 cups (300 ml/1/2 pint) brown sauce or gravy (see page 29)

GARNISH:
12 black olives, pitted
4 green cabbage leaves, blanched, refreshed and patted dry

METHOD
1. Butterfly the 4 thick scallops to obtain wider scallops.
2. Combine all the stuffing ingredients in a bowl and divide into four balls. Place one ball in the center of each of the scallops and tie with strings, as for Beef Olives (see page 50).
3. Heat the oil in a pan and fry the rolls for 5 minutes until brown. Transfer to a flameproof casserole dish. Pour in the vermouth and brown sauce, cover with a lid and braise at 350°F (180°C/Gas mark 4) for 16-20 minutes.
4. Remove the meat rolls from the casserole, discard the strings. Serve the meat on the blanched cabbage leaves. Pour a pool of sauce next to the meat and sprinkle over the pitted olives.

CHEF'S TIPS:
If you have not tasted French Provençal Tapenade, you have not lived. It still comes as a surprise to me that black olives are not more popular. The combination of ground black olives, anchovy tenderloins and capers, in my opinion, can beat even foie gras. This delicate spread served on cocktail crackers or toasted French bread is a pure delight. In this recipe the Tapenade paste is used to stuff the pork tenderloin.

Pork Rib Chops with Baby Eggplants and Plums

Serves: 2
Preparation time: 5 minutes,
plus 20 minutes to degorge the eggplants
Cooking time: 35 minutes

INGREDIENTS

2 pork back rib chops, trimmed of rind and fat
2 tbsp olive oil
salt and pepper

SAUCE:
2/3 cup (150 ml/1/4 pint) dry white wine
generous 1/2 cup (100 g/4 oz) sugar
1 tsp tomato paste
1 tsp yeast extract
1 tsp grated fresh ginger root
1 large tomato, skinned, deseeded and chopped
4 baby eggplants
4 large plums

GARNISH:
fresh tarragon leaves

METHOD

1. Season the pork chops. Heat the oil in a pan and shallow fry the chops for 6 minutes on each side. Remove the meat from the pan and keep warm. Discard a little oil from the pan and add the wine, 1/2 cup(100 ml/4 fl oz) water, sugar, tomato paste and yeast extract. Boil the sauce for 4 minutes, then add the ginger, seasoning and, lastly, the chopped tomato.
2. Prick the baby eggplants with a fork and rub them with salt. Leave for 20 minutes to allow the bitter juices to be drawn out. Wash away the salt and the juices and pat dry the eggplants.
3. Gently stew the baby eggplants in the sauce for 15 minutes, then add the plums and simmer for 8 minutes until soft.
4. Pour a pool of the sauce on to each plate, place a pork chop in the center and serve each portion with 2 eggplants and 2 plums. Garnish the sides of the plates with a few tarragon leaves.

CHEF'S TIPS:
This dish has an attractive garnish of baby eggplants and large plums. The sauce that is served with the pork is flavored with ginger and has a sweet and sour taste.

Ginger: is the washed and dried rhizomes of the plant, *Zingiber officinale*. There are several varieties with different degrees of pungency. Jamaican ginger, which is peeled; African ginger, which is smaller, darker and covered with an outer skin. The oil is found in the skin so that gingers without the skin are milder and less aromatic. The ginger with the skin left on has a harsher flavor. Jamaican ginger is generally considered to be the best.

Barbecue Spare Ribs Chinatown

Serves: 4
Preparation time: 15 minutes, plus minimum 20 minutes marinating (preferably overnight)
Cooking time: 20 minutes, plus 1 hour

INGREDIENTS

2 lb (1 kg) pork spare ribs

MARINADE:
1 tsp tomato paste
2/3 cup (150 ml/1/4 pint) fresh pineapple juice
3 tbsp soy sauce
3 drops chili or Tabasco sauce
4 tbsp clear honey
4 tbsp vinegar (brown malt or wine)
1/2 tsp Chinese five spice powder
2 garlic cloves, chopped
1-inch (2.5cm) piece of fresh ginger root, grated
1/2 tsp allspice
salt
1/3 cup (75 ml/3 fl oz) sake or dry sherry

SERVE WITH:
rice, boiled
celery, boiled and cut slantwise
carrots, boiled and cut slantwise
sesame seeds, to sprinkle

METHOD

1. Place the pork in a large saucepan and cover with 4 1/2 cups (1 liter/1 3/4 pints) cold water. Bring the water to a boil and then simmer for 20 minutes. Remove the scum as it rises to the top; in this way you will have a clear broth that can be used as stock for soups.
2. Remove the meat from the water and strain the stock.
3. Combine all the marinade ingredients in a large bowl. Soak the spare ribs for at least 20 minutes or overnight, if possible. Place the marinade in the fridge to produce a stronger flavor.
4. Transfer the ribs and marinade to a casserole dish and braise in the oven at 350°F (180°C/Gas mark 4) for 1 hour. Turn the meat over several times during cooking. If too much sauce evaporates during braising, add a cupful of the pork stock. Do not allow the ribs to become dry. Serve the pork with rice, boiled celery and carrots and sprinkled with sesame seeds.

CHEF'S TIPS:

For this recipe you can use the cheaper cuts of pork – ribs from the belly or the better quality neck chops that have leaner meat. There are three different stages to the cooking of spare ribs. First the meat is simmered for 20 minutes, then it is marinated for at least 20 minutes and, finally, it is braised in the oven for approximately 1 hour. The type of marinade used may vary according to taste from a simple sweet and sour dressing to a very spicy sauce.

The most important ingredient for the marinade and the one which gives it the characteristic spare rib taste, is the Chinese five spice powder. The powder is a combination of cloves, cinnamon, anise seeds, mace and allspice and is available from Asian stores and larger supermarkets.

Pork Chops in Orange and Lemon Sauce

Serves: 4
Preparation time: 12 minutes,
plus 2 hours marinating
Cooking time: 45 minutes

INGREDIENTS

4 x 8-oz (225 g) pork chops

MARINADE:
juice of 2 lemons
juice of 2 oranges
1 tbsp honey
1 tbsp soy sauce
3 tbsp cider vinegar
2 tbsp oil
1 onion, finely chopped
1/2 tsp coarsely ground black pepper
1 garlic clove, crushed
1 tsp cornstarch mixed with 2 tbsp water

GARNISH:
1 lemon, sliced
a few cloves
1 tbsp chopped lemon grass (optional)

METHOD

1. Place the lemon and orange juice in a large, shallow baking dish and add the honey, soy sauce, vinegar, oil, chopped onion, pepper and garlic. Mix together well to make the marinade.
2. Place the pork chops side by side in the marinade, basting each one with the liquid. Cover the dish and let stand for 2 hours at room temperature. The chops should be turned and basted frequently with the marinade during this standing time.
3. Bake the chops at 350°F (180°C/Gas mark 4), covered in the marinade, for 45 minutes or until the meat is tender, basting occasionally.
4. Stir the cornstarch mixture into the sauce 15 minutes before the end of the cooking time.
5. Garnish the skin of each lemon slice with a few cloves. Serve each pork chop garnished with a lemon slice and a spoonful of sauce. Pour any remaining sauce into a sauce boat to accompany the chops. If liked, sprinkle with the lemon grass.

CHEF'S TIPS:
Pork chops are more substantial than spare ribs, as they have more meat, and the lemon and honey flavors give the dish a delicate, subtle flavor.

Lemon grass is a herb with a lemon flavor which can be used like mint or parsley. It is now sold fresh in many large supermarkets.

Serve with plain boiled rice and seasonal green vegetables.

Pig's Trotters in Ginger Sauce

Serves: 4
Preparation time: 30 minutes
Cooking time: 2 hours

INGREDIENTS

4 pig's trotters, cut into 2-inch (5 cm) pieces, or boned
8 oz (225 g) fresh ginger root, sliced
2/3 cup (150 g/5 oz) brown sugar
2/3 cup (150 ml/1 1/4 pint) cider vinegar
1 tsp salt
good pinch of coarsely ground black pepper

GARNISH:
4-8 small baby turnips, quartered or turned
4-8 baby beets, peeled and quartered or turned
4 scallions, finely chopped
fresh parsley

METHOD

1. Soak the trotters in 3 cups (750 ml/1 1/4 pint) cold water with 1 tablespoon of the vinegar and leave for 15 minutes. Rinse and drain. Put the trotters in a saucepan, covered with fresh water and bring to a boil then drain. Repeat this operation twice, changing the water each time. This operation is done to ensure that the trotters are clean.
2. Cover the blanched trotters with fresh water. Add all the ingredients, including the remaining vinegar, except the garnish, and simmer for 2 hours. By the end of this time the sauce should be like a syrup.
3. While the trotters are cooking, boil the beets and turnips in salted water for 15 minutes. Drain and add to the stew at the end of the cooking time.
4. Serve garnished with scallions and parsley.

CHEF'S TIPS:

In my long experience as a chef, I have found that most gourmets love pig's trotters whether they are broiled, French style, or served in a vinaigrette, as sold in every charcuterie in France, Italy and Germany. I have cooked pig's trotters in dozens of different ways and all have been appreciated by my customers. In this recipe, the trotters are cooked in a ragôut with turnips, baby beets, fresh ginger root and vinegar.

Vinegar: Modern cooking makes full use of aromatic vinegar. A wide variety of vinegars are readily available – wine, cider, malt – and all of these may be flavored with herbs, spices and fruits. Wine vinegars tend to be the mildest and are generally preferred for cooking. Balsamic is the most aromatic vinegar and the most expensive.

Indonesian Liver

Serves: 4
Preparation time: 12 minutes
Cooking time: 30 minutes

INGREDIENTS

1 lb (450 g) pigs' liver, sliced
    and cut into strips
1 1/4 cups (300 ml/1/2 pint) canned coconut milk or fresh
    coconut water (if neither of these are available, use a
    mixture of 1 1/3 cups (100 g/4 oz) unsweetened shredded
    coconut infused in 2 cups (450 ml/3/4 pint) boiling water to
    make coconut milk)
2 tbsp oil
1 large onion, cut into rings
1/2 tsp ground coriander
1 clove garlic, crushed
1/2 tsp chili powder
1/2 tsp turmeric
2 tbsp flour
2 tbsp soy sauce
2 tbsp peanut butter
salt

SERVE WITH:
rice
pinch of saffron or turmeric

METHOD

1. If making your own coconut milk, prepare this first: place the unsweetened shredded coconut in a small bowl. Add 2 cups (450 ml/3/4 pint) boiling water and let stand for 15 minutes. Strain through a cheesecloth or a fine strainer. This will make approximately 1 1/4 cups (300 ml/1/2 pint).
2. Heat the oil in a frying pan, add the onions and cook until lightly browned. Remove half the onions for garnishing and keep warm. Stir the coriander, garlic, chili powder and turmeric into the pan and cook over a low heat for 1 minute.
3. Toss the liver in the seasoned flour, shaking off the excess. Add the liver to the pan and cook until browned. Stir in the soy sauce, peanut butter and salt.
4. Stir in the coconut milk and bring to a boil, stirring. Cover and simmer for 30 minutes. Garnish with the fried onions.
5. Serve the liver on a bed of rice, which has been cooked in water to which a pinch of saffron or turmeric was added at the start of cooking.

CHEF'S TIPS:
This dish can also be made using lambs' or calves' liver. The tenderness of the meat will depend on the length of time it is cooked. In French cookery, pigs' livers are used in terrines, pâtés and sausages. Fried pigs' liver is also a popular dish.

Glazed Ham with Maple Syrup

Serves: 6-8
Preparation time: 20 minutes,
 plus 6 hours soaking the ham
Cooking time: 2 hours

INGREDIENTS

4 lb (2 kg) ham

GLAZING:
2/3 cup (150ml/1/4 pint) maple or corn syrup, or 1/2 cup
    (100 g/3 1/2 oz) brown sugar
1 tbsp mustard powder
1 tsp mix of ground ginger cinnamon and black pepper
24 cloves

GARNISH:
3 oranges, sliced, but unpeeled
24 pitted red or candied cherries

METHOD

1. Soak the ham for 6 hours. Remove the ham from the liquid, place in a large saucepan and cover with clean cold water. Bring the ham to a boil and simmer for 1 hour 40 minutes. Let cool in its own liquid. When cold, remove the ham from the liquor, peel away the rind and cut off the excess fat, leaving just a thin covering.
2. Score the remaining fat with a sharp knife making vertical and horizontal lines at 2-inch (5 cm) intervals, in a crisscross pattern of squares. Stud the corners of the squares with cloves.
3. Combine the spices and mustard powder with the brown sugar or syrup. Sprinkle or pour over the ham. Place the ham in a roasting pan and bake at 400°F (200°C/Gas mark 6) for 10 minutes.
4. If served hot, cut in thick slices and serve with spinach or braised celery. If served cold, garnish with the orange slices and cherries threaded on wooden toothpicks.

CHEF'S TIPS:

Before boiling a ham, always soak it in cold water for 6 hours during which time the water should be changed twice. When the ham has been soaked, place it in a large saucepan and cover it with fresh cold water, bring to a boil and simmer. The water should be kept simmering for the whole cooking time. The length of time needed to cook the ham is calculated on the basis of 20 minutes per 1 lb (450 g) plus 20 minutes extra, for joints up to 10lb (5 kg). Never allow a ham to boil too fiercely. Glazed ham is equally delicious served hot or cold.

A garnish of macedoine (diced, cooked vegetables) in mayonnaise, or potato salad, would be ideal served with ham as part of a buffet.

Peperonata of Ham

Serves: 4
Preparation time: 15 minutes
Cooking time: 25 minutes

INGREDIENTS

1 1/2 lb (675 g) cooked ham, cut into cubes
2 tbsp olive oil
1 medium onion, chopped
8 baby onions, peeled
4 carrots, cut into cubes
2 garlic cloves, chopped
1 sprig of thyme
2/3 cup (150ml/1/4 pint) port wine
2/3 cup (150ml/1/4 pint) water
2 large sweet tomatoes, skinned, deseeded and chopped
1 small chili pepper, deseeded and sliced
1 tbsp orange rind
salt and pepper
1 3/8 cups each split, deseeded and cut into small squares
    red and yellow bell peppers

METHOD

1. Heat the oil in a wok or shallow frying pan and stir-fry the ham and chopped onions for 2 minutes.
2. Add all the other ingredients and simmer for 25 minutes. Season to taste.

CHEF'S TIPS:

Ham is the great stand-by and it does not need much imagination to make good use of cooked ham. In my home town of Boulogne-sur-mer almost every café, including my father's, featured ham and French fries on its menu to attract the day-trippers. Delicious as these simple dishes are, ham can form the basis of many more exciting and unusual recipes. It can be made into mousses or terrines, used in omelettes, or stuffed with whipped cream cheese or avocado and tomato fillings. Ham can be made into turnover pastries, used as a filling for pancakes or vol au vents and is an important ingredient in many complex sauces, including the famous Réforme sauce in which it is served with beets, tongue, truffles and dill pickles to enrich a lamb or pork rib chop.

Serve with rice or pasta or boiled potatoes.

Bacon and Blue Cheese Pasta Bake

Serves: 4
Preparation time: 12 minutes
Cooking time: 35 minutes

INGREDIENTS

1 1/2 cups (350 g/12 oz) derinded and chopped bacon slices
2 tbsp (25 g/1 oz) margarine
1 garlic clove, crushed
2 cups (100 g/4 oz) sliced mushrooms
1/4 cup (25g/1oz) all-purpose flour
1 1/4 cups (300 ml/ 1/2 pint) milk
1 cup (75 g/3 oz) grated blue cheese
black pepper
8 oz (225 g) dried fettucine or tagliatelle
1 2/3 cup s(150 g/5 oz) chopped mozzarella cheese

METHOD

1. Melt the margarine in a large saucepan and add the bacon and garlic. Cook until the bacon has colored. Add the mushrooms and cook for 1-2 minutes. Stir in the flour. Remove the pan from the heat and gradually stir in the milk, mixing well.
2. Return the pan to the heat and bring to a boil, stirring constantly, until a smooth, glossy sauce has formed. Add the blue cheese and seasoning.
3. Meanwhile, cook the pasta, according to package instructions. Drain well. Toss the pasta with the sauce. Pour into a baking dish, sprinkle with the mozzarella cheese and cook in a hot oven at 400°F (200°C/Gas mark 6) for 10-15 minutes, until browned.

CHEF'S TIPS:
Good pasta dishes are popular with children and adults alike. So many blue cheeses are now sold in the supermarkets that you can just take your pick.

Serve with a mixed green salad.

Bacon Omelet

Serves: 2
Preparation time: 12 minutes
Cooking time: 5 minutes

INGREDIENTS

4 bacon slices, derinded and chopped
1 tbsp oil
1 1/3 cups (225 g/8 oz) peeled and chopped potatoes,
    cooked until tender
2 cups (100 g/4 oz) sliced mushrooms
2 tomatoes, chopped
1 tbsp chopped fresh parsley
3 eggs, beaten
2 tbsp milk
black pepper

SERVE WITH:
salad
crusty bread

METHOD

1. Heat the oil in a non-stick frying pan and cook the bacon until colored. Add the potatoes and cook for a further 2-3 minutes. Stir in the mushrooms and tomatoes and sprinkle over the parsley.
2. Beat together the eggs, milk and seasoning. Pour over the bacon mixture and cook gently, easing the cooked egg mixture away from the sides of the pan to allow the uncooked mixture to take its place. Brown under a preheated broiler.
3. Serve immediately with salad and crusty bread.

CHEF'S TIPS:
An omelet is a quick, easy and delicious dish that can be ready in minutes. The secret of a good omelet is to have the additional ingredients prepared in advance and the eggs added only at the last minute. Omelets should always be served immediately.

Swiss Potatoes with Bacon

Serves: 4
Preparation time: 10 minutes
Cooking time: 15-20 minutes

INGREDIENTS

1 lb (450 g) potatoes, peeled (leftover mashed potatoes could
be used instead)
1 tbsp oil
1/2 cup (100 g/4 oz) derinded and chopped bacon
1 small onion, finely chopped
1 garlic clove, crushed
1/2 cup (75 g/3 oz) corn kernels
2 tbsp snipped fresh chives
black pepper

METHOD

1. Cook the potatoes for 8 minutes in a large pan of boiling salted water. Drain, let cool, then grate.
2. Heat the oil in a large non-stick frying pan. Add the bacon, onion and garlic and cook until colored. Mix in the potatoes, corn kernels, chives and seasoning. Cook on one side for 3-4 minutes then turn. Continue cooking until browned, turning occasionally. Serve immediately.

CHEF'S TIPS:

Ham and potato complement each other well and most countries, where bacon is eaten, have their variation of dishes that combine these two ingredients. This recipe is for rosti potatoes, a favorite dish in Switzerland.

Bacon, Cheese and Celery Fondue

Serves: 4
Preparation time: 10 minutes
Cooking time: 10 minutes

INGREDIENTS

6 bacon slices, derinded and chopped
1 tbsp (15g/ 1/2 oz) margarine
1 garlic clove, chopped
3 celery sticks, very finely chopped
2/3 cup (150ml/ 1/4 pint) white wine
1 tsp English mustard
2 cups (225 g/8 oz) grated mature Cheddar cheese
4 tsp cornstarch mixed with 2 tbsp water
black pepper

TO SERVE:
cooked bacon rolls
cauliflower florets
chunks of crusty bread

METHOD

1. Melt the margarine in a fondue or saucepan. Add the bacon and garlic and cook for 2-3 minutes. Stir in the celery and cook for 2 minutes. Stir in the wine, mustard and cheese and cook gently until the cheese has melted.
2. Stir in the cornstarch mixture. Bring to a boil, stirring continually, and simmer uncovered for 2-3 minutes, until thickened. Serve immediately with bacon rolls, cauliflower florets and chunks of bread, to dip.

CHEF'S TIPS:
Fondue consists basically of melted cheese mixed with beer, wine or milk – the choice is yours. Flavor it with kirsch or with caraway seed liqueur, Kümmel, as the Scandinavians might. Fondue is a good party dish, which can be adapted to suit children, teenagers or adults.

There are many good reasons why we use alcohol in cooking:

1. To provide aromatic flavor and to retain the natural flavor of herbs and spices used in conjunction with it.
2. Wine, apple cider or beer are used for their acidic properties to balance flavor and to marinate meats.
3. The higher the alcohol content, the more pronounced the aromatic fragrance will be.

Wines or fortified drinks up to 18 proof, like port, sherry and Madeira, are added to sauces or soups at the last moment, since any prolonged boiling would evaporate the alcohol and diminish the flavor.

Toad in the Hole

Serves: 4
Preparation time: 15 minutes,
plus 20 minutes for the batter to rest
Cooking time: 30 minutes

INGREDIENTS

4 slices of bacon, derinded
4 pork sausages
1 medium onion, sliced in rings
2 cups (100 g/4 oz) sliced field or wild mushrooms
1 tbsp Worcestershire sauce

POPOVERS:
1 cup (100 g/4 oz) strong bread flour
1/2 tsp salt
2 eggs, beaten
1 1/4 cups (300ml/1/2 pint) water and milk, mixed

GARNISH:
1 tbsp chopped fresh parsley

METHOD

1. Combine all the ingredients for the popovers in a bowl: first mix the flour and salt, make a well in the center and break in the eggs. Gradually add the liquid, beating the mixture until smooth. Let the batter rest for 20 minutes.
2. Broil the bacon and reserve the drippings.
3. Put 2 teaspoons of the bacon drippings in each of four 4-inch (10 cm) diameter baking pans. Heat the greased pans in the oven for 10 minutes. (For successful popovers, it is important that the drippings in the pans are really hot).
4. Heat the remaining drippings in a frying pan and shallow fry the sausages for 5 minutes, then remove them from the pan. In the same fat stir-fry the onion for 3 minutes, until soft. Add the mushrooms and cook for 1 minute. Remove the mushrooms and onions from the pan and place them in a bowl.
5. Wrap each sausage in a slice of broiled bacon. Drizzle some Worcestershire sauce over the cooked mushrooms and onions.
6. Pour half the batter into the pans and bake for 10-15 minutes at 400°F (200°C/ Gas mark 6). Then place one wrapped sausage and a spoonful of the mushroom and onion mixture onto each. Cover with the rest of the batter and bake for a further 10-15 minutes. (Baking the batter in layers like this ensures that the sausages remain well embedded.) Sprinkle with chopped parsley before serving.

CHEF'S TIPS:

This combination of sausage and popovers, although popular, does not receive the appreciation it deserves, because it is so often very badly made. The secret of good popovers is to always use strong bread flour and never be tempted to replace it with self-rising flour.

Parsley is a member of the *Petroselinum crispum* family of herbs. It should be freshly chopped just before using, to retain its distinctive flavor. Parsley can be added at the last moment to all soups and stews, sprinkled over fried fish cooked in butter or over cooked vegetables like potatoes and cauliflower.

Honey Baked Knuckle of Bacon

Serves: 2
Preparation time: 15 minutes,
plus 3 hours soaking
Cooking time: 2 1/2 hours

INGREDIENTS

2 shanks of ham
16 cloves
3 tbsp clear honey
2 1/2 cups (600 ml/1 pint) apple cider

SAUCE:
1 1/4 cups (300 ml/1/2 pint) brown sauce or gravy (see page 29)
4-6 small potatoes
2 1/3 cups (225 g/8 oz) sliced green cabbage
4 small carrots
salt and pepper
1 tsp caraway seeds

METHOD

1. Soak the shanks in cold water for 3 hours. Place the shanks in a large saucepan, cover with fresh water and bring to a boil, reduce the heat and continue to simmer for 2 hours. When cooked, remove the shanks from the water and peel away the rind.
2. Stud the shanks with cloves, brush with the honey and place in a roasting pan. Bake for 30 minutes at 400°F (200°C/Gas mark 6) basting frequently with the cider until it is all used.
3. Boil the cabbage and the other vegetables separately, flavored with the caraway seeds.
4. Place each shank on a plate on a bed of cooked cabbage leaves, surrounded with carrots and potatoes. Stir any leftover cider liquor in the roasting pan into the brown sauce, and serve sauce separately.

CHEF'S TIPS:
Knuckle of ham is always well received and is featured in most fashionable restaurants. This dish was created, with his customary flair, by Paul O'Sullivan. The ham, glazed with honey and studded with cloves, is served on a bed of small potatoes, carrots and green cabbage flavored with caraway seeds.

Caraway: Caraway seeds are the dried fruit of the herb *Carum carvi*. The leaves of the plant are also used. The flavor is strong and highly aromatic. Caraway is commonly used to flavor Scandinavian brown breads and cakes and also to enhance the flavor of certain meats, fish, pickles and sauces.

Tenderloin of Bacon with Grapefruit

Serves: 4
Preparation time: 15 minutes,
plus 1 hour marinating
Cooking time: 20 minutes

INGREDIENTS

12 oz (350 g) bacon tenderloin, cut into 1/2-inch (1 cm) slices
5 tbsp oil

MARINADE:
4 tbsp pink grapefruit juice
2 tbsp finely chopped fresh tarragon, or 1 tbsp dried tarragon
salt and black pepper

DRESSING:
3 tbsp oil
2 tbsp pink grapefruit juice
1 tsp clear honey
2 tsp finely chopped fresh tarragon, or 1 tsp dried tarragon
salt and black pepper

VEGETABLES:
8 oz (225 g) small potatoes, scrubbed
1 cup (100 g/4 oz) topped and tailed green beans

GARNISH:
1 pink grapefruit, peeled and sliced

METHOD

1. Place the pieces of bacon between two sheets of plastic wrap and flatten them with a rolling pin or meat mallet.
2. Lay the bacon in a shallow dish. Mix 4 tablespoons of the oil with the grapefruit juice, tarragon and seasoning and pour over the bacon. Cover and marinate in the fridge for 1 hour, turning occasionally.
3. For the dressing: shake the oil, grapefruit juice, honey, tarragon and seasoning in a screw-top jar.
4. Cook the potatoes and green beans in boiling salted water until tender.
5. Remove the bacon from the marinade and gently pan-fry in the remaining oil until golden brown on each side.
6. Drain the cooked vegetables, toss in the dressing and place on serving plates. Arrange the bacon and grapefruit slices around the vegetables and serve immediately.

CHEF'S TIPS:

Bacon tenderloin is now available in most large supermarkets. In this recipe the tenderloin is thinly sliced and daintily presented with segments of sweet grapefruit. The Florida, seedless grapefuit is particularly recommended for flavor. Citrus fruits and bacon complement each other perfectly.

Bacon with Pineapple Malaysian Style

Serves: 4
Preparation time: 12 minutes,
plus 15 minutes to soak the bacon
Cooking time: 12 minutes

INGREDIENTS

1 lb (450 g) lean bacon, derinded with some of the
    fat removed, cut into strips
2 tbsp oil
1 large onion, chopped
1 green bell pepper, deseeded and cut into small squares
1 small can pineapple chunks (with juice reserved)
1 tsp five spice powder
pinch of ginger
1 tbsp sake (rice wine) or sherry
1 tbsp cider vinegar
3 tbsp soy sauce
1 1/3 cups (225 g/8 oz) drained and sliced water chestnuts
2 tsp cornstarch mixed with 2 tbsp water
salt and black pepper

SERVE WITH:
rice, boiled
carrots, boiled

METHOD

1. Soak the bacon in cold water for 15 minutes.
2. Heat the oil in a wok or shallow frying pan and stir-fry the bacon for 5 minutes. Remove the bacon from the pan and in the same oil, stir-fry the onion, bell pepper and pineapple.
3. Return the bacon to the pan and add the pineapple juice, five spice powder, ginger, sake or sherry, vinegar, soy sauce and sliced water chestnuts. Stir in the cornstarch mixture and cook for 4 minutes. Season to taste.
4. Serve with boiled rice and boiled carrots.

CHEF'S TIPS:
When bacon is to be used in this kind of Asian dish, it should be desalted in cold water for 15 minutes before use.

Bacon-Stuffed Cabbage Leaves

Serves: 4
Preparation time: 15 minutes
Cooking time: 15 minutes

INGREDIENTS

1 cup (225 g/8 oz) diced bacon
1 cup (225 g/8 oz) skinned and diced breast of chicken
scant 1 cup (150 g/5 oz) peeled shrimp
5 tbsp oil
5 tbsp soy sauce
1 tsp sugar
2 tbsp cornstarch
1/2 cup (100 g/4 oz) dried egg noodles
1 large onion, chopped
1/2 cup (100 g/4 oz) white cabbage, shredded
3 tbsp oyster sauce
1 clove garlic, crushed
1/2 tsp each of ground pepper and ginger
4 mushrooms, sliced
2 tbsp chopped fresh parsley

METHOD

1. Place the chicken, bacon and shrimp in a bowl. Mix together the soy sauce, sugar and 1 tablespoon of the cornstarch and pour over the chicken, bacon and shrimp.
2. Stand the noodles in a bowl of boiling water for 5 minutes. Drain and stir 1 tablespoon of the oil over the noodles to prevent them sticking together.
3. Heat 2 tablespoons of the oil in a large frying pan. Add half the onions and the cabbage and fry for 2 minutes. Stir in the noodles and oyster sauce. Heat well, then transfer onto a serving plate and keep warm.
4. Heat the remaining oil in a frying pan and fry the rest of the onions, the garlic, ginger and black pepper for 1 minute. Add the bacon, chicken, shrimp and mushrooms (reserving the marinade) and stir-fry for 5 minutes.
5. Mix the reserved marinade with the remaining tablespoon of cornstarch. Add to the frying pan together with the chopped parsley. Bring to a boil, stirring constantly. Spoon the sauce over the noodles and serve.

CHEF'S TIPS:

Spanish paella, in which seafood, poultry and pork are cooked with rice, may well have its origins in China, certainly dishes that combine seafood and meat are common in Asiatic cuisine. Nasi Goreng is another example of a dish in which anything edible, as long as it tastes good, can be mixed together.

Bacon Satay

Serves: 4
Preparation time: 15 minutes,
plus 2 hours marinating
Cooking time: 15 minutes

INGREDIENTS

1 1/2 lb (675 g) ground ham or bacon
1 cup (100 g/4 oz) finely chopped peanuts
1 egg
1/2 tsp chili powder or Tabasco sauce

PEANUT SAUCE:
1 tbsp oil
1 medium onion, chopped
2 garlic cloves, crushed
1 1/4 cups (150 g/5 oz) salted peanuts
2 tbsp soy sauce
1 tbsp tomato paste
1/2 tsp ground cumin
1 small chili pepper, deseeded and chopped
juice and grated rind of 1 lemon
salt, to taste
1 tbsp sugar or honey

METHOD

1. To make the peanut sauce: heat the oil in a frying pan and stir-fry the onion, garlic and peanuts for 5 minutes. Add all the remaining ingredients, and 1 1/4 cups (300 ml/1/2 pint) water, and simmer for 10 minutes. Process the sauce in a blender until it forms a thin purée. Reheat until it boils again. Add a little more water if it is too thick.
2. Combine the ground ham or bacon, peanuts, egg and chili pepper or Tabasco sauce into a thick mixture. Divide the mixture into small balls the size of plums. Thread onto wooden skewers. Brush the meat balls with the satay sauce and refrigerate for 2 hours.
3. Cook the meat on a barbecue or under the broiler for approximately 8 minutes until cooked through. Continue to brush with the peanut sauce, during cooking.

CHEF'S TIPS:
Soak wooden skewers in water for 1 hour before using – this prevents them from burning too easily.

Pork kebabs are popular in Asia where a lot of pork is eaten. Muslims make their kebabs with lamb or chicken and Westerners use all kinds of meat for their barbecues. The peanut sauce, which is served with the bacon kebabs in this recipe, is rich in protein. Instead of using ground meat, you could cut the meat into 3/4-inch (2 cm) cubes.

Serve with the peanut sauce, a mixed salad and plain boiled rice.

Pork and Pineapple with Yellow Rice

Serves: 2
Preparation time: 10 minutes,
plus 1 hour marinating
Cooking time: 20 minutes

INGREDIENTS

8 oz (225 g) lean pork
2 tsp cornstarch mixed with 2 tbsp water
2 tbsp oil
salt and pepper

MARINADE:
2/3 cup (150 ml/5 fl oz) fresh pineapple juice
2 tbsp soy sauce
1-2 tsp five spice powder
1 tsp tomato paste
1 small piece fresh ginger root, grated

GARNISH:
wedge of fresh pineapple
3 celery sticks
2 small carrots
1 medium onion

SERVE WITH:
generous 1/2 cup (100 g/4 oz) long grain rice
1 tbsp turmeric powder
3 drops egg yellow food coloring (optional)
1 tbsp olive oil
2 slices of fresh pineapple, cut in wedges

METHOD

1. Cut the meat into strips 1 1/2-inch (3.5 cm) long. Cut the pineapple and vegetables for the garnish into strips the same length.
2. Combine the pineapple juice, soy sauce, five spice powder, tomato paste and ginger for the marinade in a bowl, and soak the meat for 1 hour.
3. Heat the oil in a wok or shallow pan and stir-fry the meat and garnish for 8 minutes. Add the marinade and cornstarch mixture. Season to taste.
4. Boil the rice for 20 minutes with turmeric and yellow coloring. Drain. Season to taste and stir in oil.
5. Mold the rice in a star shape and garnish with a border of pineapple wedges. Place the meat mixture on the side of the plate.

CHEF'S TIPS:
Stir-fried dishes are popular and quick to produce. Fresh pineapple contains a tenderizing enzyme that makes the meat less chewy and the fresh juice is an ideal marinade. Turmeric is used to color the rice, plus a few drops of egg yellow food coloring, for a brighter color. Saffron could be used for a more subtle shade.

Pork Noisettes with Lentils

Serves: 4
Preparation time: 10 minutes,
plus 2 hours soaking for lentils
Cooking time: 30 minutes

INGREDIENTS

4 x 5-oz (150 g) boneless pork chops, rind and fat removed,
    tied into noisettes
2 tbsp oil

GARNISH:

1 cup (225 g/8 oz) green lentils, soaked for 2 hours
1 medium carrot, cut into small cubes
salt and pepper
1 tbsp butter
4 medium-sized apples, cored and skin scored
2 tbsp tomato catsup

SAUCE:

2/3 cup (150 ml/ 1/4 pint) apple cider
1 small shallot, chopped
1 1/4 cup (300ml/1/2 pint) brown sauce or gravy (see page 29)
2 tbsp heavy cream
2 mint leaves, chopped
salt and pepper
pinch of mixed spice

METHOD

1. Heat the oil and pan-fry the pork noisettes for 6 minutes. Remove from pan and keep warm.
2. Pour off most of the fat, retaining meat juices and a little of the fat. Stir in the cider and shallot and boil for 8 minutes. Stir in the brown sauce and simmer for 5 minutes. Stir in cream and mint and season to taste.
3. Fill the center of the apples with a little tomato catsup and bake for 20 minutes at 400°F (200°C/Gas mark 6).
4. Meanwhile, boil the soaked lentils for 20 minutes. Add the carrots 5 minutes before the lentils are cooked. Drain, season and stir in the butter
5. Place pork on plates, accompanied by the baked apple and lentils.

CHEF'S TIPS:
Boneless pork chops can be prepared more quickly than a roast. Tie them neatly with string to make noisettes. The best fruit accompaniment for pork is baked apple which will remain firm after cooking. Acid apples tend to disintegrate and are best for making a purée sauce.

Stir-Fried Pork with Rice Noodles

Serves: 2
Preparation time: 10 minutes,
plus 1 hour marinating
Cooking time: 15 minutes

INGREDIENTS

1/2 lb (225 g) lean pork loin, cut in thin slices
1 tbsp oil

MARINADE:
2/3 cup (150 ml/1/4 pint) watermelon juice
2 tbsp soy sauce
1 small chili pepper, deseeded and chopped
1 tsp tomato paste
salt and pepper

GARNISH:
1 1/4 cups (150 g/5 oz) sliced slantwise celery
2 1/2 cups (150 g/5 oz) sliced mushrooms
2 small carrots, grooved with a rinder and sliced
5 oz (150 g) rice noodles
a little oil or butter

METHOD

1. Thin the pork slices down further with a meat mallet. Cut each slice into four pieces.
2. Mix together the marinade ingredients and pour into a deep container. Soak the meat for 1 hour. Drain and save the marinade for the sauce.
3. Heat the oil in a wok or pan and stir-fry the meat for 6 minutes then add the celery, mushrooms, carrots and reserved marinade and cook for 5 minutes. Season to taste.
4. Meanwhile, soak the noodles in boiling water for 5 minutes. Drain well and reheat in a little oil or butter.
5. Form the noodles into a nest on each plate and arrange the meat and garnish in the center.

CHEF'S TIPS:
Pork lends itself to recipes using smaller cut pieces of meat for one mouthful bites. Rice noodles only need to be soaked in boiling water for 5 minutes and then tossed in oil or butter for 2 minutes.

To prepare watermelon juice: process the flesh of a 225 g (8 oz) slice to a purée. Remove seeds. It is an enzyme in the watermelon that helps tenderize the meat.

Roast Pork with Peaches

Serves: 8
Preparation time: 30 minutes
Cooking time: 1 hour 40 minutes

INGREDIENTS

1 x 4-lb (2 kg) blade roast (rind and fat removed and chined,
    rib ends trimmed)
salt and pepper

GARNISH:
4 fresh ripe peaches
2/3 cup (150 g/5 oz) cream cheese
4 strands of chives, snipped with scissors

GRAVY:
1 small onion, quartered
1 celery stick, quartered
1 tbsp cornstarch mixed with 2 tbsp water

METHOD

1. Season the roast and place on a rack in a deep roasting pan. Roast in a hot oven at 400°F (200°C/Gas mark 6) for 30 minutes. Drain off the excess fat, add the onion, celery and 2 1/2 cups (600 ml/1 pint) water. Reduce heat to 350°F (180°C/Gas mark 4) and roast for a further 1 hour. Baste the meat every 15 minutes and turn it round.
2. Remove the roast when it is cooked. Place the pan on the top of the stove and boil down the liquid. Stir in the cornstarch mixture and boil the liquid, stirring for 4 minutes, until thickened and cleared. Strain and serve separately.
3. Scald the peaches in boiling water. Peel them, cut in halves, and stone.
4. Mash the cream cheese with the chives, and fill the cavities of the peaches with this mixture.
5. Place slices of the meat with a pool of gravy and the stuffed peaches on each plate. If required for a cold buffet, brush the meat with semi-set aspic jelly, when cold (see page 18). Use the same garnish, if liked.

CHEF'S TIPS:
This recipe uses the cut of pork known as roast or rib part, where chops are taken. More usually, this roast is cut from a lamb carcass. The joint should have the chine bone loosened or removed for easier carving. You can ask your butcher to do this preparation for you.

Great British Breakfast

Serves: 2
Preparation time: 15 minutes
Cooking time: 12 minutes

INGREDIENTS

2 eggs
2 tbsp (25 g/1 oz) butter, softened
2 tbsp heavy cream
salt and pepper
4 slices of bacon, rindless
4 dried prunes, pitted
6 small pork chipolata sausages
8 slices of black pudding
2 small tomatoes
4 small potatoes in the skin, boiled and sliced
oil and butter, for cooking

GARNISH:

sprigs of parsley

SERVE WITH

toast

METHOD

1. Spread the inside of 2 ramekin dishes with the soft butter and crack an egg into each. Place the ramekins in a deep baking pan half-filled with water and poach the eggs for 3-4 minutes, so that the yolk is still soft and the white lightly firm. Pour some of the cream around the top and serve in the ramekins.
2. Brush the bacon with a little oil and broil for just 2 minutes. Cool and wrap each slice around a pitted prune. Spear rolls onto wooden toothpicks. Broil for another 2 minutes until crisp.
3. Broil the sausages for 8 minutes and black pudding for 2 minutes.
4. Make an incision in the skin of the tomatoes and scald in boiling water for 30 seconds. Remove the skin only and keep warm.
5. Fry the potato slices in a mixture of butter and oil until golden. Season and drain.
6. To serve, place the ramekin with the poached egg in the center of a large platter and surround with alternate black pudding, potato slices, sausages, tomatoes and stuffed bacon rolls. Garnish with the parsley, whose fragrance will mingle with the bacon aroma.

CHEF'S TIPS:

One of the most glorious and most popular early meals in Britain and Ireland must be the typical Victorian breakfast. It consists of pork items such as sausages, black pudding and bacon slices with eggs, potatoes, tomatoes, mushrooms, fried bread and sometimes lamb rib chops. The taste for black pudding or blood sausages has never diminished – on the contrary, it has spread among the young generation who appreciate the spicy content and texture from the best products made with less fat.

In my version of the perfect breakfast, I have introduced an egg poached in a little cream and fresh, scalded tomatoes, which both contribute to a balanced meal.

ALL ABOUT LAMB

Introduction

Lamb is a popular meat to serve on all occasions, from the humblest to the most grand. It is the essential ingredient for tasty, nutritious, inexpensive stews.

Where once it was only possible to buy large joints of lamb, the meat is now packaged in a variety of convenient forms – ready-ground for moussaka, burgers and stuffings; small or large chops and rib chops; tenderloin and roasts.

SIGNS OF QUALITY IN LAMB

When buying mutton, the chief points to remember are as follows.
1. The flesh should be firmer than beef;
2. The meat should be deep red in color;
3. The fat should be firm and white;
4. The meat should not be sticky to touch;
5. There should be no unpleasant smell.

When buying lamb, the chief points to remember are as follows.
1. The flesh should be firm;
2. The fat should be white;
3. The veins at the neck end should have a bluish tint;
4. There should be no unpleasant, rancid, goaty smell.

CARVING LAMB

In the hands of an expert, carving can look deceptively easy. It is, however, a skill that needs to be mastered. It is very important that you use a sharp carving knife, with a 10-inch (25 cm) long blade. Always sharpen the knife before carving with a traditional steel or an electric knife sharpener. An electric carving knife is also a valuable addition to the kitchen, since it allows you to carve the meat very thinly – this is not only more attractive, but also helps make the meat go further. Always use a carving fork with a thumb guard and, if possible, place the joint on a spiked carving dish so that it does not slip.

Let meat stand for about 15 minutes before carving it. Carve thin, consistent slices in order to obtain the best flavor. When possible, cut the lamb against the grain – this will give you more tender slices. You will probably find that it is much easier to carve if you are standing up. Always use a long, even sawing action and keep the blade at the same angle. Do not press down on the meat too much as this will squeeze out the juices. Serve the carved meat on very warm plates.

Each joint needs to be carved differently depending upon the position of the bones and the way in which the meat and fat are distributed. There are no hard and fast rules, but the following guidelines will help.

LEG OF LAMB: Carve the leg with the round side uppermost, inserting the knife near the knuckle. Make the first cut down to the bone diagonally. Cut out a thick wedge-shaped slice. Then carve slices from either side of the cut. Turn the joint over and carve in long slices, parallel to the leg bone.

SHOULDER OF LAMB: Carve the shoulder downwards towards the knuckle end. Turn over and carve downwards in long slices.

LOIN ROAST: Have your butcher cut through the sections of the backbone so that it can be divided into chops.

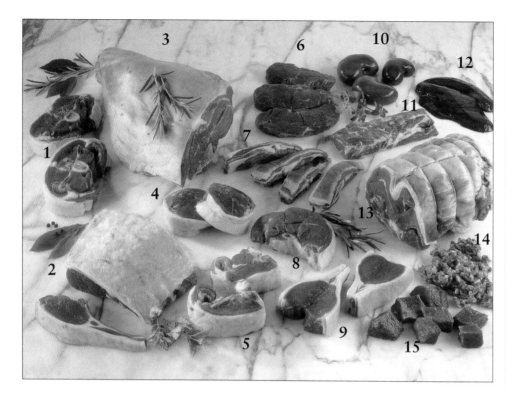

British Lamb Retail Cuts

1. Double loin chop (Barnsley chop)
2. Best end
3. Leg
4. Noisette
5. Loin chop
6. Leg steak
7. Breast riblet
8. Chump chop
9. Valentine steak
10. Kidney
11. Neck fillet
12. Liver
13. Rolled shoulder
14. Mince
15. Cubes

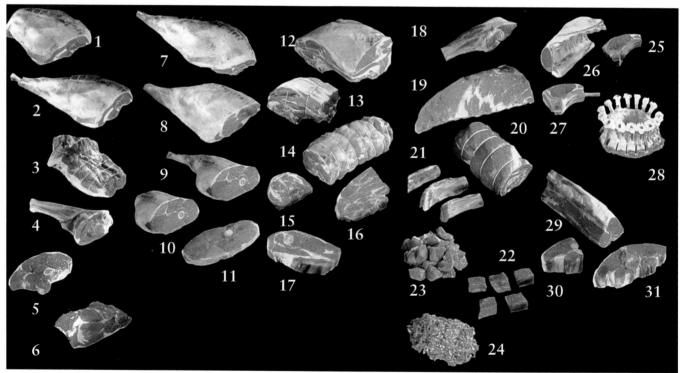

American Lamb Retail Cuts

1 American style roast	6 Boneless sirloin roast	9 Shank portion roast	13 Pre-sliced shoulder	17 Arm chop	21 Riblets	26 Rib roast	30 Loin chop
2 French-style roast	7 Whole leg	10 Center leg roast	14 Boneless shoulder roast	18 Shank	22 Cubes for kebabs	27 French rib chop	31 Double loin chop
3 Boneless leg roast	8 Short cut leg, sirloin off	11 Center slice	15 Neck slice	19 Spareribs	23 Lamb for stew	28 Crown roast	
4 Hind shank		12 Square-cut shoulder, whole	16 Blade chop	20 Boneless rolled breast	24 Ground lamb	29 Loin roast	
5 Sirloin chop					25 Rib chop		

Peppered Leg of Roast Lamb Imperial

Serves: 6
Preparation time: 20 minutes
Cooking time: 1-1 1/2 hours

INGREDIENTS

4lb (2 kg) leg of young lamb
   (with pelvic bone removed)
1/3 cup (25 g/1 oz) mixed and crushed dried red, black
   and green peppercorns
8 garlic cloves - 2 finely chopped,
   6 cut in slivers
2 tbsp olive oil
1 tsp salt
1 sprig rosemary
lamb's caul or a slice of fat for roasting
3 tbsp oil for roasting

SAUCE:
1 tsp all-purpose flour
1/4 cup (50 ml/2 fl oz) raspberry vinegar
scant 1/4 cup (50 g/2 oz) redcurrant jelly
2/3 cup (150 ml/1/4 pint) lamb or veal stock
1 small piece ginger root, peeled and chopped
2/3 cup (150 ml/1/4 pint) light cream
a few green peppercorns, bottled in brine

VEGETABLE CAKES:
2 large potatoes, peeled and grated
1 carrot, cut into julienne strips
1 leek, cut into julienne strips
oil, for frying

METHOD
1. Make a paste of the dried peppercorns, chopped garlic cloves, olive oil and salt.
2. Remove the outer layer of skin from the lamb. Make six incisions in the surface of the leg and insert the six slivers of garlic and a little rosemary.
3. Rub the peppercorn paste over the leg. Wrap it in lamb's caul, or a slice of fat (to keep moist) and cover with a piece of oiled foil.
4. Roast in a hot oven at 400°F (200°C/Gas mark 6) for 25 minutes, then reduce the heat to 375°F (190°C/Gas mark 5) for a further 35 minutes, if you require the meat to be pink. If the roast is to be well-done, allow another 20 minutes of cooking time. Baste the roasting joint frequently with a little oil. Once the meat is brown, uncover the foil and continue to baste with 2-3 tablespoons water (this will create steam without further browning).
5. Remove the cooked lamb from the oven and keep warm. Discard the excess fat, leaving 2 tablespoons only in the roasting pan. Place the pan on top of the stove and make the sauce.
6. Add the flour to the fat to make a roux and cook until light brown. Stir in the vinegar, red currant jelly, stock and ginger. Boil for 10 minutes. Pour the sauce through a strainer into a saucepan. Stir in the cream and season to taste. Add a few green peppercorns, plus 1 teaspoon of the brine.
7. Carve the lamb and serve with the sauce and vegetable cakes.

VEGETABLE CAKES
1. Mix together the potatoes, carrot and leek, then squeeze the mixture to get rid of the excess moisture.
2. Shape into small heaps and fry in a shallow pan in hot oil. When golden on both sides, remove from the pan.

CHEF'S TIPS:
This magnificent roast was a favorite with the visiting dignitaries at the Imperial Hotel in Cork, Ireland where John Morrin, the head chef, created this dish. The leg of lamb needs to have the pelvic bone removed, so ask your butcher to bone it for you.

The pepper sauce makes a welcome change from the usual gravy, generally served with roast lamb.

Serve with small turned potatoes, carrots and leeks.

Roast Leg of Lamb with Apricots

Serves: 6-8
Preparation time: 15 minutes
Cooking time: 70 minutes

INGREDIENTS

3 lb (1.5 kg) boneless lamb leg roast
oil, for basting and deep frying

STUFFING:
scant 1 cup (150 g/5 oz) dried apricots
    (soaked if necessary)
2 cups (100 g/4 oz) fresh breadcrumbs
1 small onion, finely chopped
4 tbsp (25 g/1 oz) grated fresh ginger root
1 tsp ground cinnamon
1 egg, beaten
salt and freshly ground pepper
apricot halves, to garnish

DAUPHINE POTATOES:
150 ml (5 fl oz) choux paste
2 lb (1 kg) Duchesse potatoes

CHOUX PASTE:
1/4 cup (50 g/2 oz) butter
1 cup (100 g/4 oz) strong bread flour
2 eggs, beaten

DUCHESSE POTATOES:
2 lb (1 kg) potatoes, boiled and drained
1/2 cup (100 g/4 oz) butter
2 egg yolks
salt and pepper

METHOD

1. First, prepare the stuffing. Cut the apricots into small pieces and mix with the breadcrumbs, chopped onion, ginger and cinnamon. Combine with the egg and season to taste.
2. Spread the stuffing along the center of the saddle and roll the meat up carefully. Secure with string.
3. Place the saddle in a roasting pan, brush with oil and roast in a hot oven at 400°F (200°C/Gas mark 6) for about 70 minutes to serve pink.
4. Carve and garnish with the apricot halves. If liked, serve with the Dauphine potatoes.

POTATOES
1. First make the choux paste. Melt the butter with 1/2 cup (100 ml/4 fl oz) water, and bring to a boil. Remove from the heat and quickly tip in all the flour. Beat until smooth, and the paste forms a ball in the center of the pan. Let cool slightly, then beat in the eggs.
2. Mash the Duchesse potatoes with the butter and egg yolks. Season to taste.
3. Mix the choux paste and the duchesse potatoes together. Mold the mixture into even-size pieces with the aid of two spoons and place on waxed paper.
4. Drop the molded mixture into deep hot oil and fry until crisp and golden brown. Drain.

CHEF'S TIPS:
A saddle of lamb is a joint that can be served for any celebration. A saddle can be boned and stuffed to provide more portions. A simple salad of lettuce and fresh apricots would make the ideal side garnish. Serve this joint with an orange sauce.

Peppered Lamb Rib Roast with Coriander

Serves: 4
Preparation time: 15 minutes
Cooking time: 30 minutes

INGREDIENTS

2 lamb rib roasts, trimmed
2 tbsp oil
6 tbsp whole green peppercorns
    (fresh or canned in brine)
3 tbsp coriander seeds
2 tbsp clear honey

POTATO CAKES:
1 lb (450 g) potatoes, peeled
1/4 cup (50 g/2 oz) butter
salt and pepper
a little flour, for dusting
oil, for frying

GARNISH:
fresh cilantro leaves

METHOD
1. Put the lamb on a wire rack in a roasting pan.
2. Brush the lamb lightly with oil and roast at 400°F (200°C/Gas mark 6) for 20 minutes.
3. Meanwhile, lightly crush the peppercorns and coriander seeds and mix together well.
4. When the lamb has been cooking for 20 minutes remove it from the oven, brush it with honey and coat it with the peppercorns and coriander seeds. Roast for a further 10 minutes to serve pink.
5. Garnish with a few fresh cilantro leaves and serve with the potato cakes.

POTATO CAKES
1. Boil the potatoes, then, when cooked, mash with the butter. Season and mix well.
2. Mold into four cakes and dust with flour.
3. Shallow fry in hot oil, until golden brown on both sides.

CHEF'S TIPS:
This lamb rib roast, neatly trimmed and skinned, is delicious served with snow peas and kidney beans. Potato cakes make a perfect accompaniment.

Indonesian Lamb

Serves: 4
Preparation time: 15 minutes, plus 1 hour marinating
Cooking time: 25 minutes

INGREDIENTS

2 lamb rib roasts, trimmed
2 tbsp oil, for frying

MARINADE:
1 1/4 cups (300 ml/1/2 pint) tomato juice
1 oz (25 g) fresh coriander
generous 1/3 cup (50g/2oz) sugar
1 chili pepper, deseeded and chopped
juice of 1 lemon
2 garlic cloves, chopped
1 small piece of ginger root, chopped
1 tbsp oil
1 tsp salt
2/3 cup (150 ml/1/4 pint) strong stock

SAUCE:
1 tbsp finely chopped galangal root or
    powder or ginger
1/2 cup (100 ml/4 fl oz) coconut cream or
    coconut milk*
1 cup (100 g/4 oz) macadamia nuts or
    almonds
2/3 cup (150 ml/1/4 pint) stock
salt, to taste
thinly sliced cucumber, to garnish

METHOD

1. Process the marinade ingredients in a food processor or blender and soak the lamb for 1 hour.
2. Heat the oil in a frying pan and brown the lamb for 5 minutes. Transfer the meat and marinade to a lidded casserole dish. Cook at 325°F (160°C/Gas mark 3) for 25 minutes.
3. Mix the galangal root or ginger, nuts and coconut milk or cream with the stock. Simmer in a pan and add the cooking liquor from the lamb. Check seasoning and pour through a strainer.
4. To serve, place two rib chops per portion on a plate. Garnish with slices of cucumber and a pool of sauce.

CHEF'S TIPS:

The sauce is traditionally made from coconut* and candle nut, grown mostly in Australia and the Pacific islands, but you can substitute almonds or macadamia nuts. Serve fried rice or Nasi Goreng and cucumber with the lamb.

Galangal, also called laos, is available from specialist Thai food stores. It is a member of the ginger family so some finely chopped fresh ginger root could be substituted.

*Canned coconut cream is best for the sauce but, if unavailable, soak 1/4 cup(2 oz/50 g) creamed coconut in 1/2 cup
(100 ml/4 fl oz) boiling water, pour through a strainer and use the milk.

Rib Roast of Lamb Eucalyptus

Serves: 4
Preparation time: 15 minutes
Cooking time: 30 minutes

INGREDIENTS

2 rib roasts of lamb, trimmed
a little oil
1 1/4 cups (300 ml/1/2 pint) stock
2 red bell peppers, split and deseeded

EUCALYPTUS BUTTER:
1 cup (225 g/8 oz) butter, softened
4 drops of eucalyptus oil
pinch of black pepper

GARNISH:
1 cup (50 g/2 oz) macadamia nuts

METHOD

1. Brush the lamb with oil and roast in a hot oven at 400°F (200°C/Gas mark 6) for 25 minutes to serve pink. Let rest for 10 minutes.
2. Mix the eucalyptus oil and black pepper into the softened butter.
3. Brush the bell peppers with oil then broil until blistered. Peel off the skin.
4. Remove most of the fat from the roasting pan, leaving 1 tablespoon of the fat and the meat juices. Add the stock or water, boil for 2 minutes and then beat in the eucalyptus butter. Season the sauce and strain.
5. Carve the roast into chops. Serve on a plate with a pool of the sauce and the broiled red bell peppers. Sprinkle the macadamia nuts over the lamb.

CHEF'S TIPS:

This recipe uses an extract of the eucalyptus tree that is grown in the sheep-rearing areas of Australia. The eucalyptol found in the leaves is a powerful antiseptic as well as a strong flavoring agent and gives this dish its distinct quality. You can buy eucalyptus oil at drug stores.

A simple salad and boiled potatoes can be served with the lamb. Broiled bell peppers make a good garnish for this dish. Bell peppers, or capsicums, can be red, yellow, green or purple in color. The red have the strongest flavor.

Macadamia Lamb Flavored with Celery and Anise Seeds

Serves: 4
Preparation time: 15 minutes
Cooking time: 15 minutes

INGREDIENTS

1 1/2 lb (675 g) loin of lamb roast,
    trimmed
1 tbsp oil and 2 tbsp (25 g/1 oz) butter,
    for searing the lamb
1 cup (100 g/4 oz) seasoned flour
1 egg
1/2 cup (50 g/2 oz) chopped macadamia nuts
2/3 cup (50g /2oz) mixed celery and anise
    seeds

SAUCE:
2 tbsp oil
2 shallots, chopped
1/4 cup (50 ml/2 fl oz) sweet red vermouth
1 1/4 cups (300 ml/1 /2 pint) stock
1 tbsp (15g/ 1/2 oz) butter
salt and pepper

METHOD

1. Heat the oil and butter in a frying pan and sear the lamb until brown all round. Let cool.
2. Cut the loin into two pieces. Roll the meat in the seasoned flour and beaten egg and coat one half of the loin with macadamia nuts and the other half with celery and anise seeds.
3. Pour the fat left in the frying pan over both halves and roast in a hot oven at 400°F (200°C/Gas mark 6) for 10-12 minutes.
4. To make the sauce: heat the oil in a pan and sauté the shallots for 1 minute. Add the vermouth and stock and boil to reduce by half. Whisk in the butter and season to taste.
5. To serve, place one slice from the macadamia coated loin and one slice from the seed coated loin on each plate. Pour some sauce around the meat and arrange a selection of lightly cooked vegetables .

CHEF'S TIPS:
In nouvelle cuisine, the traditional method of using a roux of butter and flour to thicken a sauce, is replaced by whisking pieces of butter into the sauce at the end of its cooking time to emulsify and thicken it. Replacing flour with butter may seem to contradict the nutritional principle of reducing the fat and calorific content of a sauce whenever possible. If this is a particular concern, use a purée of vegetables to give the sauce an attractive texture.

Roast Lamb with Provençal Herbs

Serves: 4
Preparation time: 15 minutes,
plus 30 minutes marinating
Cooking time: 40 minutes

INGREDIENTS

1 1/2 lb (675 g) boneless lamb roast
2-3 tbsp oil
salt, to season

MARINADE:
2 tbsp olive oil
2 drops rosemary oil (optional)
2 drops lavender oil (optional)
1 tsp spearmint leaves, chopped
1 tbsp mixed herbes de Provençe
1 glass of dry sherry

SAUCE GLAZE:
1/4 cup (50 ml/2 fl oz) raspberry vinegar
1 1/4 cups (300 ml/1/2 pint) reduced or
    concentrated brown sauce or stock*
    (see pages 29 and 46)
1/4 cup (50 ml/2 fl oz) medium sherry
1/4 cup (50 g/2 oz) unsalted butter
4 fresh strawberries, to garnish

METHOD

1. Mix the marinade ingredients together and spoon over the lamb. Let rest for 30 minutes.
2. Heat the oil in a pan and sear the meat on all sides for 5 minutes. Season with salt and roast at 350°F (180°C/Gas mark 4) for 40 minutes to serve pink.
3. Remove the meat from the oven, but keep warm. Place the roasting pan on top of the stove. Add the vinegar to the meat juices and boil until reduced. Pour in the brown sauce or stock and sherry. Pour the sauce through a strainer. At the last moment, whisk in the butter. Slice the lamb.
4. To serve, place the meat slices on a plate with the sauce and garnish with the strawberries.

CHEF'S TIPS:
Using the thick part of a boneless leg saves both time and money because it is a prime cut and, therefore, quick to cook. The mingled scent of rosemary, marjoram, basil, wild thyme and mint (spearmint is particularly good) makes this a wonderfully aromatic dish. To make your own aromatic oils, flavor good quality oil with fresh herbs, such as rosemary and lavender. Use 2 cups (50 g /2 oz) herbs to 2 1/2 cups (600 ml/1 pint) oil. Seal and keep for one week before using.

*A quick stock can be made by adding 2 teaspoons yeast extract to 1 1/4 cups (300 ml/1/2 pint) boiling water.

Lamb with Anise and Ginger Sauce

Serves: 6
Preparation time: 20 minutes,
plus 1 hour marinating
Cooking time: 2 hours

INGREDIENTS

3 1/2 lb (1.6 kg) boneless lamb leg roast, trimmed and trussed

MARINADE:
2/3 cup (150 ml/1/4 pint) Madeira wine
juice of 1 lime
1 small piece of ginger root, chopped
2 tsp salt
1 pinch of chili powder

SAUCE:
1 tbsp sesame oil
1 star anise
1/4 cup (50 ml/2 fl oz) soy sauce or yeast extract
2 tbsp (25 g/1 oz) honey
2 1/2 cups (600 ml/1 pint) stock, ideally veal stock, or water
2 tsp cornstarch mixed with 4 tbsp water

METHOD

1. Combine the marinade ingredients in a bowl and spoon over the lamb. Marinate for 1 hour.
2. Bring 4 1/2 cups (1 liter/1 3/4 pints) of water to a boil and simmer the lamb for about 10 minutes. Remove the meat from the liquid and cut it into 1-inch (3 cm) thick slices. Place these slices in a Dutch oven.
3. Heat oil in a frying pan, add the star anise and cook for 30 seconds to develop the flavor. Add all the ingredients for the sauce, except the cornstarch. Pour the sauce over the lamb and add the ginger and onion from the marinade. Cover with a lid and braise in a moderate overn at 375°F (190°C/Gas mark 5) for 1 1/2 hours.
4. Remove the meat from the oven and keep warm. Pour the liquid through a strainer into a small saucepan. Boil for 10 minutes. Mix the cornstarch with the water in a cup and add to a boiling gravy to thicken it. Cook for 4 minutes to clear the starch.
5. Serve on a platter with a pool of the sauce.

CHEF'S TIPS:

Serve with braised fennel and fried sweet potato French fries.

The lamb in this Asiatic dish is well flavored and is cooked through rather than served pink. The French fries which garnish the lamb are made from the sweet potato. The sweet potato can be cooked like the Western potato, but is not, in fact, related to it. It does, as its name implies, taste sweet.

Boneless Lamb Leg Roast Braised with Spinach

Serves: 2
Preparation time: 15 minutes
Cooking time: 20 minutes

INGREDIENTS

2 x 6-oz (175 g) 1-inch (2.5 cm) thick pieces of boneless leg roast
2 tbsp walnut or peanut oil

SAUCE:
4 scallions, sliced
1/2 cup (100 ml/4 fl oz) red wine
1 tbsp red wine vinegar
1 pinch of dry thyme
1/2 cup (100 ml/4 fl oz) lamb stock
2 tbsp rose or cranberry jelly
1/4 cup (50 g/2 oz) butter

SERVE WITH:
8 oz (225 g) spinach or seakale
1/4 cup (50 ml/2 fl oz) heavy cream
salt and pepper
grated nutmeg

METHOD

1. Place all the ingredients for the sauce, except the butter, in a pan and boil for 10 minutes. When the sauce is reduced by half, whisk in the butter to emulsify it. Season to taste.
2. Heat the oil in a frying pan and sear the meat on all sides for 5 minutes. Transfer the meat to a hot oven at 400°F (200 °C/Gas mark 6) and cook for 8 minutes. Remove the meat from the oven and slice.
3. Boil the seakale in salted water for 7 minutes, or the spinach, without water, for 5 minutes. Drain well and reheat in the heavy cream. Season with the salt, pepper and grated nutmeg.
4. To serve, arrange four thin slices, or one thick slice, of the meat on each plate and serve with a spoonful of the creamy seakale or spinach and a spoonful of the sauce.

CHEF'S TIPS:

This Australian recipe makes use of the lean meat produced from the larger breeds of sheep that are native to that country. The dish should be served with leaf spinach or seakale, if available. Remember that spinach should always be well washed before cooking.

The leaves of seakale, like the leaves of Belgian endive, are usually bitter. Lightly boil the leaves in salted water with lemon juice. In this recipe the bitterness of the seakale or spinach contrasts with the sweetness of the rose jelly. Flower jellies are sometimes sold at country markets, where there are often good homemade food stalls. Cranberry jelly or rosehip syrup can be substituted.

Roast Lamb with Spinach Galettes

Serves: 4
Preparation time: 15 minutes
Cooking time: 30 minutes

INGREDIENTS

1-lb (450 g) boneless leg roast
2 tbsp oil
salt and black pepper

SAUCE:
2/3 cup (150 ml/1/4 pint) medium Port wine
1 1/4 cups (300 ml/1/2 pint) strong stock (made
    from bones – see page 46)
2 tsp wholegrain mustard

GARNISH:
1 lb (450 g) leaf spinach, washed thoroughly
1 lb (450 g) potatoes, peeled and sliced
1/4 cup (50g/2oz) butter
1 garlic clove, crushed

METHOD

1. Heat the oil in a frying pan and sear the meat until brown on all sides. Transfer the meat to a roasting pan and cook at 375°F (190°C/Gas mark 5) for 20 minutes.
2. When cooked, season to taste. Remove the meat from the pan, drain off the excess fat leaving 1 tablespoon of the oil and meat juices. Boil for 3 minutes to reduce and concentrate. Add the port and stock and boil for a further 5 minutes. Check seasoning and pour through a strainer.
3. Cook the spinach without water for 6 minutes. Press the spinach to remove as much moisture as possible. Season and add garlic and a little butter. Fill four individual ramekin dishes with the spinach, leaving enough room for the potato slices.
4. Boil the potatoes for 3 minutes. Remove and drain. Arrange the cooked slices of potato so that they overlap each other, on top of the spinach in the ramekin dishes. Brush with remaining butter and bake for 10 minutes until golden brown.
5. Turn the cooked galettes out on to the plates, potato side up. Add the mustard to the sauce. Slice the lamb and serve with a little sauce poured over the meat and the rest in a separate jug.

CHEF'S TIPS:
Using a boneless roast from the thick part of the leg is both more economical and time saving than cooking a whole leg roast.

The garnish of spinach, with a topping of sliced potatoes, is simple and effective and can be prepared within minutes.

Rib Roast on Couscous

Serves: 4
Preparation time: 15 minutes
Cooking time: 25 minutes

INGREDIENTS

2 lamb rib roasts, trimmed
2 tsp ground anise seeds
3 tbsp oil
salt and pepper
1 1/3 cups (225 g/8 oz) couscous
1/4 cups (50 g/2 oz) butter
2 1/2 cups (600 ml/1 pint) lamb stock
1 medium onion, chopped
1 red bell pepper, deseeded and chopped
1 chili pepper, deseeded and chopped

GARNISH:

watercress

SERVE WITH:

zucchini, broiled

METHOD

1. Coat the lamb with the anise seeds and half the oil, season and roast in the oven at 400°F (200°C/Gas mark 6) for 20 minutes.
2. Rub the couscous with butter, like making a crumble mixture. Place in a roasting pan with stock and bake for 10 minutes. After 5 minutes, stir the couscous with a fork to avoid lumps forming.
3. Heat remaining oil in a pan and stir-fry the onion, bell pepper and chili pepper for 6 minutes over a low heat. Mix the vegetables with the couscous.
4. Carve the lamb into chops and serve two per portion with the couscous. Garnish with watercress and serve with the broiled zucchini.

CHEF'S TIPS:
The couscous is the main attraction of this particular dish. The couscous semolina should be rubbed with butter and cooked with the minimum of stock or water. Packages of couscous with clear cooking instructions are now available in most large supermarkets.

Poached Lamb with Horseradish Cream

Serves: 4
Preparation time: 15 minutes,
plus 1 hour to make the stock
Cooking time: 30 minutes

INGREDIENTS

1 lb (450 g) chump or fillet end leg, boned
4 1/2 cups (1 liter/ 1 3/4 pints) stock (made from bones,
    1 carrot, 1 leek and 3 chicken bouillon cubes)
salt and pepper

SAUCE:
2/3 cup (150 ml/1/4 pint) heavy cream
1 tbsp horseradish relish
salt and pepper

GARNISH:
32 small onions, peeled

METHOD

1. To make the stock: boil the lamb bones with the carrot, leek and stock cubes in 4 1/2 cups (1 liter/ 1 3/4 pints) water. Cook for 1 hour and then strain. Season to taste.
2. Poach the lamb in this stock for 20 minutes.
3. Slice the meat and keep it hot in the stock.
4. Beat the heavy cream and mix it with the horseradish. Season to taste.
5. Boil the onions in some of the stock for 10 minutes.
6. To serve, pour a spoonful of the horseradish cream onto each plate and place thin slices of lamb around it with eight small onions, per portion.

CHEF'S TIPS:

In this recipe the meat is poached, as in a fondue, and it is therefore possible to cook it according to individual taste — rare, medium or well-done. When buying your lamb, have the butcher give you the bones, for making the stock.

Serve with boiled potatoes, sprinkled with chopped mint.

Limerick Irish Stew

Serves: 4-6
Preparation time: 20 minutes
Cooking time: 1 1/2 hours

INGREDIENTS

2-3 lb (1-1.5 kg) neck or shoulder of
    lamb, left on the bone and chopped
bouquet of parsley, thyme and a bay leaf –
    tied together with string
2 large onions, finely chopped
freshly ground black pepper and a little salt
4 carrots, chopped into bite-sized pieces
3 leeks, chopped into bite-sized pieces
1 small turnip, chopped
a few small potatoes, peeled and chopped
1-1 1/3 cups (75-100 g/3-4 oz) shredded cabbage
parsley, finely chopped
dash of Worcestershire sauce

SERVE WITH:
brown soda bread

METHOD

1. Remove the meat from the bone and trim off all the fat. Keep the bones. (You can have the butcher do this for you.)
2. Place the meat in a pot, cover with cold salted water and bring to a boil. Drain and then rinse the lamb (this removes any scum).
3. Put the meat, bones, bouquet of herbs, onions, seasoning, carrots, leeks and turnips in a fresh pot and cover with water. Simmer gently for 1 hour. Skim off the scum as it rises. (This is very important for the final flavor and appearance of the stew).
4. Add the potatoes and continue to cook for a further 20 minutes. For the last 5 minutes, add the cabbage.
5. When the meat and vegetables are cooked, remove the bones and bouquet of herbs. Stir in the chopped parsley and a dash of Worcestershire sauce.
6. Serve in deep bowls with the brown soda bread.

CHEF'S TIPS:
This version of Irish stew is probably the best I've ever tasted. It comes from Limerick, an area of Ireland famous for its gastronomy, and has a rich, creamy flavor. Use stewing lamb, from the neck or shoulder.

Lamb Shanks with Vegetables

Serves: 6
Preparation time: 15 minutes
Cooking time: 1 1/2 hours

INGREDIENTS

6 lamb shanks with bones sawn,
    so that the shanks stand upright
salt and black pepper
2-3 tbsp olive oil
4 garlic cloves, crushed
4 sprigs of fresh thyme
2 sprigs of fresh rosemary
4 1/2 cups (1 liter/1 3/4 pints) lamb stock
6 red skinned potatoes, peeled and diced
1 lb (450 g) pumpkin, peeled and diced
1 each medium-sized leek, carrot and
    celery stick, cut into julienne sticks
2/3 cup (150 ml/1/4 pint) crème frâiche

METHOD

1. Heat the olive oil in a pan, season the shanks and brown. Transfer the meat to a casserole dish and add the garlic, herbs and stock. Cover and cook at 350°F (180°C/Gas mark 4) for 1 1/2 hours or until the meat is tender.
2. Remove the shanks from the liquid and keep warm.
3. Cook the potatoes and the pumpkin in the stock until tender. Remove and keep warm.
4. Blanch the julienne vegetables in the stock for 1 minute.
5. Pour the stock through a strainer into a pan, add the crème fraîche and boil until reduced by half. Add all the cooked vegetables and heat through.
6. To serve, stand the shanks on a plate, fill the center with the vegetables and the sauce.

CHEF'S TIPS:
Although this is a very economical dish, it is arguably as tasty as the best Irish stew, using the shank end of leg (knuckle) or the shoulders.

Serve with braised chicory.

Lamb Tagine

Serves: 4
Preparation time: 15 minutes
Cooking time: 30 minutes

INGREDIENTS

1 lb (450 g) lean lamb, trimmed and cubed
salt and freshly ground black pepper
1 medium onion, sliced
1 medium fennel bulb, roughly chopped
3/4 cup (225 g/8 oz) potatoes, peeled and roughly diced
1/2 tsp ground ginger
pinch of saffron, soaked in a little hot water
1 strip of orange rind
2 cups (450 ml/3/4 pint) chicken stock
1 1/4 cups (150 g/5 oz) topped and tailed snow peas
2/3 cup (150 g/5 oz) canned apricot halves in juice, drained and
    quartered
1 tbsp cornstarch mixed with 3 tbsp cold water
1 tbsp lemon juice

GARNISH:
4 apricot halves, sliced fanwise
tomato strips, to garnish

METHOD

1. Place the lamb in a non-stick pan, season and gently sauté for 5 minutes, stirring occasionally.
2. Add the onion, fennel, potatoes, ginger, saffron and orange rind. Sweat for 3-4 minutes, then add the stock.
3. Bring to a boil then reduce to a gentle simmer and cook for 20-25 minutes. Stir in the snow peas and apricots and cook for a further 2-3 minutes.
4. Add the mixed cornstarch to the pan and stir well until thickened. Add the lemon juice and season to taste. Garnish with the apricots and tomato strips.

CHEF'S TIPS:
The Tagine is an Arab dish popular in North Africa and usually garnished with wheat semolina, couscous. The aniseed taste of the fennel, the ginger and the saffron give this dish a truly exotic flavor.

Indian Lamb with Apricots

Serves: 4
Preparation time: 15 minutes
Cooking time: 1 hour

INGREDIENTS

1 lb (450 g) boned shoulder or leg of lamb,
    trimmed of fat and cut into 1-inch (2.5 cm) cubes
2 tbsp oil
2 tbsp fresh curry powder
2 medium onions, diced
2 tsp freshly grated ginger root
1 garlic clove, crushed
1 tsp chili powder
1/2 tsp turmeric
2 tsp ground coriander
4 tomatoes, chopped
juice of 1 lemon
1 tsp sugar
12 dried apricots (soaked in warm
    water to soften then drained)

METHOD

1. Heat the oil in a heavy pan, gently sauté the curry powder until fragrant.
2. Add the onions and fry until softened. Then add the ginger and garlic and cook for a further 2 minutes. Next, add the chili, turmeric, coriander and tomatoes and cook for 8 minutes until the sauce thickens.
3. Add the lamb, stir into the sauce, and cook gently over a low heat for about 45 minutes.
4. Finally stir in the lemon juice, sugar and apricots and cook for a further 5 minutes.

CHEF'S TIPS:

Lamb is frequently used in Indian cooking. This dish makes use of the combination of apricots and lamb, so popular in Asian and Arabic cuisines. If you buy the no-need-to-soak dried apricots, they do not require soaking.

Serve with boiled long grain rice and popadums.

Braised Shoulder of Lamb in Red Wine

Serves: 4
Preparation time: 15 minutes
Cooking time: 2 1/2 hours

INGREDIENTS

1 half shoulder of lamb
2 slices of bacon
3 tbsp olive oil
2 garlic cloves, cut into slivers
1 medium red onion,
    chopped in big cubes
1 carrot, cut into big chunks
1 stick celery, sliced

SAUCE:
1 tbsp flour
2/3 cup (150 ml/1/4 pint) stock
2/3 cup (150 ml/1/4 pint) Spanish red wine
1 tbsp tomato paste
sprigs of fresh rosemary
1 tsp cornstarch mixed with3 tbsp water (optional)
salt and ground black pepper

METHOD

1. Fry the bacon in 2 tablespoons of the olive oil for 1 minute, then add the garlic, onion, carrots and celery. Fry for a further 5 minutes until browned. Stir in the flour and cook over a low heat until browned.
2. Remove from the heat and gradually stir in the stock, wine and tomato paste. Bring to a boil to thicken. Cover and simmer for 10 minutes. Pour the sauce through a strainer and discard the bacon and vegetable mixture.
3. Seal and brown the lamb shoulder in the remaining olive oil in a casserole dish on the stove top. Add the prepared sauce and sprigs of rosemary. Bring to a boil, cover and simmer for about 2 1/2 hours until tender.
4. If desired, thicken the sauce with the cornstarch mixed with the water. Adjust seasoning to taste.

CHEF'S TIPS:

A succulent half shoulder joint of lamb is ideal for this recipe. Alternatively, it would be possible to use a whole shoulder, boned, stuffed and rolled for easy carving. Use equal quantities of ground lamb and breadcrumbs or cooked rice, for a delicious stuffing (optional).

Serve with rice and a julienne of mixed bell peppers.

Kashmir Lamb Rogan Josh

Serves: 4
Preparation time: 15 minutes
Cooking time: 1 1/2 hours

INGREDIENTS

1/3 cup (75 ml/3 fl oz) oil
1 1/2 lb (675 g) boned lean shoulder of lamb, diced
10 cardamom pods, shelled
1 bay leaf
10 whole black peppercorns, crushed
1 tsp ground cumin
1 tsp salt
1 tsp ground cloves
1/3 cup (75 ml/3 fl oz) sweetened pineapple juice

MARINADE:
1 small piece of fresh ginger root, peeled and grated
1/3 cup (50 g/2 oz) pineapple cubes
2/3 cup (150 ml/1/4 pint) plain thick yoghurt
1 red chili pepper with seeds
1 tbsp paprika powder
1 tbsp tomato paste
1 tsp sugar

METHOD

1. Process all the marinade ingredients with 1 1/4 cups (300 ml/1/2 pint) water to a thin purée and set aside. If time allows, the lamb can be marinated in this mixture overnight.
2. Heat the oil in a large metal casserole dish and cook the meat for 7 minutes until brown. Add the spices and stir well for 1 minute. Remove the surplus oil, if any remains.
3. Stir in 2 1/2 cups (600 ml/1 pint) water and the pineapple juice and add the marinade. Bring to a boil.
4. Cover and cook gently for 1 1/2 hours or cook in a moderate oven at 350°F (180°C/Gas mark 4).

CHEF'S TIPS:

There are many different recipes for Rogan Josh. This particular recipe is milder than many, since Kashmir Hindus do not eat onion or garlic. For the best flavor, place the lamb in the marinade and leave overnight in the fridge, before cooking.

Serve with boiled rice and sweet corn kernels mixed together.

Japanese Braised Lamb

Serves: 4
Preparation time: 15 minutes
Cooking time: 1 hour

INGREDIENTS

1 1/2 lb (675 g) shoulder of lamb, trimmed and diced
1 tbsp oil
4 tbsp (25 g/1 oz) peeled and chopped fresh ginger root
2/3 cup (150 ml/1/4 pint) soya milk
10 baby onions, skinned
2 1/2 cups (600 ml/1 pint) stock
2/3 cup (150 ml/1/4 pint) sake rice wine or sherry
scant 1/4 cup (50 g/2 oz) honey
1/4 cup (50 ml/2 fl oz) soy sauce
2 cups (225 g/8 oz) peas
salt and pepper, to taste

METHOD

1. Heat the oil in a frying pan and brown the lamb over a high heat. Transfer the meat to a colander and pour over boiling water to degrease the meat.
2. Place the lamb in a deep pan with half the ginger, the soya milk and 2/3 cup (150 ml/1/4 pint) water, cover with a drop lid.* Bring to a fast boil. Reduce the heat and simmer for 30-40 minutes.
3. Remove from the heat, strain and rinse the meat under cold running water to cool.
4. Blanch the onions in lightly salted water and refresh under cold water.
5. Drain the lamb and place in a deep pan. Add the stock, sake or sherry and the remaining ginger. Cover with a drop lid and bring to a fast boil. Reduce the heat and simmer for 10 minutes.
6. Add the honey and simmer for a further 5 minutes. Then add the soy sauce and simmer for 5 minutes more.
7. Add the onions and peas and simmer for a final 2 minutes.

CHEF'S TIPS:

A shortage of fish has encouraged the traditionally fish-eating population of Japan to increase their consumption of meat. Japanese dishes are becoming more westernized and more lamb is imported from Australia and New Zealand. This recipe should use soya milk as the Japanese don't use dairy milk.

Serve with rice. English mustard may be served as an accompaniment.

*Wooden drop lids are recommended, but if these are not available, improvise with vented foil. Cut a diameter slightly larger than the pot and pierce the center to allow steam to escape. Place so that the outer edges of the foil press against the sides of the pan and put on the food or liquid.

Kidneys on Potato Rostis

Serves: 2
Preparation time: 20 minutes
Cooking time: 20 minutes

INGREDIENTS

2 tbsp oil
4 lambs' kidneys, trimmed, defatted and halved

POTATO ROSTIS:
1 lb (450 g) potatoes
1/4 cup (50 g/2 oz) butter
salt and pepper

SAUCE:
2 shallots, chopped
1 tsp yeast extract
1 tsp tomato paste
1 1/4 cups (300 ml/1/2 pint) lamb stock or water
1 tbsp cornstarch mixed with 3 tbsp water
salt and pepper

GARNISH:
watercress

METHOD

1. First prepare the rostis. Boil the potatoes in their skins for 15 minutes until just tender. Let cool, then peel and grate. Season with salt and pepper. Divide the mixture into two.
2. Heat half the butter in a small frying pan and fry half the grated potato on both sides until golden. Press the mixture to make it more compact like a thick pancake. Turn out and keep warm, then make a second potato cake with the remaining potato.
3. Heat oil and sauté the kidneys for 5 minutes. Remove and keep hot.
4. In the same pan, stir-fry the shallots for 2 minutes until soft, but not brown. Add the yeast extract and tomato paste, stock or water and boil for 12 minutes. Thicken the sauce with the cornstarch mixture. Season to taste and simmer for 4 minutes.
5. Reheat kidneys in the sauce for 1 minute without boiling.
6. To serve, place the rostis on serving plates, top with the kidneys and surround with a pool of sauce. Garnish with watercress.

CHEF'S TIPS:
Kidneys are popular as a light entrée for a lunch or dinner menu, although this could also be served as a breakfast dish – with Swiss potato rostis, grated potato cakes.

Lamb Fritters Tokyo Style

Serves: 4
Preparation time: 30 minutes marinating
Cooking time: 10 minutes

INGREDIENTS

1 1/2 lb (675 g) lean lamb from leg, loin or shoulder,
    cut into 1-inch (2.5 cm) cubes
3 red bell peppers, cored, deseeded
    and cut into leaf shapes
2 green bell peppers, cored, deseeded
    and cut into leaf shapes
cornstarch, for dredging
salt

MARINADE:
1/3 cup (75 ml/3 fl oz) dark soy sauce
1/3 cup (75 ml/3 fl oz) sake or brandy
3 tsp juice from ginger*

COATING:
6 egg whites, beaten to a soft snow
scant 3/4 cup (75 g/3 oz) cornstarch
2 tbsp (15 g/1/2 oz) finely chopped scallions
3 tbsp finely chopped fresh ginger root
oil, for deep frying
lemon wedges, to garnish

METHOD

1. Mix the marinade ingredients together and soak the lamb for 30 minutes.
2. For the coating: sprinkle the cornstarch onto the beaten egg whites, add the scallions and ginger and mix in well. Preheat the oil to 330°F (175°C).
3. Roll the lamb chunks in cornstarch, dip in the coating mixture and deep fry gently.
4. Deep fry the bell peppers for 30 seconds only. Remove from the oil and dust with salt.
5. Arrange the lamb and bell peppers on serving plates and garnish with the lemon wedges.

CHEF'S TIPS:

Like the Chinese, the Japanese use small quantities of good quality meat in their cooking. Tempura, a fried dish, is very popular in Japanese cuisine. The use of side dishes of pickle, chutney and savory sauces can make this quick and simple recipe seem more elaborate.

Serve with salad or with rice and baby carrots.

*To obtain ginger juice, process the chopped ginger and a little water in a blender or food processor. Pour through a very fine strainer or cloth to extract the juice. Allow for the water when measuring for the recipe.

Surf and Turf Kebab Pacific

Serves: 4
Preparation time: 15 minutes
Cooking time: 10 minutes

INGREDIENTS

4 x 6-oz (175 g) loin of lamb, eye only
16 jumbo shrimp, peeled
2 large green bell peppers, deseeded and
    cut into 1-inch (2.5 cm) squares
3 tbsp oil
1 tbsp sesame oil

SAUCE:
1 tbsp sunflower oil
2 large red bell peppers, deseeded and chopped
1-2 fresh green chili peppers, deseeded and chopped
1 medium onion, chopped
1/2 tsp crushed Szechwan peppercorns
14-oz (400 g) can chopped tomatoes
2 tbsp dry sherry

METHOD

1. First, make the sauce: heat the oil in a pan and fry the red bell peppers, chili peppers, onion and Szechwan peppercorns until tender. Place in a blender or processor with the tomatoes and sherry and process until smooth. Reheat when required.
2. To make the kebabs: cut each lamb fillet into six equal pieces. Thread three pieces of lamb and two prawns on to each skewer, interspaced with green bell peppers. Two kebabs serve one portion.
3. Place the kebabs under a hot preheated broiler and cook for about 8-10 minutes, turning occasionally and brushing with the oils.
4. Serve the kebabs with the Szechwan sauce.

CHEF'S TIPS:

Cuts of lamb suitable for kebabs: Use the thick part of the leg, trimmed and cubed to make kebabs. Loin of lamb is also ideal for kebabs. These kebabs use the lean eye piece only of the loin. Enhance the Asian flavor of this striking dish by serving it with stir-fried julienne of vegetables presented in pastry boats.

These kebabs could also be barbecued and served with a mixed green salad.

Crushed black peppercorns can be used if Szechwan peppercorns are unavailable, but they do not give such an authentic flavor.

Lamb Rib Chops Spanish Style

Serves: 4
Preparation time: 20 minutes
Cooking time: 30 minutes

INGREDIENTS

12 lamb rib chops, trimmed
2 red bell peppers, deseeded and diced
3-4 zucchini, diced
oil
2 medium onions, diced
8 garlic cloves, peeled and blanched
2 cloves of garlic, crushed
1 tbsp flour
scant 1 cup (200 ml/7 fl oz) tomato sauce
scant 1 cup (200 ml/7 fl oz) light stock
salt and freshly ground pepper
2 medium eggplants, thinly sliced
10 barquettes (small pastry cases)

METHOD

1. Sauté the bell peppers, zucchini and onions in hot oil for 8 minutes until soft and slightly browned. Set aside.
2. Sauté the blanched cloves of garlic in hot oil until lightly browned. Remove and set aside.
3. In the same oil sear the lamb on both sides over a high heat. Remove the chops and place in a warm oven with the garlic cloves.
4. Add the crushed garlic to the pan, stir in the flour and cook briefly. Slowly pour in the tomato sauce and stock, stirring continuously, to make a smooth sauce. Season with salt and pepper, and simmer gently for 20 minutes.
5. Deep fry the eggplant slices in hot oil for 1 minute. Remove and drain. Place the zucchini mixture in the pastry barquettes.
6. Arrange three lamb chops on each plate with the filled barquettes and eggplant slices. Spoon a little sauce over the lamb and garnish with the sautéed garlic. Serve immediately.

CHEF'S TIPS:
If liked, the lamb can be seared with a hot skewer for special effect.

One of the regular customers at our restaurant in Paris, the Ducastaing, habitually ordered 12 rib chops for his main meal. He certainly would not have considered one daintily presented rib chop sufficient. In my own restaurant in Park Lane, London, I insisted that three prime rib chops constituted a fair portion.

Garlic and shallots can be fried or roasted and served like nuts to garnish a dish, as in this recipe.

Mango Bango Chops

Serves: 4
Preparation time: 15 minutes
Cooking time: 15-20 minutes

INGREDIENTS

8 small lamb sirloin chops, trimmed
1 tbsp oil
1 tsp cumin seeds
2 cups (450 ml/3/4 pint) lamb stock
4 tbsp mango chutney
2 tsp cornstarch mixed with 3 tbsp cold water
1 tbsp light brown sugar
salt and pepper

GARNISH:
fresh mango slices

METHOD

1. Heat the oil in a large frying pan and fry the chops for about 10-12 minutes to serve pink. Set aside and keep warm.
2. Add the cumin to the pan and fry gently for 1-2 minutes. Drain away any excess fat from the pan and deglaze with a little stock.
3. Stir in the mango chutney and remaining stock, bring to a boil and reduce slightly.
4. Add the mixed cornstarch to the sauce and boil to thicken, stirring. Simmer for 1 minute. Just before serving, stir in the brown sugar and season to taste.
5. Serve the chops with the sauce and garnish with fresh mango slices.

CHEF'S TIPS:

Turn lamb sirloin chops into a more exotic dish by serving them with tropical fruit. In this recipe the meat is accompanied by mango chutney and is garnished with slices of fresh mango.

You do not need to have an enormous appetite to eat two sirloin chops and I would consider two small chops to be a sensible serving for most people.

Lamb Steaks with Plum Sauce

Serves: 4
Preparation time: 12 minutes,
plus 30 minutes marinating
Cooking time: 30 minutes

INGREDIENTS

4 x 5-oz (140 g) shoulder steaks

MARINADE:
1 medium red onion, chopped
2 garlic cloves
2/3 cup (150 ml/1/4 pint) soy sauce
1/2 cup (100 ml/4 fl oz) tomato juice
juice and rind of 1 lime
1 tsp Chinese five spice powder
salt and pepper
generous 1/2 cup (150 g/5 oz) red plum jam

GARNISH:
2 sliced limes

METHOD

1. Place all the ingredients for the marinade, using just half the red plum jam, in a blender and process until smooth. Season with salt and pepper.
2. Spoon the marinade over the steaks, ensuring that they are well coated. Cover and refrigerate for at least 30 minutes.
3. Pour off the excess marinade from the steaks and set aside. Place the steaks in a single layer on a wire rack in a roasting pan and cook for 20 minutes at 425°F (220°C/Gas mark 7).
4. Remove the meat from the oven and brush with a little of the remaining warmed plum jam and cook for a further 4 minutes.
5. Meanwhile, place the reserved marinade in a pan with any remaining plum jam. Bring to a boil and simmer for 10 minutes. Garnish the plum glazed steaks with the slices of lime and serve with the sauce.

CHEF'S TIPS:
The shoulder steak is prepared in a way that is similar to the classic spare rib recipe. The marinade makes the lamb special - it not only flavors the meat, but it also helps to keep it succulent.

A pilaf of rice served with garlic flavored sautéed tomatoes would make a delicious accompaniment.

Lamb Loin Roast Provençal with Ratatouille

Serves: 4
Preparation time: 35 minutes
Cooking time: 25 minutes

INGREDIENTS

4 x 6-oz (175 g) noisettes or medallions
2 tbsp oil
salt and pepper

RATATOUILLE:
2 zucchini, sliced
2 small eggplants, diced
salt and pepper
2 tbsp oil
4 large tomatoes, skinned, deseeded and diced
2 garlic cloves, crushed
8 small mushrooms

SAUCE:
2/3 cup (150 ml/1/4 pint) white wine
2/3 cup (150 ml/1/4 pint) brown sauce or stock
  (see pages 29 and 46)
1/4 cup (50 g/2 oz) unsalted butter, softened

METHOD

1. Brush the lamb with the oil and season.
2. Prepare the ratatouille: sprinkle salt over the eggplants and zucchini. Let rest for 30 minutes. Rinse and pat dry with paper towels.
3. Heat the oil in a pan and stir-fry the zucchini and eggplants for 3 minutes. Add the tomatoes, garlic, mushrooms and season. Simmer for 15 minutes.
4. Pan-fry the lamb, according to taste – rare, medium or well-done. Remove from the pan and keep warm. Discard the excess fat, but retain one tablespoonful and the meat juices. Boil for 1 minute, then add the wine. Continue to boil until the liquid is reduced by half and then add the brown sauce or stock. Season to taste. Finally, whisk in the butter to emulsify the sauce.
5. To serve, cut each piece of lamb into three pieces, place the meat on a pool of sauce and garnish with the ratatouille.

CHEF'S TIPS:

The loin is the finest and most tender part of the lamb. Boneless, fatless loin noisettes or medallions are the choicest of all lamb cuts and the most expensive. More importantly, they make the tastiest entrées or broils. Gourmets tend to prefer the meat to be juicy, succulent and underdone or pinkish. It is, however, always a matter of taste, and those preferring their meat more well-done need only cook it for a few minutes longer.

The lamb is served with a ratatouille mixture of zucchini, eggplants and tomatoes. Potato cakes also make a good accompaniment (see page 105).

Medallions of Lamb Steaks with Vegetables

Serves: 3
Preparation time: 15 minutes
Cooking time: 10-15 minutes

INGREDIENTS

3 boneless leg steaks or chump steaks
salt and crushed peppercorns

SAUCE:
2/3 cup (150 ml/1/4 pint) white port wine
1 1/4 cups (300 ml/1/2 pint) white sauce,
    thickened with cream (see page 38)
1/2 cup (50 g/2 oz) chopped macadamia nuts or
    walnuts
2 tbsp (25 g/1 oz) butter
1 cup (25 g/1 oz) snipped fresh chives

SERVE WITH:
1/2 cup (50 g/2 oz) snow peas, blanched for 10 seconds
3 baby carrots, boiled for 20 seconds
1 cup (100 g/4 oz) celery, cut into sticks and
    blanched for 30 seconds
1/2 cup (50 g/2 oz) green beans, cut in half
    and blanched for 20 seconds

GARNISH:
4 sprigs of rosemary

METHOD

1. Season the meat with salt and crushed peppercorns. Sauté in a non-stick pan for 3-4 minutes on each side. Remove the lamb from the pan and keep warm.
2. Sauté the blanched vegetables for the garnish in the same pan for 1 minute. Season.
3. To make the sauce: boil the port in a saucepan for 30 seconds, add the white sauce and nuts and simmer for 5 minutes. Add the butter and chives.
4. To serve, place a pool of the sauce on each plate, top with lamb steaks and surround with the vegetables. Garnish with the rosemary.

CHEF'S TIPS:
This recipe uses portions of lamb cut from the thick part of the leg. This could be boneless leg steaks or boned chump chops, called steaks. The meat can be cooked to order to suit individual taste. The dish is served with a selection of vegetables.

Lamb Steaks with Mixed Bell Peppers

Serves: 4
Preparation time: 12 minutes
Cooking time: 6 minutes

INGREDIENTS

4 thin leg steaks
2 red bell peppers
2 yellow bell peppers
4 zucchini
2 tbsp oil
1 tbsp sesame oil
6 basil leaves, chopped
salt and pepper

METHOD

1. Cut the bell peppers in half, deseed and broil skin side up until the skin begins to blister, remove from the broiler and peel. Cut the bell peppers and zucchini into strips. Heat the oil in a frying pan and stir-fry the vegetables for about 4 minutes, until tender. Sprinkle with the basil and seasoning.
2. Remove the vegetables from the pan and keep warm. In the same oil, fry the steaks for 2-3 minutes on each side. Season to taste.
3. Arrange the steaks attractively on serving plates with the vegetable strips.

CHEF'S TIPS:

This is a real *repas en vitesse*. A meal virtually prepared in minutes. Use different colored bell peppers for a more attractive dish.

Serve with cooked pasta sprinkled with grated cheese.

Boneless Loin Medallions Florentine

Serves: 2
Preparation time: 5 minutes
Cooking time: 12 minutes

INGREDIENTS

2 boneless loin steaks or medallions, tied neatly with string
salt and pepper
2 tbsp oil
1 lb (450 g) fresh spinach, washed
6 cloves of garlic

SAUCE:
1 shallot, chopped
3 tbsp medium sherry
1 chicken bouillon cube
2 tsp cornstarch mixed with 2 tbsp water
2 cups (100 g/4 oz) cleaned and sliced small mushrooms
2 wild mushrooms, cleaned and sliced
4 scallions, bulbs only

METHOD

1. Brush the lamb with a little of the oil and season to taste.
2. Cook the cleaned spinach, without water, for 6 minutes. Remove from the pan and squeeze out the surplus moisture.
3. Heat the remaining oil and pan-fry the meat for 12 minutes. Remove from the pan and keep warm.
4. Fry the cloves of garlic in the same oil for 30 seconds, then remove and reserve. Discard most of the oil, but retain 1 tablespoonful. Stir-fry the shallot for 1 minute. Stir in the sherry and boil for 2 minutes. Stir in the cornstarch mixture, 1/2 cup (100 ml/4 fl oz) water and the bouillon cube and boil, stirring, for a further 3 minutes. Add the sliced mushrooms and scallions and cook for 1 more minute. Season to taste.
5. Serve the lamb with the spinach, mushroom sauce and garlic cloves.

CHEF'S TIPS:
Here's proof that even if only cooking for two people, it's possible to prepare something nutritious and interesting in very little time.

The garlic will aid your digestion, the spinach will improve your blood and you will enjoy the lamb all the more.

Italian-style Lamb with Sambucca

Serves: 4
Preparation time: 10 minutes,
plus 1 hour marinating
Cooking time: 30 minutes

INGREDIENTS

2 lamb rib roasts, trimmed

MARINADE:
1/4 cup (50 ml/2 fl oz) olive oil
1 tbsp fennel seeds
1 tsp crushed peppercorns

SABAYON SAUCE:
4 egg yolks
2 tbsp (25 ml/1 fl oz) Sambucca liqueur
1/2 cup (100 ml/4 fl oz) dry white wine or vermouth
salt

METHOD

1. Mix the ingredients for the marinade together, coat the roasts and leave to marinate for 1 hour. Place in a roasting pan and roast for 16-20 minutes at 400°F (200°C/Gas mark 6). Remove the meat from the oven and let rest.
2. Meanwhile, prepare the sabayon sauce. Whisk all the ingredients together in a metal bowl over a saucepan half filled with boiling water. The mixture should thicken like custard.
3. Slice the roasts into chops and place three on each serving plate, pour a pool of sauce next to the meat and garnish with vegetables.*

CHEF'S TIPS:

The sabayon sauce served with this rib roast of lamb is enhanced by the addition of Sambucca liqueur with its intense and distinctive aniseed flavor. Have the butcher remove the fell and fat from the lamb.

*For an attractive garnish, coat some large mushrooms with a mixture of olive oil, thyme, black pepper and anise seeds and broil. Serve the mushrooms with blanched baby carrots, turnips and tomatoes with the roasted rack.

Lamb Rib Chops with Redcurrants

Serves: 4
Preparation time: 10 minutes
Cooking time: 10-14 minutes

INGREDIENTS

8 lamb rib chops, trimmed
1/2 cup (50 g/2 oz) seasoned flour
egg wash - 2 eggs beaten with 1/2 cup (100 ml/4 fl oz) milk
4 cups (225 g/8 oz) fresh breadcrumbs
3/4 cup (75 g/3 oz) grated Parmesan cheese
oil, for frying

SAUCE:
1 1/2 cups (75 g/3 oz) thinly sliced small mushrooms
2 tbsp (25 g/1 oz) butter
1 1/2 tbsp (25 g/1 oz) redcurrant jelly
3/4 cup (175 ml/6 fl oz) port wine

GARNISH:
sprigs of fresh redcurrants (optional)

METHOD

1. Coat the lamb chops in the flour, egg wash and breadcrumbs and then dust lightly with the Parmesan cheese.
2. To serve the lamb pink, shallow fry the chops over a moderate heat for about 6-8 minutes. Drain well before serving.
3. To make the sauce: fry the mushrooms in the butter until tender, but not too brown. Drain well. Meanwhile, gently heat the redcurrant jelly with the port to make a smooth sauce. Stir in the mushrooms and serve with the chops.
4. Garnish with sprigs of fresh redcurrants, if available.

CHEF'S TIPS:
Redcurrant jelly is the traditional accompaniment for roast lamb. Serve the lamb with green beans, asparagus, peas or Brussel sprouts to balance the flavor and color of the dish.

Roulade of Lamb Napoli

Serves: 10
Preparation time: 25 minutes
Cooking time: 30 minutes

INGREDIENTS

FILLING:
3 lb (1.5 kg) boned shoulder of lamb, finely diced
1 1/3 cups (225 g /8 oz) chopped bacon
1/3 cup (75 g/3 oz) unsalted butter
2 garlic cloves, crushed
2 cups (100 g/4 oz) chopped mushrooms
2 lb (1 kg) fresh spinach, blanched
2 cups (225 g/8 oz) grated Parmesan cheese
1/2 tsp cayenne pepper
1/4 tsp ground nutmeg
1/4 tsp dried sage
1/2 tsp dried thyme
1/4 tsp dried rosemary
2 eggs, beaten
salt and freshly ground pepper

DOUGH:
5 1/2 cups (625 g/1 lb 6 oz) all-purpose flour
1/2 tsp salt
6 eggs, beaten

TO FINISH:
1/2 cup (50 g/2 oz) grated Parmesan cheese
2/3 cup (150 g/5 oz) melted unsalted butter

METHOD

1. To make the filling, sauté the lamb and the bacon in butter for 5 minutes. Add the mushrooms and garlic and sauté for 5 more minutes. Stir in the blanched spinach and then pass through a fine meat grinder, or grind in a food processor. Set aside.
2. When the mixture is cool, mix in the cheese, herbs, spices and eggs. Season well with salt and pepper.
3. For the dough: sift the flour and salt into a mixing bowl, stir in the eggs and knead to a smooth dough.
4. Divide the dough into two equal portions and roll out into rectangular sheets about 1/8-inch (3 mm) thick. .
5. Divide the filling equally between the two sheets. Spread evenly, leaving a 1 1/2-inch (3.5 cm) border around the edges.
6. Roll up each sheet of dough and wrap securely with cheesecloth, tying the ends with string.
7. Place in a roasting pan and cover with cold salted water. Bring to a boil and then simmer on the top of the stove for 20-25 minutes. Turn off the heat and allow the roulade to cool in the water.
8. To serve, remove the cheesecloth. Slice the roulade into portions and place on a greased cookie sheet. Brush with the melted butter, sprinkle with the Parmesan and broil for 5 minutes. Serve immediately.

CHEF'S TIPS:
This is an ideal winter dish satisfying enough to feed a hungry crowd and cleverly using vegetables to stretch the meat. This is delicious served wih a tomato sauce flavored with basil.

Japanese Lamb Packages

Serves: 8
Preparation time: 20 minutes, plus 1 hour marinating
Cooking time: 10 minutes

INGREDIENTS

FILLING:
3 lb (1.5 kg) cooked shoulder of lamb, cut into fine strips
2 garlic cloves, crushed
5 tsp sugar
1 tsp freshly grated ginger root
2/3 cup (150 ml/1/4 pint) soy sauce
2/3 cup (150 ml/1/4 pint) dry sherry
1/4 cup (50 ml/2 fl oz) oil
2/3 cup (150 ml/1/4 pint) chicken stock
2 tsp cornstarch

PANCAKES:
4 cups (450 g/1 lb) strong bread flour
1 tsp salt
6 eggs
4 1/2 cups (1 liter/1 3/4 pints) milk
scant 1 cup (200 ml/7 fl oz) oil
scallions, to tie packages

SAUCE:
1 1/4 cups (300 ml/1/2 pint) soy sauce
2/3 cup (150 ml/1/4 pint) dry sherry
3 tsp sugar
2 tsp freshly grated ginger root

METHOD

1. For the filling: mix the garlic, 1 teaspoon of the sugar, ginger, soy sauce and sherry together. Add the lamb, mix well and set aside for 1 hour.
2. Remove the lamb from the marinade and sauté in hot oil for 5 minutes, drain and set aside.
3. Put the remaining marinade into the pan, add the remaining sugar and the stock and bring to a boil. Mix a little water into the cornstarch and add to the pan, stirring until it thickens. Pour on top of the lamb, mix well and chill.
4. To make the pancakes: sift the flour and salt into a bowl, add the eggs and beat well, pouring in the milk gradually. Stir in the oil. Set aside for several hours, then whisk again before use.
5. Lightly grease a large pancake or omelet pan and heat to a high temperature. Spoon enough mixture into the pan to completely coat the base. Cook for 1 minute, turn the pancake over with a wide spatula, and cook for 1 minute more. Remove the cooked pancake from the pan and set aside. Continue to cook pancakes until all the mixture is used up. There should be about 16 pancakes.
6. To make the sauce: combine all the ingredients in a pan over a low heat and stir until the sugar dissolves. Set aside.
7. Arrange a portion of the filling in the center of each pancake, bring up the edges, completely encasing the filling, and tie with scallion.
8. Place on a cookie sheet and warm through in a moderate oven at 350°F (180°C/Gas mark 4) for 10 minutes. Serve immediately, allowing two packages per person. Serve the sauce separately.

CHEF'S TIPS:

These rolls are made from wanton dough, like Chinese spring rolls, or, for speed, you could use ready-made phyllo leaves. When making the pancakes, always use strong bread flour for the best results. Make the batter in advance.

Char-grilled Lamb Steaks on Warm Potato Salad

Serves: 2
Preparation time: 20 minutes
Cooking time: 12 minutes

INGREDIENTS

2 thick lamb steaks (taken from the leg or loin)
1 tbsp oil (walnut if available)
salt and black pepper

SALAD:
8 oz (225 g) pumpkin, peeled and sliced
8 oz (225 g) small potatoes
generous 1 cup (100 g /4 oz) shredded red cabbage
1 red bell pepper, cut into thin strips
1 small onion, chopped
1 tbsp snipped chives

DRESSING:
3 tbsp olive oil
1 tbsp wine vinegar
1 tsp Dijon mustard
salt and pepper

GARNISH:
1 bunch of garden cress

METHOD

1. Brush the oil all over the lamb and season well. Barbecue or char-grill to requirement – rare or medium.
2. Boil pumpkin until tender. Boil potatoes in their skins. Drain. When cool enough to handle, peel and slice them. Combine all the vegetables in a bowl.
3. Whisk the dressing ingredients. Pour over the salad vegetables and toss.
4. Place a large spoonful of the salad on each plate and top with the lamb. Garnish with a small bunch of garden cress.

CHEF'S TIPS:

A potato salad with a good French vinaigrette tastes even better when served hot and is an ideal accompaniment for any broil. This grilled or barbecued meal takes very little time to prepare and cook, so makes a very quick and easy dish for anyone in a hurry.

Lamb Pasanda

Serves: 4
Preparation time: 20 minutes
Cooking time: 35 minutes

INGREDIENTS

3 tbsp (35 g /1 1/2 oz) unsalted butter
1 large onion, crushed
1 lb (450 g) lean lamb (from leg or shoulder), cubed
2 garlic cloves, chopped
1-inch (2.5 cm) piece of ginger root, peeled and finely chopped
1/2 tsp each: turmeric, ground coriander, cumin and nutmeg
pinch of cayenne pepper
2/3 cup (150 ml/1/4 pint) light cream
2/3 cup (150 ml/1/4 pint) plain yoghurt
salt, to taste
1/4 cups (25 g/1 oz) finely chopped almonds
1 tsp garam masala

GARNISH:
1 1/4 cups (150 g/5 oz) toasted almonds or
    peanuts

METHOD

1. Heat the butter in a sauté pan and gently stir-fry the onion until soft, but not brown.
2. Add the lamb to the pan and cook for 5 minutes, tossing and stirring continually. Sprinkle in all the spices and stir well. Finally, add 1 1/4 cups (300 ml/1/2 pint) water, cover with a lid and simmer for 30 minutes or until the meat is tender.
3. Stir in the cream and yoghurt, season to taste and add the chopped nuts and garam masala. Heat through gently without boiling.
4. Garnish with the toasted nuts.

CHEF'S TIPS:

A deliciously spicy dish with a creamy sauce. It is always better to buy spices in small quantities, since they tend to lose their flavor very rapidly if they are not kept in airtight jars and used within a few months.

Serve with boiled rice and chappatis or popadums.

Lamb Corfu

Serves: 4
Preparation time: 10 minutes,
plus 6 hours marinating
Cooking time: 30 minutes

INGREDIENTS

4 x 6-oz (175 g) lamb loin steaks
1-2 tbsp oil, for frying

MARINADE:
1/2 cup (100 ml/4 fl oz) olive oil
juice of 2 lemons
salt and pepper
handful fresh cilantro leaves, chopped

SAUCE:
1/2 cup (100 g/4 oz) unsalted butter, softened
1 tsp ground coriander
1 tbsp olive oil
1 medium red onion, chopped
4 lemon segments
1/2 cup (100 ml/4 fl oz) clear honey
2 tsp yeast extract
salt and pepper

SERVE WITH:
green salad, with lemon dressing

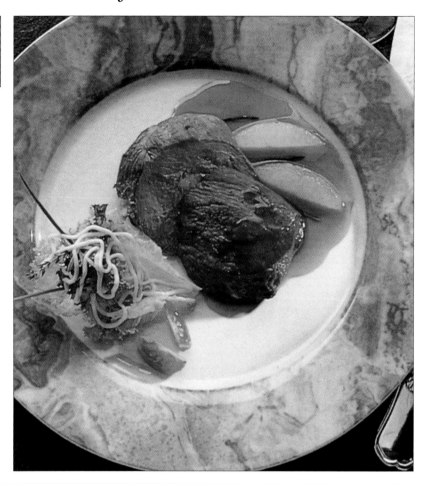

METHOD

1. Combine the marinade ingredients in a large bowl and soak the lamb for 6 hours.
2. Heat the oil in a pan and seal the meat all round for 5 minutes. Transfer to a roasting pan and cook in the oven at 400°F (200°C/Gas mark 6) for 10 minutes.
3. For the sauce: beat the butter and coriander to the consistency of cream. Heat the oil in a pan and stir-fry the onion for 2 minutes, then add the lemon segments, honey and yeast extract. Boil for 3 minutes to reduce. Season and stir in the beaten butter.
4. Serve the lamb with the sauce and the green salad with a lemon dressing.

CHEF'S TIPS:
Lamb is widely used in Greek cuisine. After poultry it is the most readily available meat, and lemon and rosemary are traditionally used to flavor it, although this recipe uses cilantro as a flavoring.

Sheep's Tongue in Red Pickle

Serves: 2
Preparation time: 15 minutes, plus marinating overnight
Cooking time: 2 hours

INGREDIENTS

2 sheep's tongues
2 3/4 cups (225 g/ 8 oz) shredded red cabbage
1 beet, shredded
1 red onion, shredded
1 1/4 cups (300 ml/1/2 pint) red wine
1 tbsp wine vinegar
1 small leek
1 carrot, peeled
1 onion, skinned
1/3 cup (25 g/1 oz) salt
salt and a few crushed peppercorns
6 juniper berries
2 3/4 cups (225 g/8 oz) shredded green cabbage
12 small onions

METHOD

1. In a bowl, marinate the red cabbage, beet and red onion in the red wine, vinegar and 1 1/4 cups (300 ml/1/2 pint) water and leave overnight.
2. Boil the sheep's tongue in 2 quarts (1.7 liters/3 pints) of water with the leek, carrot, onion and salt for 1 1/2 hours until tender. Remove the tongue from the water and peel off the outer skin. Cut into slices and return to the stock to keep warm.
3. Boil the red cabbage mixture for 30 minutes. Season with the salt, peppercorns and the juniper berries. Boil the green cabbage and small onions separately.
4. Serve the tongue on a plate with the boiled small onions and green cabbage. The red cabbage should be served on a side plate.

CHEF'S TIPS:

Sheep's tongue is a great delicacy in Arab and Muslim countries. If you can overcome your initial apprehension, sheep's tongue is simple to prepare and is highly nutritious and easy to digest. This dish can be eaten either hot or cold.

Serve with boiled new potatoes.

ALL ABOUT VEAL

Introduction

In our family restaurants, we always featured the best veal dishes. My father entrusted much of my training in butchery and charcuterie to two of his regular meat suppliers – Jules and Dupont. I have vivid memories of the many tasty cooked dishes one could buy from their charcuterie shops.

Veal is a very popular meat in both North America and Europe – highly praised by gourmets and appreciated by all for its versatility – you only have to consider the following dishes to understand why. Calves' liver and sweetbreads are considered gastronomic delights when cooked in butter or prepared in a creamy sauce as a filling for vol-au-vents. The classic dishes of Viennese Schnitzel and Escalope Marsala are always popular today. A fillet of veal en croûte, pot roasted with artichoke hearts and truffles is a great luxury, and a medallion of veal, taken from the loin, is equal to the best beef Tournedos. The recent application of Asiatic styles of stir-frying to the cooking of veal, with exotic vegetables, cut julienne-style, and the addition of fruit juices and coconut milk instead of cream and wines, has helped to extend the repertoire of veal cookery. The fact that veal is not only less fatty than beef, but also more tender and easily digestible appeals in this health-conscious time.

In this chapter I invite you to try a selection of classical and modern dishes using veal, based on a variety of different cooking styles. It is always the sauce which makes the dish and I must stress the value of veal bones and knuckles as essential ingredients in the making of the most succulent stocks and sauces.

Veal lends itself to being blended with a wide variety of flavors, garnishes, spices and herbs. The texture of veal meat makes it ideal for forcemeat, pâtés, terrines, mousses, quenelles, dumplings, kromeskies, burgers and pies. The choice of uses and dishes is quite extensive.

The best French calves for veal production come from Brie, Nivers and Touraine. The calves are kept indoors in a scrupulously clean environment, and fed exclusively on a diet of milk, sometimes supplemented with eggs, which keeps the flesh white. In recent times there has been some controversy surrounding this. In Britain, however, and in some other countries, the young calves are kept with their mothers and allowed to eat grass. This means that the flesh tends to be pink rather than white. It is possible for the meat from these calves to be as white as that from the calves kept inside, if it is soaked in salted water prior to being cooked. Veal from calves under three months old is called 'crevard' and veal between three and six months is called 'd'éclat' by the French.

SIGNS OF QUALITY IN VEAL
When buying veal, the chief points to remember are as follows.
1. The flesh should be pale pink, firm in structure with a pleasant smell
2. The meat should be moist when cut
3. The bones should be pinkish and porous with a certain amount of blood inside. The extremities of shoulder blade and breastbone should be flexible
4. The fat should be white and slightly pinkish, firm in and around the pelvic cavity and in the region of the kidneys, but there should be very little surface fat
5. Connective tissue should be gelatinous, not hard, sinewy or bubbly (i.e. full of air)

The butchery cuts of veal are the same as beef, but they have different names in English and in 'kitchen' French.

VEAL

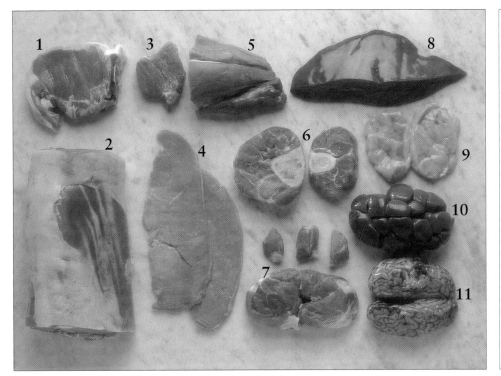

Braised Veal Knuckles in Sweet Ginger

Serves: 2
Preparation time: 30 minutes, plus overnight
to marinate
Cooking time: 1 hour

INGREDIENTS

2 x 12-oz (350 g) veal knuckles
    with the bone attached
2 tbsp oil

MARINADE:
1/4 cup (25g/1 oz) fresh peeled and chopped
    ginger root
1/2 cup (100 ml/4 fl oz) wine vinegar
2 scallions, chopped
1 1/4 cups (300 ml/1/2 pint) sweet white
    wine
6 black peppercorns, coarsely ground
1 tsp salt

STOCK:
4 oz (100g) piece of ginger root, broiled
    slightly
4 tbsp soy sauce or 1 tsp yeast extract
2/3 cup (150 ml/1/4 pint) vinegar
2 tbsp sugar
2 tsp cornstarch mixed with 2 tbsp water
salt and pepper

METHOD

1. Trim round each knuckle to 2-inch (5 cm) from the bare bone.
2. Combine marinade ingredients in a bowl. Place the knuckles in the marinade and let soak overnight in the fridge.
3. Heat the oil in a large saucepan, drain the knuckles and fry for about 10 minutes until brown.
4. Put 2 1/2 cups (600 ml/1 pint) water, the ginger, soy sauce or yeast extract, vinegar and sugar for the stock in a saucepan, add the marinade and bring to a boil.
5. Place the knuckles in a Dutch oven, pour over the hot marinade and stock liquor. Cover with a lid and braise for 1 hour at 325°F (170°C/Gas mark 3).
6. Pour the liquor through a strainer and thicken it with the cornstarch and water to make a sauce. Boil for 4 minutes. Check the seasoning.
7. Place the knuckles on the plates with a some of the sauce poured around.

CHEF'S TIPS:
Brown Veal Stock
Use the same ingredients as above, but roast veal meat and bones for 30 minutes before simmering them in water. Shallow fry a selection of vegetables for 6 minutes, drain and add them to the knuckles. Remove the meat after 2 hours of slow simmering for use in another dish. Continue to simmer the bones and vegetables for a further 2 hours. Pour the liquid through a strainer. Grind the meat for pies, or sauce to serve with pasta. Use the stock for all light veal sauces for entrees, veal chops, sweetbreads etc. A salad of rice, celery and mushrooms in a vinaigrette dressing would be a suitable accompaniment for this dish, alternatively the usual root vegetables can be used (see page 47).

Rack of Veal Stuffed with Kidneys

Serves: 6
Preparation time: 20 minutes
Cooking time: 45 minutes

INGREDIENTS

1 calf's kidney, trimmed and cut into strips
1 tsp dry mustard mixed with 1 tbsp seasoned flour
1 tbsp oil
2 tbsp (25g/1 oz) butter
2-lb (1 kg) boneless veal rib roast
oil and butter, to coat
2 carrots, diced
1 cup (150 g/5 oz) diced onions
1 1/4 cups (150 g/5 oz) sliced celery
4 1/2 cups (1 liter/1 3/4 pints) veal stock
1 tbsp tomato paste
5 juniper berries or 1 tbsp gin
salt and black pepper
1 tsp cornstarch mixed with 3 tbsp vermouth

GARNISH:
sprigs of wild thyme

BERNY POTATOES
4 lb (2 kg) potatoes, peeled
1/2 cup (100 g/4 oz) margarine or butter
salt and pepper
4 egg yolks
2 oz (50 g) truffle, finely chopped*
1/2 cup (50 g/2 oz) flour, for dusting
2 eggs, lightly beaten
1 1/2 cups (175 g/6 oz) flaked almonds
oil, for deep frying
parsley, to garnish

METHOD

1. Season the kidney strips, then dust with mixed flour and dry mustard.
2. Heat the oil and butter and stir-fry the kidney strips for 4 minutes. Remove and let cool.
3. Place the boneless roast on its back, skin downwards. Arrange the kidney pieces along the inside. Roll up and tie with string. Brush with the oil and butter. Place on a trivet of bones in a shallow baking dish, without the lid. Roast at 400°F (200°C/ Gas mark 6) for 20 minutes to brown the meat.
4. Add the vegetables to the meat after it has browned. Pour in the veal stock, add the tomato paste, gin or berries and seasoning. Cover with a lid, lower the oven to 350°F (180°C/Gas mark 4) and braise for 20-25 minutes.
5. To serve, remove the string and cut the meat into thick slices. Pour the liquid into a saucepan and boil for 3 minutes. Thicken slightly with the cornstarch and vermouth mixture. Cook for 4 minutes to clear the starch. Strain the sauce. Check seasoning. Garnish with thyme.

BERNY POTATOES
1. Boil the potatoes. Drain, pat dry and pass through a strainer into a bowl. Add butter or margarine and seasoning.
2. Return the mixture to the saucepan, add the egg yolks and mix well away from the heat until the mixture leaves the bottom of the pan clean. Let cool, then add the finely chopped truffle.
3. Mold the mixture into small balls. Dip in the flour and egg wash and coat with almonds. Shape like an apricot.
4. Fry in deep hot oil until golden brown. Drain and serve garnished with parsley.

CHEF'S TIPS:
Use calf's trotters or bacon rind with the roast veal to make the sauce thicker and to improve the flavor. Calf's kidney is the most delicate entrée. It can be cooked quickly on its own, without any garnish, but serve it with a sauce lightly flavored with sweet mustard, a little cream and a good sprinkling of fresh chopped parsley and tarragon for a really delicious dish.

*It is the truffle in the potato recipe which gives the dish the name 'Berny'. However any chopped mushrooms could be substituted.

Loin of Veal Sangiovese

Serves: 4
Preparation time: 20 minutes
Cooking time: 25 minutes

INGREDIENTS

2 lb (1 kg) veal loin roast or tenderloin

FILLING:
4 slices of prosciutto ham
4 slices of Bel Paese cheese
4 chicken livers, trimmed and scalded in
    boiling water
1 tsp coarsely ground black pepper
1 pinch of crumbled dried sage

SAUCE:
1 1/4 cups (300 ml/1/2 pint) Chianti wine
1 small shallot, chopped
1 sprig of thyme
1 1/4 cups (300 ml/1/2 pint) brown stock
1 tsp cornstarch mixed with 3 tbsp dry
    Italian vermouth
salt and pepper

METHOD

1. Cut the veal down the center and open out like a butterfly. Flatten the veal with a meat mallet or rolling pin. Place the slices of ham, the cheese and the livers on top. Sprinkle with pepper and ground sage. Roll and tie up with string. Wrap in oiled foil and bake for 25 minutes at 400°F (200°C/Gas mark 6).
2. Meanwhile prepare the sauce. Boil the chopped shallot and thyme in wine for 5 minutes, add the brown stock and thicken it with the cornstarch and vermouth mixture. Boil for 4 minutes to clear the starch and produce a glossy sauce. Check seasoning.
3. Place three slices of meat on each plate with some sauce and serve with tagliatelle.

CHEF'S TIPS:
Sangiovese is the principal red grape of Tuscany, Italy, from which Chianti wine is produced. Chianti forms the basis of the delicious sauce, which accompanies the meat. The veal itself has an extravagant filling of liver, Italian ham and Bel Paese cheese. Tagliatelle boiled *al dente* and tossed in butter, with a garnish of cilantro, and a little balsamic vinegar does justice to this dish.

Stuffed Veal Breast Mediterranean

Serves: 6
Preparation time: 20 minutes
Cooking time: 45-50 minutes

INGREDIENTS

2 lb (1 kg) rolled veal breast roast, boned
2 pig's cauls to wrap the joint (bacon
  slices can be used instead)
2 tbsp (25 g/1 oz) butter
1 tbsp oil
salt and pepper
1 sprig of thyme
1 tsp cornstarch mixed with 3 tbsp of vermouth

VEGETABLES:
1 carrot, coarsely diced
1 onion, coarsely diced
1 stick of celery, coarsely diced
2 tomatoes, chopped

STUFFING:
1/2 cup (100 g/4 oz) ground veal or sausage meat
1/2 cup (100 g/4 oz) ground liver (or use black pudding
  mixture)
2 cups (100 g/4 oz) chopped mushrooms
2 tbsp (25 g/1 oz) golden raisins

1 egg
1 tbsp chopped mixed herbs
3 black olives, pitted and diced
3/4 cup (75 g/3 oz) deseeded and finely diced red and
  green bell peppers
1 zucchini, peeled and finely diced

GARNISH:
1 tbsp oil
1 cup (100 g/4 oz) diced red and green bell peppers
2 small zucchini, diced

RATATOUILLE:
2 tbsp olive oil
1 small onion, sliced
2 garlic cloves, crushed
4 zucchini, sliced
2 eggplants, peeled and sliced
4 large tomatoes, skinned, deseeded and roughly
  chopped
1 tbsp chopped fresh basil

METHOD

1. Untie the meat and open it out ready to stuff.
2. In a bowl, combine the ingredients for the stuffing. Place the stuffing along the inside of the breast. Roll over and wrap the rolled joint in pig's caul or bacon slices. Tie up with strings.
3. Heat the oil and butter in a large pan and brown the meat for 10 minutes. Remove the meat from the pan and place it in a Dutch oven with the breast bones. In the frying pan brown the vegetables slightly and add to the meat. Cover with 2 1/2 cups (600 ml/1 pint) water. Add the thyme and seasoning. Cover with a lid and braise for 35-40 minutes at 350°F (180°C/Gas mark 4) until cooked through.
4. Prepare the ratatouille. Heat oil in a shallow pan and stir-fry the zucchini, eggplants, onion and garlic for 5 minutes. Add the tomatoes and simmer for a further 10 minutes. Season and sprinkle with basil.
5. Prepare the garnish for the sauce. Heat the oil and stir-fry the bell peppers and zucchini for 3 minutes only. Season and reserve.
6. Remove the meat. Make up liquor to 2 1/2 cups (600 ml/1 pint) with boiling water, for the sauce. Stir in the cornstarch and vermouth. Boil for 4 minutes to thicken the sauce, then strain. Season to taste.
7. To serve, place slices of meat on the plates, pour some of the sauce around the meat and sprinkle over the diced bell peppers and zucchini for garnish.

CHEF'S TIPS:
Always pot roast the meat with a trivet of bones and a flavoring of coarsely cut root vegetables. Be careful not to cut the vegetables too small since small vegetables will brown too quickly. Add the vegetables after the meat has been well browned for 25 minutes. Keep the level of the liquid in the casserole constant by adding stock or water to compensate for the liquid lost through evaporation.

Veal Blanquette

Serves: 6
Preparation time: 15 minutes, plus
 1 hour soaking time
Cooking time: 1 1/2 hours

INGREDIENTS

2 lb (1 kg) stewing veal, cut into 1-inch
    (2.5cm) cubes
1 carrot
1 celery stick
1 onion, studded with two cloves
1 sprig of thyme

ROUX:
1/4 cup (50 g/2 oz) butter
1/2 cup (50 g/2 oz) strong bread flour
1/2 cup (100 ml/4 fl oz) heavy cream
salt and pepper
grated mace or nutmeg

GARNISH:
4 baby carrots
4 baby turnips
8 scallions
8 small white onions
4oz (100 g) green beans

METHOD

1. Soak the meat in cold salted water for 1 hour. Drain and rinse. Drain again. Place meat in a large saucepan and boil for 10 minutes. Throw away the liquid. Refresh the meat and reboil it in 4 1/2 cups (1 liter/1 3/4 pints) clean water with the carrot, celery, onion and thyme. Simmer for 1 1/2 hours until tender. Strain and reserve liquor. Top up to make 4 1/2 cups (1 liter/1 3/4 pints) if necessary.
2. To make the roux: melt the butter and stir in the flour, cook for 15 seconds without browning. Gradually add the veal liquor. Boil for 10 minutes and then strain. Add cream and seasoning, return the meat to the sauce and reheat for 10 minutes.
3. Cook the garnish separately in boiling salted water.
4. Serve the veal stew and sauce on a large soup plate and place the vegetable garnish on top.

CHEF'S TIPS:

For all stews it is best to use shoulder or breast of veal. The meat should be cut into 1-inch (2.5 cm) cubes. The main characteristic of veal blanquette is the whiteness of the meat. The blanquette is prepared in four stages (as above) to ensure that the meat remains white.

A fricassee differs from a blanquette, in that the meat for a fricassée is seared in butter, the cooking liquid is then added and, when cooking is complete, it is thickened with cream and egg yolks.

Serve with potatoes or rice.

Veal Chops Grandma Style

Serves: 4
Preparation time: 15 minutes
Cooking time: 20 minutes

INGREDIENTS

4 x 8-oz (225 g) veal rib chops, trimmed
2 tbsp seasoned flour
1 tbsp oil
2 tbsp (25 g/1 oz) butter
1 1/4 cups (300 ml/1/2 pint) dry white wine
1 sprig of thyme
1 garlic clove
1 tsp yeast extract
1 tsp cornstarch mixed with 3 tbsp light
    cream

GARNISH:
1 tbsp oil
2 tbsp (25 g/1 oz) butter
2 slices bacon, derinded and diced
12 small onions, peeled
12 small mushrooms
16 turned potatoes (barrel
    shaped, as big as plums)
2/3 cup (150 ml/1/4 pint) stock
parsley or cilantro leaves

METHOD

1. Coat the veal chops in seasoned flour. Shake off the surplus. Heat the oil and butter in a pan and shallow fry the meat for 6 minutes on each side. Place the veal chops in a Dutch oven and just cover with the white wine. Add the sprig of thyme, whole clove of garlic and yeast extract. Cover with a lid and braise for 20 minutes at 350°F (180°C/Gas mark 4).
2. Meanwhile heat the oil and butter in a sauté pan and fry the bacon for 5 minutes until brown. Add the onions, mushrooms and potatoes and stir-fry for 10 minutes. Cover the pan with a lid – this helps to keep the flavor in. Stir and toss the vegetables until cooked. Pour in the stock and simmer for 10 minutes.
3. When the chops are cooked drain the cooking liquor into a pan and thicken slightly with the mixed cornstarch and cream. Boil for 4 minutes and strain. Check the seasoning.
4. Place the veal chops on the plates and coat with the sauce, arrange the vegetable garnish beside the chops. Sprinkle with parsley or cilantro leaves.

CHEF'S TIPS:
Veal rib chops braised in white wine are a great favorite of mine. It was often featured as the dish of the day on the menu of my father's restaurant, the Ducastaing, in Paris in the late 1930s. The garnish of small onions, baby mushrooms and dainty small turned potatoes really does make this dish.

Veal Rolls with Prosciutto and Cranberries

Serves: 4
Preparation time: 20 minutes
Cooking time: 12 minutes

INGREDIENTS

4 x 5-oz (150 g) veal scallops, cut from the
    round roast
4 x 4-oz (100 g) slices Prosciutto ham
oil, to brush

STUFFING:
2 tbsp (50 g/2 oz) butter
1 medium onion, chopped
1 1/4 cups (150 g/5 oz) cranberries, or pitted
    sour cherries
1 1/2 cups (75 g/3 oz) fresh breadcrumbs
1 tbsp chopped fresh sage
1 egg
salt and pepper

SAUCE:
1/2 cup (100 ml/4 fl oz) apple juice
1/4 cup (50 ml/2 fl oz) cider vinegar
1 tbsp cranberries or raspberries
1/2 cup (100 ml/4 fl oz) brown sauce
    (see page 29)
1/2 cup (100 ml/4 fl oz) light cream
1 tbsp sweet butter

METHOD

1. Place the veal scallops between two sheets of plastic wrap and pat lightly with a wooden mallet or rolling pin.
2. Prepare the stuffing. Heat the butter in a frying pan and shallow fry the onion until soft. Add the cranberries, breadcrumbs and chopped sage and fry for 1 minute. Remove from the heat and mix in the egg. Season to taste.
3. Place one quarter of the stuffing inside each scallop and roll them up. Wrap the rolled scallops in oiled foil, fold the foil like a package with the ends tucked underneath. Place in a baking dish and transfer to a hot oven 400°F (200°C/Gas mark 6) and bake for 8 minutes. Remove from the oven and let rest for 5 minutes.
4. Meanwhile prepare the sauce. Boil the apple juice and vinegar until reduced by half. Add the berries for color and brown sauce and cream. Boil for 5 minutes and whisk in the butter to emulsify the sauce.
5. Pour some of the sauce and put three slices of each veal roll on each plate. Garnish with the strips of Prosciutto. Brush the Prosciutto with a little oil.

CHEF'S TIPS:

Veal and ham complement each other very well. In this recipe Prosciutto is used to garnish the stuffed roulade of veal. In Australia, muntries (a type of red berry which are very sharp) would be used instead of cranberries.

Buttered noodles and a spinach salad would be ideal served with this dish. In a salad, spinach can be mixed with root vegetables. The iron content of spinach has been greatly exaggerated, but it is a nutritious vegetable and, like many vegetables, it is best cooked lightly in butter rather than boiled in water. Spinach leaves should be washed three times before cooking and well-drained to eliminate all traces of sand.

Russian Veal Kournick Pie

Serves: 4
Preparation time: 20 minutes, plus
15 minutes resting time for pastry
Cooking time: 25 minutes

INGREDIENTS

2 tbsp oil
1 1/2 cups (250 g/9 oz) ground veal
scant 1 cup (100 g/4 oz) chopped onions
1 eggplant, diced
2 cups (100 g/4 oz) chopped mushrooms
1 tbsp chopped parsley
salt and pepper
1 egg, beaten
12 oz (350 g) puff pastry (see page 29)
1 egg yolk, for glazing
1 1/4 cups (300 ml/1/2 pint) brown sauce
   (see page 29)
1/4 cup (50ml/2fl oz) medium sherry

GARNISH:
asparagus tips

METHOD

1. Heat the oil in a frying pan and stir-fry the meat and onion together for 15 minutes. Meanwhile, soak the diced eggplant in salted water for 15 minutes. Rinse and pat dry.
2. Add the eggplant, mushrooms, parsley and seasoning to the meat. Remove the mixture from the heat, let cool and mix in the beaten egg to bind the mixture.
3. Roll out the puff pastry on a floured board to 1/4-inch (5 mm) thick. With a plain cookie cutter cut out 8 x 3 3/4-inch (9 cm) rounds. Continue to roll out four of the rounds until they have a diameter of 4-inch (10 cm).
4. Place the smaller rounds on an oiled cookie sheet and spoon one-eighth of the meat mixture onto each round. Brush the sides with water and cover with the larger rounds of paste. Crimp the edges. Brush with egg wash. Let rest for 15 minutes. Bake in a hot oven at 400°F (200°C/Gas mark 6) for 20-25 minutes.
5. Mix together the brown sauce and sherry in a pan and heat through.
6. Place a pie on each plate, surround with some of the sauce and garnish with asparagus tips.

CHEF'S TIPS:

This type of pie, served as an entrée, can be made with brioche, croissant, Danish pastry or, more simply, puff pastry. You can make your own or, for speed, buy ready-prepared chilled or frozen. The meat filling must always be well cooked. It is possible to use leftovers for this dish and so it can be economical to prepare. The pie can be served hot or it can be eaten cold.

Kurrajong Veal Crêpe

Serves: 4
Preparation time: 20 minutes
Cooking time: 20 minutes, plus 1 hour resting time

INGREDIENTS

4 x 6-oz (175 g) veal steaks from the loin or
    tenderloin
1 tbsp oil
2 tbsp (25 g/1 oz) butter, for shallow frying

CREPE MIXTURE:
2 eggs
1 1/4 cups (300 ml/1/2 pint) milk
1 1/4 cups (150 g/5oz) all-purpose flour
2-3 tbsp melted butter
pinch of salt

FILLING:
1/4 cup (50 g/2 oz) butter
1 medium onion, finely chopped
4 cups (225 g/8 oz) chopped mushrooms
2 tbsp breadcrumbs (optional)
1 tbsp chopped fresh parsley
pinch of thyme
1 tsp yeast extract
salt and black pepper

SAUCE:
1 1/4 cups (300ml/1/2 pint) brown sauce
    (see page 29)
1/4 cup (50 ml/2fl oz) medium sherry

METHOD

1. First, make the crêpes. Combine all the ingredients in a bowl, using just 1 tablespoon of the melted butter, and beat well to obtain a smooth batter. Grease a large pancake pan, 10-inch (25 cm) diameter, with oil or lard. Pour about a quarter of the mixture into the pan for each pancake. Toss and cook 4 pancakes until golden on both sides.
2. Heat oil and butter in a frying pan and shallow fry the veal steaks for 5 minutes. Remove the veal from the pan, allow to cool and chill for 1 hour.
3. Fry the chopped mushrooms and onions in butter until firm and free of juice. Add breadcrumbs, if too wet. Stir in parsley, thyme and yeast extract and season to taste.
4. Place a crêpe on a clean pastry board, place a veal steak onto the crêpe and spoon some of the mushroom mixture onto the steak. Wrap up the package. Place the stuffed pancakes on a greased cookie sheet and brush with the remaining melted butter. Bake for 5 minutes in a hot oven at 400°F (200°C/Gas mark 6). Remove from the oven and let rest in a warm place for 5 minutes.
5. Mix together brown sauce and sherry in a pan. Serve the crêpes cut in half, with a spoonful of the sauce.

CHEF'S TIPS:

Veal should be cooked through and, unlike beef, it should not be served pinkish. The tenderloin tends to have a more delicate flavor and to be more tender than the loin. The skin of the meat should always be removed.

The crêpes can be served with small turned carrots and turnips, snow peas or other seasonal vegetables.

Veal Fillet Steak with Morels

Serves: 2
Preparation time: 35 minutes
Cooking time: 35 minutes

INGREDIENTS

2 x 6-oz (175 g) veal tenderloin
    steaks, 1-inch (2.5 cm) thick
1 tbsp oil
2 tbsp (25 g/1 oz) butter
1 shallot, chopped
225 g (8 oz) morel mushrooms or
    2 cups (100 g/4 oz) dried, soaked
1/2 cup (100 ml/4 fl oz) dry white wine
1/2 cup (100 ml/4 floz) veal stock
1/4 cup (50 m/2 fl oz) heavy cream
salt and pepper
juice of 1/2 a lemon

GARNISH:
fresh cilantro leaves

METHOD

1. Season the veal steaks. Heat the oil and butter in a lidded pan and shallow fry for 12-15 minutes, turning twice. Remove the meat and keep warm.
2. In the same fat, shallow fry the shallot for 2 minutes, then add the mushrooms and wine. Boil for 5 minutes.
3. Remove the mushrooms and keep warm. Add the veal stock and boil for a further 10 minutes. Stir the cream into the sauce and boil rapidly to reduce for another 5 minutes. Season the sauce.
4. Squeeze the juice of 1/2 a lemon over each steak. Place the steaks on each plate and pour a pool of sauce next to them. Serve with the morels. Garnish with the cilantro leaves.

CHEF'S TIPS:
The grenadin cut can be taken from the 'noix' or, as in this recipe, from the tenderloin. It can be prepared and cooked like a tournedo, except that it is tougher and takes longer to cook.

Morel mushrooms have a sponge like appearance. If using dried, which are more readily available, use only 2 cups (100 g/4 oz) and soak in cold water.

Serve this dish with butterfly pasta.

Veal Scallops Rijswik with Peas

Serves: 2
Preparation time: 12 minutes
Cooking time: 20-30 minutes

INGREDIENTS

2 x 6-oz (175 g) veal scallops
1/4 cup (50 g/2 oz) raw ground veal
1 cup (100 g/4 oz) peas, cooked
salt and pepper
seasoned flour
2 tbsp (25 g/1 oz) butter
1 tbsp oil
3 tbsp Dutch gin
6 tbsp beer
2/3 cup (150 ml/1/4 pint) brown sauce
    (see page 29)

TO SERVE:
2/3 cup (150 g/5 oz) long grain and wild rice,
    boiled
Duchesse potatoes (see page 104) and potato waffles

METHOD

1. Beat the scallops as thinly as possible. In a bowl combine the raw ground veal with the peas, salt and pepper. Spread this mixture over the center of each scallop. Roll up the meat and tie it with two strings, like a package. Coat in seasoned flour.
2. Heat the butter and oil in a lidded pan and cook the meat packages for 15 minutes over a low heat. Remove the meat from the pan. Discard the strings. Drain away half of the fat in the pan and deglaze the meat juices with the gin and beer. Add the brown sauce and boil for 10 minutes. Season the sauce and strain it.
3. Waffle potato batter is made by finely grating raw potatoes and adding 1 egg per 1 lb (450 g) of potatoes. Cook using a waffle iron. Duchesse potatoes are mashed potatoes mixed with egg yolks and butter. Use 1 egg yolk and 1/4 cup (50 g/2 oz) of butter per 1 lb (450 g) of mashed potatoes.
4. Place the stuffed scallop on a plate with three piped servings of duchesse potatoes, the potato waffles and a portion of rice. Serve the sauce separately.

CHEF'S TIPS:
Dutch gin is specified in this recipe becasue it has a stronger juniper flavor than other gins. It is suggested that the dish be served with rice, Duchesse potaoes and waffles, because the Dutch like a filling, starchy accompaniment.

Veal Fillet with Celery Root

Serves: 4
Preparation time: 20 minutes
Cooking time: 12 minutes

INGREDIENTS

8 small veal tenderloin pieces, beaten with a
    meat mallet or rolling pin to give thin
    scallops
2 tbsp seasoned flour
3 tbsp oil
2 tbsp (25 g/1 oz) butter
1/2 celery root, boiled and puréed
1/4 cup (50 g/2 oz) firm mashed potato
1 egg yolk
1 cup (50 g/2 oz) fresh whole wheat
    breadcrumbs

SAUCE:
3 tbsp medium or dry sherry
1/2 cup (100 ml/4 fl oz) veal stock
1 shallot, chopped
4 tbsp heavy cream
1 oz (25 g) chopped truffles
2 tbsp (25 g/1 oz) unsalted butter
salt and pepper
celery root purée, to garnish (from above)

METHOD

1. Coat the veal with seasoned flour. Heat the oil and butter in a pan and fry the veal for 8 minutes until cooked. Remove the veal from the pan.
2. Mix together the celery root (reserve some) and potato, then use the vegetable mixture to coat the veal. Roll in the egg yolks and coat with the breadcrumbs. Place the veal in the oven at 400°F (200°C/Gas mark 6) for 12 minutes, to brown the top only. Keep the veal warm while making the sauce.
3. Boil the sherry, veal stock and shallots together until the liquid has reduced by a third. Add the cream and the chopped truffles. Whisk in the butter to emulsify the sauce and season to taste.
4. To serve, pour a pool of sauce onto each plate and arrange two pieces of veal per portion in the sauce. Garnish with a spoonful of the reserved celery root purée.

CHEF'S TIPS:

In order to make a successful vegetable purée it is best to have a starchy textured base provided by puréed potatoes, to this you can add any other puréed vegetable. To serve the purée use an ice cream scoop, or shape the purée using two spoons together or pipe it if you have a star pastry tip.

To make the purée of any root or tuber vegetable really fluffy, blend in some whipped cream: use 1/2 cup (100 ml/4 fl oz) of heavy cream for each 1 lb (450 g) of vegetables. To avoid lumps in the purée always pass it through a ricer or strainer. Squeeze lemon juice over the celery root to prevent it from discoloring. To make a purée more flavorsome, simply beat in some soft cream cheese.

Serve with snow peas, Brussels sprouts, sliced peaches and herbs.

Veal Surf and Turf

Serves: 4
Preparation time: 15 minutes
Cooking time: 45 minutes

INGREDIENTS

4 x 5-oz (150 g) veal scallops, flattened
8 jumbo shrimp, shelled, deveined and raw
    (fresh or frozen)
1/4 cup (50 g/2 oz) butter
2 tbsp oil
1 1/4 cups (300 ml/1/2 pint) white wine
1 1/4 cups (300 ml/1/2 pint) veal stock
2 garlic cloves
1 small onion, chopped
juice of 1 lemon
2 cups (225 g/8 oz) broccoli, in small pieces
2 sticks of celery, cut in slices
salt and pepper

SERVE WITH:
2 carrots, thinly sliced
5 oz (150 g) black rice noodles
2 tbsp butter
a few snow peas

METHOD

1. Soak the black rice noodles for the garnish in cold water for 30 minutes, then drain.
2. Heat the butter in a shallow pan or a wok and fry the veal scallops for 3 minutes only. Remove the veal and keep warm.
3. In the same pan, add the oil to the butter and stir-fry the shrimp until red. Add the stock, wine, onion, garlic, lemon juice, broccoli and celery to the pan and simmer for 3 minutes. Season to taste.
4. Blanch the carrots and snow peas in boiling water for about 15 seconds. Heat the two tablespoons of butter and toss the drained noodles and blanched carrots together.
5. Arrange the noodles and carrots on a plate and place the shrimp, veal and snow peas on top. Strain the juice from the pan and pour a little of it over the noodles. (A few lima beans would provide further interest.)

CHEF'S TIPS:

For the best flavor, buy frozen green prawns. A stock can be made from the prawn shells, which is where most of the flavor is to be found.

The French would shallow fry the shrimp in their shells for a few minutes, add the stock and then continue to cook for a further 3 minutes. They would remove the shell from the cooked shrimp and take out the black intestinal cord from the tail of the shrimp thereby ensuring that the tail meat is clean.

This dish could also be made with breast of chicken instead of veal and crayfish or baby langoustines could replace the jumbo shrimp.

Veal Steak Alicante

Serves: 4
Preparation time: 15 minutes, plus
1 hour cooling the veal
Cooking time: 20 minutes

INGREDIENTS

1 1/2 lb (675 g) veal tenderloin, trimmed
4 1/2 cups (1 liter/1 3/4pints) concentrated
   veal stock

STUFFING:
2 tbsp chopped fresh basil
1/2 cup (50 g/2 oz) pine nuts
1 clove garlic
4 slices of Boccontini cheese*
4 slices of Italian salami
shavings of Parmesan cheese

SAUCE:
1 1/4 cups (300 ml/1/2 pint) Alicante or Chianti red wine
1 tsp cornstarch mixed with 2 tbsp water
salt and pepper

GARNISH:
sliced fresh figs

METHOD

1. Poach the whole tenderloin of veal in the stock for 10 minutes. Cool the veal in the stock for 1 hour and then slice it into four 6- oz (175 g) portions. Reserve the stock.
2. To make the stuffing, pound the basil, garlic and pine nuts together. Spread this mixture over the veal and cover with the slices of salami and cheese. Sprinkle with shaved Parmesan cheese. Place the covered pieces of veal onto an oiled cookie sheet and glaze under a broiler.
3. Boil the reserved stock with the wine until reduced by half. Thicken the sauce with the cornstarch mixed with water. Boil the sauce for 4 minutes until clear. Check the seasoning.
4. To serve, place the veal on the plates, pour a circle of sauce around the meat and garnish with the fresh figs. (A purée of fresh spinach would make an equally good garnish.)

CHEF'S TIPS:
This recipe is a modern version of the famous Veal Cordon Bleu. To make Veal Cordon Bleu, sandwich a scallop between cheese and ham, coat the package in breadcrumbs and shallow fry.

*Cheddar cheese can be used if Boccontini cheese is not available, since it also melts well under the broiler.

Hot Veal and Crab Loaf with Curry Sauce

Serves: 4
Preparation time: 15 minutes
Cooking time: 40 minutes

INGREDIENTS

4 x 5-oz (150 g) veal scallops
1 tbsp seasoned flour
2 tbsp oil
8 green spring cabbage or spinach leaves,
    blanched and refreshed in iced water

FILLING:
1 cup (150 g/5 oz) ground raw veal
1 cup (150 g/5 oz) white crabmeat,
    free from any bits of shell
2 egg whites
1/2 cup (100 ml/4 fl oz) heavy cream
    or thick yoghurt
1 small boiled onion, finely chopped
    or minced
salt and pepper
1 tsp ground ginger
1 tsp honey
juice of 1/2 lemon

SAUCE:
1 tbsp oil
1 small onion, chopped
1 garlic clove, chopped
1 tsp curry powder
1 1/4 cups (300 ml/1/2 pint) veal stock
1 tbsp canned coconut cream
1 tbsp heavy cream
salt and pepper
red, yellow and green bell peppers, cut into small squares, to garnish

METHOD

1. Flatten the veal scallops with a meat mallet. Dust each one with seasoned flour and brush with oil. Fry the scallops for 2 minutes only. Remove from the heat and let cool.
2. Prepare the filling by mixing all the ingredients together in a bowl to make a soft paste.
3. Oil a rectangular earthenware terrine and put in a layer of scallops followed by a layer of the filling. Top with a layer of the cabbage or spinach leaves. Brush with oil and cover with a lid. Bake in a moderate oven at 350°F (180°C/Gas mark 4). The terrine should be placed in a deep pan half-filled with water. Remove from the oven after 40 minutes and let cool. When completely cold, turn out and cut into neat oblong slices.
4. For the sauce, heat the oil in a pan and shallow fry the onion and garlic for 3 minutes without browning. Add the curry powder and cook for 10 seconds, then add the stock and coconut cream. Boil for 15 minutes and strain. Stir in the heavy cream and season to taste.
5. Stir-fry the squares of bell pepper in a little oil for just 2 minutes. Place two slices of the cold loaf on a plate, pour a pool of sauce around them and garnish with the bell peppers.

Calf's Liver with Grapes

Serves: 4
Preparation time: 20 minutes
Cooking time: 8 minutes

INGREDIENTS

4 x 5-oz (150 g) slices of calf's liver
seasoned flour
1/2 cup (50 g/2 oz) seedless green grapes
2 tbsp brandy
oil for frying
1 tsp all-purpose flour
1/2 cup (100 ml/4 fl oz) dry white wine
1/4 cup (50 ml/2 fl oz) cream
salt and pepper
2 tbsp chopped fresh parsley

METHOD

1. Soak the calf's liver in salted water for 10 minutes. Drain and pat dry. Coat in seasoned flour.
2. Soak the grapes in the brandy for 10 minutes.
3. Heat the oil in a pan and fry the liver: 1 minute each side for underdone meat, 3 minutes each side if the liver is to be medium to well-done. Remove from the pan and keep hot on a dish.
4. Remove the surplus oil from the pan. Stir in the flour, then the wine. Boil, stirring, for 2 minutes. Add the grapes in the brandy and the cream and boil for a further 30 seconds. Season to taste with the salt and pepper, and stir in the parsley.
5. Serve the liver with a pool of the grape sauce.

CHEF'S TIPS:

Calf's liver is very tender and only goose liver is more expensive. Most gourmets like liver underdone; it really is a matter of taste, although it is true that the longer you cook liver the tougher it will become.

Par-boiled and fried Belgian endives, fried in butter, combine well with liver and add a bitter tang to contrast with the sweet seedless grapes used in the sauce.

Sautéed potatoes, broccoli and peas or gnocchi and a mixed salad, also make good accompaniments.

Sweetbreads on Artichokes

Serves: 4
Preparation time: 12 minutes, plus 6 hours soaking
Cooking time: 20 minutes

INGREDIENTS

1 calf's sweetbread
4 artichoke hearts
juice of 1/2 lemon

SAUCE:
2 tbsp (25 g/1 oz) butter
2/3 cup (150 ml/1/4 pint) dry sake
    (rice wine) or sherry
1/2 cup (100 ml/4 fl oz) concentrated veal
    stock
1 shallot, chopped
1/2 cup (100 ml/4 fl oz) light cream
2 tbsp chopped fresh parsley and cilantro
    leaves
salt and pepper

GARNISH:
8 oz (225 g) asparagus tips
5 oz (150 g) baby carrots and turnips
melted butter, for brushing

METHOD

1. Soak the sweetbread in salted water for 6 hours. Blanch for 10 minutes and remove the skin and sinews. Cut into small pieces.
2. Heat the butter and shallow fry the sweetbread pieces for 8 minutes. Remove from the heat and keep warm.
3. To make the sauce: boil the wine and stock with the shallot until reduced by half. Whisk in the cream and add the chopped herbs. Season to taste.
4. Boil the artichoke hearts in water with the lemon juice for 20 minutes. Drain. Reheat the sweetbread in the sauce.
5. Blanch the asparagus tips, baby carrots and turnips in boiling water for 6 minutes. Drain and brush with a little melted butter.
6. Fill each artichoke with sweetbread pieces and coat with the sauce. Surround with baby carrots, turnips and asparagus tips.

CHEF'S TIPS:

For an explanation about sweetbreads see the recipe for Veal Sweetbreads Marinated in Beet Juice on page 160.

Globe artichokes, served whole, can be stuffed with chopped meat and rice or served with a simple dressing.

Jerusalem artichokes, which are, in fact, the root of a member of the sunflower plant, would also make a good garnish for veal.

Calf's Kidneys with Mustard Seeds

Serves: 4
Preparation time: 20 minutes, plus 15 minutes for soaking kidneys
Cooking time: 25 minutes

INGREDIENTS

2 x 8-oz (225 g) calf's kidneys
vinegar, for soaking
1/4 cup (50 g/2 oz) butter, melted, plus
    1/4 cup (50 g/2 oz), for gravy
2 tbsp seasoned flour
2 tbsp oil
1/2 cup (100 ml/4 fl oz) veal stock
1/3 cup (75 ml/3 fl oz) Madeira wine
2 tbsp mustard seeds
salt and black pepper

GARNISH:
2 lb (1 kg) leaf spinach, washed and drained
1 garlic clove, crushed

POMMES MACAIRE
1.15 kg (2 1/2 lb) potatoes
2 tbsp (25 g/1 oz) butter
salt and pepper
1/2 cup (15 g/1/2 oz) chopped parsley
flour, for dusting
oil, for frying

METHOD

1. Soak the kidneys in cold water with a little vinegar for 15 minutes, then rinse and pat dry. Remove the sinews and the surplus fat (the fat can be diced and used in cooking). Brush the kidneys with the melted butter. Coat the kidneys with seasoned flour.
2. Heat the oil in a pan and fry the kidneys for 5-8 minutes until brown all over. Transfer to a casserole dish and roast in the oven for 6 minutes at 350°F (180°C/ Gas mark 4). The kidneys should be slightly underdone if they are to remain tender. Remove from the oven and discard some of the fat. Keep the kidneys warm while you make the gravy.
3. Pour the veal stock and wine into the roasting pan with the mustard seeds and boil hard for 8 minutes. Whisk the remaining butter into the sauce to emulsify it. Season to taste.
4. Cook the spinach in a pan with the clove of garlic, but without any water. Season to taste. Drain the surplus juice and squeeze the spinach to make it as dry as possible.
5. Slice the kidneys and place the slices on the plates with some of the gravy and a portion of spinach.

POMMES MACAIRE
1. Scrub the potatoes and bake them in their skins. When cooked, cut in half lengthwise and scoop out all the potato from the skins and place it in a large bowl.
2. Add the butter, salt, pepper and chopped parsley and roughly mash with a spoon.
3. Divide into apricot-size portions and mold into thick cake shapes with the aid of a dusting of flour.
4. Fry in hot oil in a shallow pan until golden brown on both sides.

CHEF'S TIPS:
Calf's kidneys can be stir-fried with shallots and mushrooms and served with a sauce made up of a mixture of heavy cream, a little mustard and a drop of medium sherry. This mixture could be served on toast or in a puff pastry case.

Sweetbreads Marinated in Beet Juice

Serves: 2
Preparation time: 15 minutes, plus 2 hours preparation and marinating
Cooking time: 12 minutes

INGREDIENTS

2 whole calf's sweetbreads
oil and butter, for pan frying

MARINADE:
1 cooked beet, diced
2/3 cup (150 ml/1/4 pint) dry white wine
1 tsp wine vinegar
1 small shallot, chopped
few coriander seeds and peppercorns, crushed
1 tbsp sugar

SAUCE:
2 tbsp seasoned flour
2/3 cup (150 ml/1/4 pint) chicken or veal stock
1/4 cup (50 ml/2 fl oz) heavy cream
salt and pepper

GARNISH:
a few chives

METHOD

1. Blanch the sweetbreads for 8 minutes. Remove the outside membranes. Place the sweetbreads between two wooden chopping boards with a heavy weight to compress them for 1 hour.
2. Mix together the marinade ingredients and marinate the sweetbreads for 1 hour.
3. Remove the sweetbreads from the marinade and pat dry. Coat with seasoned flour. Heat the oil and butter in a pan and fry the sweetbreads for 4 minutes on each side. Remove from the heat and keep warm.
4. Strain the marinade. In the same fat stir-fry the shallot from the marinade for 10 seconds. Strain and add the marinade and boil for 5 minutes, then add the stock and boil to reduce by half. Stir in the cream and season to taste.
5. Pour a pool of sauce on each plate and place three slices of cooked sweetbreads in the center. Garnish with chives.

CHEF'S TIPS:
A garnish of beet, celery and parsnip strips tossed in butter would complement this dish nicely, or serve with a salad of chicory and beets and some boiled potatoes.

Char-Grilled Veal Steak with Pineapple and Butter Sauce

Serves: 2
Preparation time: 15 minutes, plus 1 hour marinating
Cooking time: 15 minutes

INGREDIENTS

2 x 11-oz (300 g) veal rib chops, trimmed
2 tbsp sunflower oil
2 egg yolks
4 tbsp butter or heavy cream
salt and pepper
2 scallions, sliced
3/4 cup (75g/3oz) pineapple, diced

PINEAPPLE MARINADE:
2 slices of fresh pineapple, mixed to a pulp in
      a food processor
1 tsp vinegar
1 tbsp sherry

GARNISH:
cilantro and basil leaves

METHOD

1. Soak the veal chops in the marinade of crushed pineapple, sherry and vinegar for 1 hour. Remove the chops from the marinade, pat dry and season. Brush with oil and char-grill for 5-6 minutes on each side.
2. Boil the marinade for 3 minutes. Place the egg yolks, marinade and butter or cream in a food blender and process together. Return to the pan and reheat while whisking until the sauce thickens to the consistency of a light white sauce. Season to taste.
3. Place a veal chop on each plate and pour a pool of sauce around it. Sprinkle with scallions and diced pineapple. Garnish with the cilantro and basil leaves.

CHEF'S TIPS:
Veal rib chops are delicious when simply char-grilled. If you are not careful, however, they can be dry unless brushed with butter and cooked slightly underdone for maximum succulence. Marinating the chops in pineapple juice gives them a better flavor, since the enzymes in the juice tenderize the meat. Fresh pineapple must be used for the marinade, as the enzymes are destroyed in the canning process.

Noisette of Veal Wrapped in Prosciutto

Serves: 4
Preparation time: 20 minutes
Cooking time: 20 minutes

INGREDIENTS

1 lb (450 g) veal tenderloin, trimmed
8 oz (225 g) Prosciutto, thinly sliced
2 tbsp seasoned flour
3 tbsp butter and oil

GARNISH:
2 leeks, white part only, cut into chunks
12 small onions
1 lb (450 g) potatoes, par-boiled, then grated
1/4 cup (50 g/2 oz) butter
1 small bunch of cilantro leaves

SAUCE:
1 1/4 cups (300 ml/1/2 pint) brown sauce
  (see page 29)
2 tbsp medium sweet Madeira wine
1/4 cup (50 ml/2 fl oz) heavy cream

METHOD

1. Wrap the Prosciutto around the trimmed veal. Tie with string, dip in seasoned flour, then pan fry in butter and oil for 8 minutes, turning to ensure it cooks evenly. Remove the veal from the pan and cut it into eight thick noisettes. Re-fry the noisettes in the butter and oil until cooked through, allow about 4 minutes for each side. Season to taste.
2. Pan fry the leeks and onions until cooked.
3. Shape the grated potatoes into biscuits then fry them in butter.
4. Place the rosti on plates and top with two noisettes of veal per portion. Garnish with the leeks and onions and flavor the brown sauce with the Madeira wine then pour some of the brown sauce and a small pool of cream around the rosti. Arrange two onions in the sauce and garnish the center of the veal with a bunch of cilantro leaves.

CHEF'S TIPS:

Leeks and potatoes complement each other so well and together they make perfect accompaniments for this dish. The potatoes are served as rosti. This is made by grating parboiled potatoes, shaping them like biscuits and frying them in butter.

Veal Scallops Vienna Style

Serves: 2
Preparation time: 12 minutes
Cooking time: 12 minutes

INGREDIENTS

2 veal scallops, flattened thinly
2 tbsp seasoned flour
1 egg, beaten with 2 tbsp milk
6 tbsp fresh white breadcrumbs
oil, for shallow frying
2 tbsp butter
juice of 1/2 lemon

GARNISH:
2 slices of lemon
fresh parsley sprigs

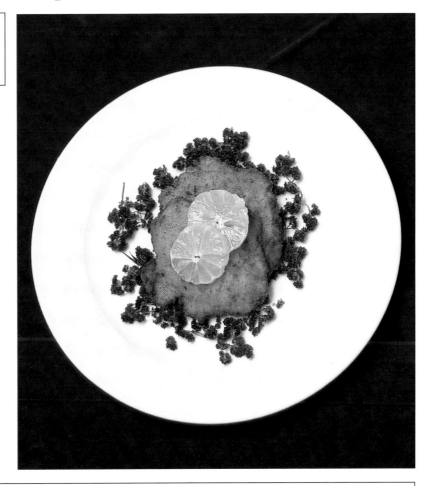

METHOD

1. Coat the veal scallops in seasoned flour. Shake off the surplus flour and dip the scallops in the beaten egg and milk and coat with the breadcrumbs.
2. Heat the oil in a pan and shallow fry the scallops for 5 minutes on each side. Drain well.
3. Place the veal on a hot plate. Immediately heat the butter in a pan until it foams, add the lemon juice and then pour over the scallops. Garnish with lemon slices and parsley.

CHEF'S TIPS:
The popularity of this classic dish does not diminish. It is important to remember that although the veal is finished off with butter, it can first be pan fried in good vegetable oil.

Alternatively, you can garnish with lemon slices, anchovies and capers.

Sweetbread Roly Poly

Serves: 4
Preparation time: 15 minutes, plus 6 hours soaking of sweetbread
Cooking time: 30 minutes

INGREDIENTS

2 tbsp butter
2 calf's sweetbreads, blanched and sliced
6 white mushrooms, sliced
2 cups (100 g/4 oz) chopped cooked wild
    mushrooms
1 medium shallot, chopped
salt and pepper
8 oz (225 g) puff pastry (see page 29)
2 cooked pancakes, 6-inches (15 cm) in
    diameter
8 spinach leaves, blanched
1 egg, beaten

SAUCE:
2 large tomatoes, skinned,
    deseeded and chopped
1 small shallot, finely chopped
1 tbsp oil
1/2 cup (100 ml/4 fl oz) reduced veal stock
1 tsp tomato paste
1 tsp honey
1/2 tsp cornstarch mixed with
    a little cold stock or water

METHOD

1. Heat the butter and gently stir-fry the sweetbreads, mushrooms and shallot for 5 minutes. Season and remove from the pan. Let cool.
2. Roll out the puff pastry to a rectangle 1/4-inch (5 mm) thick.
3. Place the 2 pancakes over the puff pastry as a double lining (this is to prevent the pastry becoming soggy) followed by the blanched, but well-dried, spinach leaves. Spread layers of the cooked mushrooms and sliced sweetbreads over the spinach leaves. Tuck the two ends of the pastry over like a package and roll up. Wet edges to seal. Brush the top of the paste with the egg wash. Let rest for 15 minutes.
4. Place on a well-oiled cookie sheet, neat side up. Bake at 400°F (200°C/ Gas mark 6) for 15-20 minutes. Cut into two portions.
5. To make the sauce, gently cook the tomatoes and shallot in the oil, to a purée. Add the stock, tomato paste and honey, and reduce. Season to taste. Thicken the sauce with cornstarch mixed with a little cold stock or water.
6. Place the roll on a plate with a pool of the sauce.

CHEF'S TIPS:

This dish is prepared in two stages: first, the sweetbreads should be sautéed with the mushrooms and finally the sweetbreads are wrapped in the already prepared pancakes and pastry. For speed, you can buy the ready-prepared chilled or frozen puff pastry. The pre-cooking treatment of the sweetbreads has already been explained in the recipe for Sweetbreads on Artichokes (see page 158).

ALL ABOUT POULTRY AND GAME BIRDS

Introduction

The term poultry used to be applied only to those birds that were raised by the farmer in the farmyard in relatively small numbers, however it now embraces any species of bird that has been commercially 'domesticated'. Turkeys, guinea-fowl and quail were all at one time strictly wild game, but today they are farmed.

GALLIFORMES BREEDS

PRINCIPAL CLASSES OF FOWL (CHICKEN/POULTRY)
The five main classes of birds bred for either meat or egg production are classified below:

1. American breeds. The best known are the Jersey White Giant, the New Hampshire, the Plymouth Rock, the Rhode Island Red, the Leg horns and the Wynadotte. These are all composite breeds that originated in North and Central America. They are medium to large birds with moderate, but colorful plumage.

2. Asiatic breeds. Presumed to be of Chinese origin, these birds are among the oldest breeds in the world. The main varieties are the Brahma, Cochin and Langham. The plumage on the birds is heavy and their skin is yellow and coarse.

3. Mediterranean breeds. The best known are the Ancona, Leg horn and Minorca. These breeds originated in Italy, Spain and Southern France. The birds have a light, closely feathered plumage of different colors and they rapidly develop to maturity.

4. English breeds. There are six main varieties: Dorking, Leg horn, New Hampshire, Plymouth Rock and Sussex and all of them are large birds. The production of these chickens is highly intensified to meet the demand for both free-range and factory-bred poultry.

5. French breeds. The principal French breeds are: Ardennaisse, Barbezieux, BourBourg, Bresse Coucou de Rennes, Crévecoeur, Faverolles, Gasconne, La Fléche, Houdan, Le Mans and Nantes.

TURKEY
Turkeys are native to the western hemisphere.

In England, Europe and North America turkey farming is now big business. The recognised varieties include the Broad-breasted Bronze and the White, the White Holland, the Beltsville White, the Bourbon Red, the Narragansett, the Black Slate and the Jersey Buff. Unlike chicken, most turkeys are bred through individual selection and mass-matings. Artificial insemination is practised in the breeding of the birds. The Broad-breasted Bronze variety is the most commonly bred.

DUCK BREEDS
The Aylesbury and Perkins ducks are bred for the quality of their meat. Magpies, Buff Orpingtons, Blue and Black Orpingtons, Rouen, Stanbridge Whites, Campbell Whites and Khaki breeds are good layers and are therefore kept for egg production.

GAME BIRDS

Guinea-fowl, Pheasant, Pigeon, Ptarmigan, Mallards (Wild Duck), Teal and Waterfowl Cornish rock hens are all considered to be two-portion birds. The following smaller birds are suitable only for one portion each: Snipe, Woodcock, Grouse and Quail.

Game birds are usually roasted at 400°F (200°C/Gas mark 6). Smaller birds can be cooked at 425°F (220°C/Gas mark 7) for between 8 and 15 minutes. 2 lb (1 kg) birds take about 30-40 minutes. Birds that are to be plain-roasted need not be marinated first, but for those which are to be pot-roasted, a preliminary soaking in wine or spirits will improve the flavor and texture of the meat.

QUAILS

In recent years the farming of quails has been intensified to meet the increase in demand from restaurants serving *nouvelle cuisine*.

Ornithologists recognise 5 genera, 7 species and nearly 20 races of quail. In the eastern and southern part of North America the Bobwhite is most common; the Scaled or Blue Quail and the Massena are found along the Mexican border; the Desert quail is native to California. All these species are ground birds and are small, averaging only 11 inches (28 cm) in length. The birds are nearly round in shape, with short tails and heavy bills and they feed on grass, seeds and clovers.

All commercially reared breeds of poultry are fed on cereals enriched with mineral and vitamin supplements to balance their diet and to produce good quality meat and eggs. Feeding geese with food stuffs that will enlarge their livers is practiced in France, North America, Israel and in certain other European countries, but not Britain.

POULTRY BUTCHERY

All butchery operations – slaughtering, plucking, drawing, trussing, cutting, boning and dissecting the birds into portions – are the same for all wild or domesticated fowl. In many parts of the world, amateur and professional cooks perform these tasks themselves, as I did when I first learned the basics of poultry husbandry in Picardy, France, in the village in which my grandparents lived. On my grandparents' farm we had a duck or chicken for lunch every Sunday. The bird was killed and trussed in preparation for cooking two days in advance.

In country markets on the Continent you can still buy live chicken, but in large parts of the United States and in Britain we are now more used to buying our poultry in plastic packages, whole or in portions and always oven-ready, from the supermarket. It is of course better to buy fresh, rather than frozen, poultry whenever possible. Frozen birds may be cheaper and more convenient, but much of the flavor is lost in the freezing and thawing processes. If you need to freeze a chicken it is better to freeze it in portions. A whole frozen turkey, for example, takes far too long to thaw. Your decision will probably depend upon whether or not you run a large kitchen and the size of your freezer.

Never refreeze poultry once it has been partially or completely thawed. Refreezing will not spoil the meat, but thawing the meat to room temperature will have allowed the dormant bacteria to be reactivated. Freezing does not, as many people imagine, kill bacteria, it simply prevents them from multiplying.

If a fresh chicken is to be kept for a day or two before it is to be cooked, it should be washed under running water, inside and out, or soaked in salted water with a little vinegar. After washing or soaking, pat the chicken dry and place it on waxed paper on a clean tray in

POULTRY

the coldest part of your refrigerator. Cover it with plastic wrap or foil to prevent it cross-contaminating any cooked food. In restaurants, separate refrigerators are kept for uncooked poultry and game. Chicken livers, hearts and gizzards should be kept in a covered container.

HYGIENE PRECAUTIONS
*All poultry should be thoroughly washed before it is cooked.
*All tools should be sterilized in hot water with detergents.
*Personal cleanliness demands that you wash your hands before and after the dissection of poultry.
*Cutting boards must also be washed with soap and bleach.
*To avoid cross-contamination avoid storing raw poultry with cooked food.

GRADING
Fowls are graded according to their age and the way in which they are fed.
1. Chicks, called *poussins* in France, are 10-12 weeks old and weigh under 1 lb (450 g).
2. Broilers or *poulet de grain* weigh from 1 1/2-2 lb (675 g-1 kg).
3. Fryers or *poulet reine* weigh from 2 1/2-3 1/2 lb (1.15-1.6 kg).
4. Roasters or *poulet gras* weigh from 3 1/2 - 5 lb (1.6-2.5 kg).
5. French Poularde are young hens that have not bred and have been specially fattened.
6. Hen, a female bird, which has laid eggs and is more than one year old.
7. Cock, a male bird, more than 1 year old, which has reproduced.

SIGNS OF QUALITY
A young chicken should have tender flesh that is elastic to the touch and not flabby.

The breast bones should be soft and flexible. The bird should have a well-rounded breast, fleshy thighs, and well-distributed fat. The legs may be white or black, according to the race, but they should never be yellow. They should be soft and pliable.

In male birds the spur should be no longer than 1 inch (2.5 cm). The short, stocky variety of chicken is preferable to the long-legged, thin kind.

The skin must be smooth and white. The parson's nose should be white, or slightly pink, with a small mass of fat covering the back.

Freshly killed birds should be hung for at least 24 hours, tied by the feet, head downwards, with a receptacle underneath to collect any remaining blood. They should be hung in a cool, airy place.

TO CUT A CHICKEN INTO PARTS
Although you can buy chicken already cut into portions at the supermarket, if you know how to dissect it yourself you will be able to get the pieces exactly as you want them. Also, whole chickens are usually cheaper per pound, so it is more economic to buy a whole chicken and cut it up as necessary.

Lay the chicken on its side with the legs away from you, the wings toward you. Lift up one wing and put the knife between the body and the wing; cut the skin at the point of the V and pull the wing bone out from the body as you cut the wing away from the socket. Follow the knife down and cut the wing off. Turn the bird over and repeat with the other wing.

Lift up one leg and slice the skin between the leg and the breast; the knife should be parallel to your work surface.

Holding the leg and thigh out from the body, use your fingers from behind, to pop the thighbone out of the socket where it is connected to the hipbone; at this point, cut off the leg and thigh piece.

Turn the chicken over and cut off the second leg and thigh piece. (If you are not planning to use the backbone, be sure to include the oysters, the little pieces of meat in spoon-shaped cavities on either side of the backbone at the front of the hip socket).

To separate the thigh from the leg, lay the piece flat on your work surface. You will see a thin line of fat going across the meat. Holding your knife perpendicular to the table, place the knife 1/16 inch (1.5 mm) between the knee cap of the leg joint and cut neatly.

Chicken legs. Place the drumstick end toward you and find the end of the thighbone. Cut around it, cutting the tendons away so that you can hold on to the top of the bone. Scrape the meat down toward the center, holding the blade perpendicular to the bone. When you come to the joint of the leg and the thigh, cut around the knee. Do not give in to the temptation to cut through it; you will need to leave the thighbone connected to use as a handle. Cut the tendons beneath the joint and keep scraping the meat down the drumstick, turning the piece constantly until you are near the very end.

Push the meat and skin back up the bone; break the bone close to the end by raising it slightly off your work surface and hitting it with the dull side of a heavy knife. You can now remove the bone from inside; leave the knuckle and an inch of bone. This boneless leg and thigh can be stuffed and baked.

Turkey legs. Turkey legs often present a problem as the drumsticks have a lot of hard tendons that make them impossible to slice. Bone them out as you would a chicken leg, then pull the tendons using a towel for a grip, or use tweezers.

PREPARATION OF CHICKEN

FOR BROILING

The bird is drawn and the wishbone removed. Cut the legs off short; then split the bird down the back with a large knife, by passing the point of the knife through the middle part of the body, while the bird is on its back on the chopping board. When cutting, begin at the neck and finish at the parson's nose. This done, flatten down with a meat mallet and remove all the ribs from the breast; trim the sides and place them on a tray with a little salad oil to marinate.

PREPARATION FOR SPATCHCOCK

This term is applied to a process of splitting the bird open for broiling or frying. The word is a compound of two words 'spat' or 'spit', and 'cock' or 'cook', indicating the style of trussing by means of a spit or skewers.

Choose a very young bird for this style of cooking. After drawing it, remove the wishbone. Cut off the drumsticks, leaving only 1/2 inch (1 cm) above the thigh joint. Insert a large knife through the opening of the neck, right inside the bird. Make an incision in the middle of the back, starting at the neck and finishing at the parson's nose. Open the chicken and flatten it with the blade of a heavy knife or rolling pin. Discard the rib bones from the breast. Insert a skewer through the wings, and another through the legs and breast skin. Let stand basted in oil and lemon juice for 2 hours before cooking.

FOR BOILING

Rub the skin with lemon juice to keep the flesh white. Cook slowly in a simmering chicken or veal stock or in boiling salted water with the white of a leek or an onion and a stick of celery. Cooking time: 1 3/4-2 hours.

HOW TO STUFF POULTRY

1. Remove the wishbone.
2. Fill the neck end with stuffing until the breast is plump. Then draw the skin over the aperture of the neck, and truss it firmly with string in the usual way, so that the breast is rounded off.
3. Another method is to fill the body from the other end with stuffing and then push the parson's nose into the vent to close it. For each bird use 4-6 oz (100-175 g) of stuffing.

CUTTING FOR SAUTE

1. Pluck, single and draw the bird and remove the wishbone.
2. Cut the neck into three equal parts.
3. Cut the legs into two pieces, separating the leg from the thigh, by placing the point of the knife at the joint.
4. Remove the wing from the stomach, by passing the knife into the joint close to the carcass, to separate the wing from the body, or cut the breast in half lengthwise, separating the breast from the back, and then trim the sides and cut into two or three portions, either lengthwise or across the breast. Cut off both ends of the middle wing.

BONING A BIRD

A boned bird is very convenient to carve for a buffet party and, if it is stuffed, it will serve more portions. You can, of course, ask your butcher to bone out a chicken for you but, if you have the time, it's not difficult to do yourself. You will need a sturdy board and a sharp, fine-bladed cook's knife. Take your time to avoid tearing the skin. It is important to keep the skin intact so the bird doesn't lose its shape.

1. Lay the bird breast down on the board, slit through the skin from the vent to the neck end to expose the backbone. Cut off the parson's nose.
2. Working on one side at a time, gently ease the point of the knife between the flesh and the bones and gradually scrape the flesh away from the rib cage. As the flesh becomes free, hold it away from the carcass, as you continue working.
3. Using a pair of sharp kitchen scissors, cut the sinew between the ball-and-socket joint, joining the thighbone to the carcass. Hold the end of the joint in one hand and cut away the flesh from the leg. Scrape the thighbone clean and then continue cleaning the drumstick until the whole leg bone is free of flesh. Remove the leg bone from the carcass and repeat this process with the other leg.
4. Cut off the lower part of each wing. Continue working the skin and flesh away from the carcass until you reach the wing joint. Cut the sinews connecting it to the carcass. Hold the exposed end of the wing bone in one hand and cut away the flesh along the bone. Pull out the bone as you work. Repeat with the other wing bone.
5. Carefully cut away the flesh from the breastbone on each side, being especially careful not to tear the skin and keeping both sides of the bird together so that the flesh remains in one piece for stuffing.
6. Lay the bird flat, ready for stuffing. Then sew up the back to seal in the stuffing and truss to reform the chicken shape.

See page 196 for Boning and Stuffing a Turkey.

HOW TO TRUSS A BIRD

Cut all the toes, except the middle one on each foot, which should be trimmed at the tip. Cut off the wing tips and trim the sides of the wings.

Remove the wishbone by pulling the flap of skin over the wishbone, then scraping the flesh over each of the forks of the bone with the point of a knife. Insert the knife under one side of the bone and cut downwards to the junction of the wing, repeat this on the other side of the bone. Once the two sides have been detached, continue to free the top of the bone. Pull the bone off the breastbone, without damaging the flesh.

Thread a trussing needle 8-9 inches (20-23 cm) with a piece of string three times the length of the bird. Hold the bird on its back, with the legs firmly against the thigh. Insert the needle through the middle of the right leg, pass it through the carcass, to come out through the middle of the other leg. Pull the needle out leaving 5 inches (12.5 cm) of the string at the other side. Turn the bird onto its breast. Push the flap of the neck skin over the opening of the neck to extend down the back. Cover it with the outstretched wings. Secure both wings and flaps together by threading the needle through the small end of one wing extremity to that of the other wing, passing through the skin and center of the backbone near the neck. Pull out the needle, taking great care not to pull the string too tightly (5 inches (12.5 cm) of string should still remain on the other side).

Having completed this operation, the two ends of string should now be joined together securely with a double knot, so that the legs will be firmly attached to the carcass. If possible, the knot should be made without cutting the string, but this is not essential.

Insert the needle through the flesh of the thigh, just underneath where the leg was pierced and where a small cavity is found. Pull the needle through the other side of the other thigh under the leg. Pull the string over this leg and reinsert the needle just above the leg into the flesh under the breastbone, to come out the opposite side, immediately above the other leg (the tip of the breastbone should be lifted before this insertion is made to avoid piercing it with the needle). This end of the string should now be joined with a double knot at the point where it was first inserted. Cut the string and you are done.

Whole Poultry and Poultry Cuts

1 Leg

2 Leg

3 Large chicken

4 Skinless breast

5 Small chicken

6 Breast with skin

7 Drumstick

Chicken Hot Pot

Serves: 4
Preparation time: 15 minutes
Cooking time: 70-80 minutes

INGREDIENTS

POACHING STOCK:
2 small onions, studded with 4 cloves
2 bay leaves
1 leek, white only
1 bunch of herbs: chervil, parsley, thyme and tarragon
2 garlic cloves, peeled
4 peppercorns
4 lb (2 kg) chicken
2 sticks of celery
1 large leek
8 baby carrots
8 small potatoes
salt and ground pepper

GARNISH:
1 tbsp chopped chervil
1 tbsp snipped chives

METHOD

1. Tie the leek with the bunch of herbs and bay leaves and place in a large pot with the onions, garlic and peppercorns. Add 10 cups (2.25 liters/4 pints) water, bring to a boil, reduce the heat and simmer for 25 minutes.
2. Add the chicken and return to a boil, then cover and simmer for a further 20 minutes.
3. Carefully lift the chicken out of the pot and remove the skin. Strain the poaching stock, discarding the vegetables and skimming any fat from the surface.
4. Cut the celery into 1 1/2-inch (4 cm) lengths, slice the leek into 1-inch (2.5 cm) thick rings, scrub the carrots and peel or scrub the potatoes. Place all these vegetables in the cooking pot with the chicken, the poaching stock, salt and pepper. Bring back to a boil, cover and simmer for 15-20 minutes, until the chicken and vegetables are tender.
5. Remove the chicken, cut into eight pieces and arrange in four warmed soup bowls. With a perforated spoon, remove the vegetables from the stock and divide among the four bowls.
6. Season the stock to taste and ladle over the chicken. Sprinkle with chervil and chives and serve immediately.

CHEF'S TIPS:

David Wilson has built up a formidable reputation for his fine cooking at the Peat Inn, Fife, in Scotland. The basic stock he uses in this dish is suitable as a foundation for any soup or sauce where a distinctive chicken flavor is required.

You may vary the vegetables used in this recipe, depending upon individual preference or the season, but remember to cut them evenly in size.

Stuffed Chicken Moroccan-Style with Lemon

Serves: 4
Preparation time: 20 minutes
Cooking time: 1 hour

INGREDIENTS

4 lb (2 kg) chicken
3 tbsp olive oil
1/4 cup (50 g/2 oz) melted butter
1 cup (225 ml/8 fl oz) chicken stock

STUFFING:

3/4 cup (75 g/3 oz) cooked long grain rice
1 small red onion, chopped
juice and grated rind of 1 lemon
1 small chili pepper, chopped
2 tsp freshly chopped mint
2 tsp turmeric
2 tsp cumin
salt and black pepper

GARNISH:

1 lemon, cut into wedges

METHOD

1. Combine all the stuffing ingredients in a bowl, including 1 tablespoon of the olive oil, but reserving half of the spices. Stuff the chicken at the neck end only, not in the cavity. Sew with strings or thread a skewer into the neck flap of the skin to prevent the stuffing from escaping. Surplus stuffing can be baked separately in a small dish and served as extra garnish. Put a wedge of lemon into the cavity.
2. Mix the remaining 2 tablespoons of oil with the remaining spices in a cup. Brush the outside of the chicken with this mixture. Sprinkle over salt and black pepper and pour over the melted butter. Cover loosely with foil and roast at 400°F (200°C/Gas mark 6) for 1 hour. Turn the chicken over during the cooking time. Baste often with the fat and juices and the chicken stock. Remove the foil for the last 15 minutes of the cooking time to let chicken brown. To check whether the chicken is cooked, pierce the thighs with a skewer. The chicken is ready when the juices run clear and are not pink.
3. Carve the chicken into four or five portions.
4. To make the gravy: collect the juices from the roasting pan and boil them with the chicken neck and winglets for 15 minutes with enough chicken stock to make up 1 1/4 cups (300 ml/1/2 pint) gravy. Strain and check the seasoning. Remove the surplus fat.
5. Garnish with lemon wedges.

CHEF'S TIPS:

A teaspoon of yeast extract added to the gravy will give it a stronger flavor.

Removing the wishbone from the chicken before roasting will make carving the breast easier. This spicy dish can be served with boiled navy beans, fennel, celery and carrots. Use the neck and winglets to make a delicious gravy.

Sprouting seeds or bean sprouts would also make an ideal accompaniment for this dish. Introduced into our gardens from Asia, there are numerous varieties of sprouting seeds that are especially good from alfalfa, fenugreek and mung beans, as well as the better known soy bean sprouts.

Caribbean Chicken

Serves: 4
Preparation time: 15 minutes, plus 2 hours marinating
Cooking time: 15 minutes

INGREDIENTS

8 chicken drumsticks, skinned
2 limes
1 tsp cayenne pepper
2 medium mangoes
1 tbsp oil
2 tbsp dark brown sugar (optional)

METHOD

1. Slash the drumsticks with a sharp knife at intervals and place in a large bowl.
2. Grate the peel of the limes and reserve. Squeeze the juice from the limes and pour over the chicken with the cayenne pepper. Cover and chill for at least 2 hours or overnight, if possible
3. Peel and slice the mangoes, discarding the pit. Drain the chicken drumsticks and reserve the marinade.
4. Heat the oil in a wide, heavy pan and sauté the chicken, turning frequently, until golden.
5. Stir in the marinade, lime rind, mango and sugar. Cover and simmer gently, stirring occasionally, for 15 minutes or until the chicken juices run clear when the flesh is pierced.

CHEF'S TIPS:
Corn kernels can be mixed with red bell peppers, carrots and peas as a macédoine, or with a batter to make fritters. On their own they make a good garnish for mixed broils or fried chicken. Corn cobs can also be served whole with melted butter.

Tomatoes are a popular and versatile fruit. They can as easily be turned into jam or they can be made into a sauce to serve with pizzas or a sauce to accompany chicken. Tomatoes can be broiled or stuffed with rice or mushroom duxelle and served as a garnish for any kind of mixed broil or they can be served in a salad with avocados or with cucumber. As an appetizer, tomatoes are delicious and refreshing.

Chicken in Broth with Garlic Mayonnaise

Serves: 4
Preparation time: 15 minutes
Cooking time: 1 hour

INGREDIENTS

3 1/2 lb (1.5 kg) chicken
salt and black pepper
4 shallots, peeled
1 leek, trimmed, washed and patted dry
2/3 cup (150 ml/1/4 pint) dry white wine
2 1/2 cups (600 ml/1 pint) chicken stock or water
1 package saffron

MAYONNAISE:
8 garlic cloves
1 tsp Dijon mustard
1 pinch chili powder
2 egg yolks
2/3 cup (150 ml/1/4 pint) mixed olive and groundnut oils
salt and black pepper

GARNISH:
chives, snipped
small leeks

METHOD

1. Season the chicken inside and out and place it in a flameproof casserole dish with the shallots, leek, wine, stock and saffron. Bring to a boil and cook gently in the oven at 375°F (190°C/Gas mark 5) for 1 hour, until the juices from the chicken run clear when the meat at the thigh is pierced with a skewer.
2. Meanwhile make the mayonnaise. Crush or pound the garlic in a mortar or heavy bowl. Add salt, pepper, mustard, chilli powder and egg yolks. Gradually whisk the mixture while pouring in the oil in a small thread; as the mixture thickens, increase the flow of the oil.
3. Remove the chicken from the liquid, peel away the skin and cut the bird into eight portions.
4. Add about half a cup of the chicken liquid to the mayonnaise. Pour a pool of this sauce on to each plate and place two pieces of the chicken upon it. Sprinkle with chives and garnish with small leeks, which have been lightly cooked in boiling water for 6 minutes.

CHEF'S TIPS:
Shaun Hill, chef-proprietor of the Merchant House restauraunt in Ludlow, England, has gained a large following for his regional cuisine. This chicken dish, devised by Mr. Hill, is redolent of my own Provençal background, is simple, yet it has the style of a grand dish. It demonstrates what I believe to be so often true – that 'simplicity is the mistress of a genius'. Serve with small potatoes.

Roast Farm-Bred Pigeons

Serves: 2
Preparation time: 10 minutes
Cooking time: 45 minutes

INGREDIENTS

2 young pigeons, trussed and seasoned inside and out
2 bacon slices
2 tbsp oil

MARINADE:
2/3 cup (150 ml/1/4 pint) fresh cantaloupe juice and purée
3 tbsp soy sauce
1 tsp Cajun seasoning (with chili)

SAUCE:
1 tbsp oil
1 small shallot, chopped
2 tbsp soy sauce
1 tsp grated ginger
2/3 cup (150 ml/1/4 pint) stock
1 tsp cornflour mixed with 3 tbsp cold water
salt and pepper

GARNISH:
4 slices of fresh cantaloupe melon, cut into wedges
a few chives

METHOD

1. Wrap the bacon slices around the pigeon breasts. Heat the oil in a sauté pan and brown the bird for 10 minutes. Transfer into a casserole and add the marinade ingredients. Cook at 400°F (200°C/Gas Mark 6) for 15-20 minutes. Remove the pigeons from the oven when cooked. Take off the bacon slices and boil them, with the remaining marinade, until it is reduced by half.
2. To make the sauce: heat the oil in a frying pan and stir-fry the shallots for 30 seconds. Add the soy sauce, ginger and stock and boil for 10 minutes. Pour in the reduced marinade from the pigeons, check seasoning and thicken the sauce with the cornflour and water mixture. Boil for 4 minutes to clear the starch.
3. Cut the birds in half and place on a dish, cover with the sauce and garnish with the wedges of fresh melon and chives.

CHEF'S TIPS:
Farm-bred young pigeons can be as tender and tasty as spring chickens. Any other young bird: grouse, partridge, pheasant, guinea fowl or wild duck, may be used in this recipe. Fresh, ripe cantaloupe or yellow fleshed melons are recommended as a garnish. Wild pigeons are to be braised for 1 hour as they have tougher meat.

Meat and Poultry Fondue

Serves: 6-8
Preparation time: 40 minutes
Cooking time: 5-6 minutes

INGREDIENTS

1 lb (450 g) lamb tenderloin (or pork, or beef fillet, or all three)
8 oz (225 g) boneless chicken breast, skinned
1 cup (50 g/2 oz) Chinese dried mushrooms
1 lb (450 g) bok choy or spinach
2-3 cakes bean curd
9 oz (250 g) vermicelli (green bean thread)
8 3/4 cups (2 liters/3 1/2 pints) stock or water

SERVE WITH:
dipping sauce (see point 1 of method)

METHOD

1. The dip sauce can be a very simple mixture of soy sauce with crushed garlic, finely chopped scallions, ginger or chili peppers. Alternatively, there are a number of commercially prepared sauces on the market which would be ideal – crushed yellow bean sauce, black bean sauce, chili and garlic sauce or hoisin, for example.
2. Trim any excess fat from the meat and cut into very thin slices. Arrange the slices of meat on a plate or put them on small individual dishes.
3. Soak the mushrooms in warm water for 30-40 minutes, then squeeze dry, discard the hard stalks and cut into thin slices. Cut the green leaves and bean curd into small pieces. Soak the vermicelli for 3-5 minutes until soft. Arrange everything neatly on one plate or in individual dishes.
4. Add a few pieces of mushroom to the stock or water and bring to a fast boil.
5. When ready, the guests should use chopsticks or a fork to pick up a piece of meat and place it in the boiling liquid for a short time. Usually, once the color of the meat changes, it is done. The meat should then be removed from the pot, dipped in the sauce and eaten while still piping hot.
6. When all the meat has been eaten, add the vegetables to the pot, let them boil for a few minutes, then ladle out the contents into individual bowls. Season with the remains of the dip sauce and serve as a most delicious soup to finish the meal.

CHEF'S TIPS:
The meat fondue was invented by Chinese and Korean cooks. Fondue is very popular as a party dish since it has the advantage of allowing each guest to cook the meat to suit their individual preferences.

Malaysian Chicken with Almonds and Mango

Serves: 4
Preparation time: 15 minutes
Cooking time: 30 minutes

INGREDIENTS

2 tbsp oil
4 large boneless chicken breast halves, skinned
    and cut in half
1 medium onion, sliced
2 tsp mild Malaysian curry blend
1 tsp cornstarch
1 1/4 cups (300 ml/1/2 pint) chicken stock
2/3 cup (150 ml/1/4 pint) light cream or natural yoghurt
2 tbsp (1 oz/25 g) canned coconut cream
1 large mango, sliced
1/4 tsp salt

GARNISH:
toasted almonds, shredded

METHOD

1. Heat the oil in a frying pan and cook the chicken and onion until lightly colored.
2. Sprinkle in the curry blend and stir gently for 1 minute. Add the cornstarch and cook for a further minute.
3. Stir in the stock and bring to a boil, stirring.
4. Cover and simmer gently for 30 minutes until the chicken is tender.
5. Stir in the cream or yoghurt, coconut and mango slices. Season to taste.
6. Serve on a plate sprinkled with toasted shredded almonds.

CHEF'S TIPS:
The predominant flavor of this dish is derived from the addition of coconut cream. This dish really has more in common with a fricassee than it has with a curry.

Serve with sautéed zucchini.

Nasi Goreng

Serves: 4
Preparation time: 15 minutes
Cooking time: 25 minutes

INGREDIENTS

1 3/4 cups (350 g/12 oz) long grain rice
2 tbsp sesame oil
1 lb (450 g) turkey breast fillets, skinned and diced
1 large carrot, peeled and sliced
1 red bell pepper, deseeded and diced
3 mushrooms, diced
2 tsp Chinese five spice powder
1/2 tsp ground coriander
1/2 tsp ground ginger
1 garlic clove, crushed
1 small chili pepper, sliced
4 tbsp soy sauce
1 tsp honey
2 1/4 cups (175 g/6 oz) fresh bean sprouts
8 shelled cooked shrimp
6 scallions, to garnish

METHOD

1. Cook the rice in boiling salted water for about 15 minutes until just tender. Drain.
2. Heat the oil in a large frying pan or wok and stir-fry the turkey for 5 minutes. Add the carrots, bell pepper and mushrooms for the final minute. Stir in the spices and garlic and cook for a few seconds more, stirring constantly.
3. Add the remaining ingredients and the cooked rice and cook over high heat for a further 4-5 minutes.
4. Serve garnished with scallions. Cut down ends with scissors, then soak in iced water to make brushes.

CHEF'S TIPS:
This dish is a kind of pilaf with Chinese spices.

Mushrooms, or fungi, are now available in our shops in a wide variety of shapes, textures and flavors. In recent years, it has become 'fashionable' to use wild mushrooms; although they remain quite expensive they have always been used in Asian cookery. Dry mushrooms have a stronger flavor, but they must be soaked in cold water to be reconstituted to their original weight. Chinese mushrooms such as black sekate are popular as are the chanterelles, oyster mushrooms, ceps and morels. There is probably nothing nicer than a simple dish of fresh field mushrooms cooked with a little garlic and thyme. Mushrooms make a delicious garnish for broils, stews or pies.

Chicken with Fennel

Serves: 4-5
Preparation time: 20 minutes
Cooking time: 60 minutes

INGREDIENTS

4 chicken portions, skinned
1 tsp paprika
black pepper, freshly ground
1 tbsp oil
1 garlic clove, crushed
scant 1 cup (150 g/5 oz) derined and chopped lean bacon
1 small leek, sliced
1 medium fennel bulb, chopped
2 1/2 cups (150g/5oz) mushrooms, quartered
1lb (450 g) small potatoes, scrubbed, cut into even-sized pieces
1 tbsp tomato paste
bouquet garni
2 1/2 cups (600 ml/1 pint) chicken stock
1 1/4 cups (150 g/5 oz) green beans, trimmed
4 medium tomatoes, skinned and quartered
1 tbsp cornstarch mixed with a little cold water

GARNISH:
fresh parsley, chopped

METHOD

1. Sprinkle half the paprika lightly over the chicken and season with black pepper.
2. Heat the oil in a large flameproof casserole dish and add the chicken, garlic and bacon. Sauté for 5 minutes to seal the chicken. Remove from the pan and set aside
3. In the same pan, fry the leek, fennel and mushrooms for 3-4 minutes, then stir in the remaining paprika, potatoes, tomato paste and bouquet garni. Replace the chicken in the casserole, pour over the stock and season well.
4. Cover and cook in the oven at 350°F(180°C/Gas mark 4) for 40 minutes.
5. Remove the casserole from the oven and stir in the beans, tomatoes and cornstarch. Return to the oven and cook for a further 20 minutes. Make sure that you remove the bouquet garni.
6. Garnish with the chopped parsley.

CHEF'S TIPS:

The fennel lends a distinctive aniseed flavor to this casserole. If the chicken is to be really succulent, it is important that the dish should be cooked at a low temperature for a relatively long cooking time.

Serve with crusty bread or potatoes.

Dopiaza Chicken with Leeks and Yoghurt

Serves: 4
Preparation time: 12 minutes
Cooking time: 1 1/2 hours

INGREDIENTS

8 chicken thighs
1/4 cup (50 ml/2fl oz) oil
1lb (450 g) chopped leeks, use white part only
2 tbsp medium Bombay curry blend
2/3 cup (150 ml/1/4 pint) natural yoghurt, mixed
   with 1 tsp cornstarch
2/3 cup (150 ml/1/4 pint) chicken stock
1 tbsp tomato paste
juice of 1/2 lemon

METHOD

1. Place the chicken in a large Dutch oven.
2. Heat the oil in a frying pan and brown half the leeks. Add the curry blend and cook for 2 minutes, stirring continually.
3. Remove the pan from the heat and stir in the yoghurt, cornstarch, stock, tomato paste and lemon juice. Pour over the chicken, cover and cook in the oven at
   350°F (180°C/Gas mark 4) for 1 1/2 hours or until the chicken is tender. After the first 30 minutes, add the remaining leeks.

CHEF'S TIPS:

This Indian dish is cooked slowly at a low temperature with the addition of leeks at two stages during the cooking process. Leeks are used in preference to onions in this recipe because of their mild flavor. The yoghurt also helps to make the sauce quite mild, despite the inclusion of curry powder.

The nouvelle cuisine school of gastronomy has taken the previously humble leek and greatly increased its repertoire – young leeks are now even being used for wrapping galantines and terrines. However, leeks still make a good simple garnish for chicken or beef. If preferred they may be served in a light cheese sauce.

Serve this dish with rice or small potatoes.

Breast of Chicken Alabama

Serves: 4
Preparation time: 15 minutes, plus 30 minutes chilling
Cooking time: 12 minutes

INGREDIENTS

4 boneless chicken breast halves, skinned
pinch of cayenne pepper or chili powder
salt
1 large egg, beaten
1 1/4 cups (150 g/5 oz) crushed roasted peanuts
2 tbsp unsalted butter
3 tbsp oil (preferably groundnut)
1 garlic clove, crushed
2 tbsp lemon juice
2 tbsp white wine

GARNISH:
slices of lemon
fresh parsley, chopped

METHOD

1. Flatten the chicken breast halves gently with the side of a knife, season with cayenne pepper or chili powder and salt to taste. Coat the chicken breasts in the egg, shaking off any excess, then coat thoroughly with the peanuts. Chill for 30 minutes.
2. Melt 1 tablespoon of the butter with the oil together in a frying pan and sauté the chicken for 5 minutes on each side or until cooked and golden brown. Place the chicken on a warmed serving dish.
3. Add the remaining butter to the pan and cook the garlic for 2 minutes. Pour the lemon juice and white wine into the pan to deglaze and pour over the chicken.
4. Garnish with the lemon slices and parsley.

CHEF'S TIPS:

There is an almost infinite variety of stuffed breast of chicken dishes. This particular recipe is a version of the popular Chicken Kiev, using peanut butter with garlic and a pinch of cayenne pepper or chili powder. Peanuts are extremely rich in protein and in this dish they supplement the food value of the chicken, making the meal highly nutritious.

Serve with a seasonal salad and small potatoes.

Breast of Chicken Stuffed with Shrimp

Serves: 4
Preparation time: 15 minutes
Cooking time: 40 minutes

INGREDIENTS

4 x 8-oz (225 g) chicken breast halves, skinned, with under fillet
flour, to coat

STUFFING:
4 uncooked jumbo shrimp, shelled
1 lb (450 g) leaf spinach
2 tbsp (25 g/1 oz) butter
black pepper and salt
flour, to coat

SAUCE:
2 tbsp oil
1 shallot, chopped
shrimp shells (from above)
1 garlic clove, chopped
2/3 cup (150 ml/1/4pint) dry white wine
1 package of saffron
1/2 cup (100 ml/4 fl oz) light cream
salt and white pepper, to season

METHOD

1. Lift the under fillet from the chicken and place the supremes and fillets between two slightly oiled sheets of plastic wrap. Beat gently with a meat mallet or rolling pin to thin the flesh, but not too much.
2. Wash the spinach three times. Drain and pat dry. Blanch eight spinach leaves for 15 seconds in a deep roasting pan, half-filled with water, keeping the leaves flat. Remove with a slice, drain and pat dry in a clean dish towel. Place the dried leaves flat on a pastry board. Wrap two leaves around the tail of each of the shrimp. Season the outside with black pepper and salt and roll in flour.
3. Place two shrimp in each of the thinned chicken breast halves, cover with a piece of the under fillet and roll up like a cigar. Coat the stuffed chicken with flour. Wrap each breast half individually in oiled foil and bake in a hot oven at 400°F (200°C/Gas mark 6) for 20 minutes.
4. Cook the remaining spinach in a little butter, with no water, for 5 minutes. Squeeze out the surplus water and season.
5. To make the sauce: heat the oil in a frying pan and stir-fry the shallots, garlic and shrimp shells for 5 minutes. Add the white wine and saffron and boil for a further 3 minutes. Stir in the cream, season and strain.
6. Cut the chicken supremes into slices and place on a bed of spinach. Pour a pool of the saffron sauce around the chicken.

CHEF'S TIPS:

It seems that serving chicken stuffed with shellfish is becoming popular all over the world. In this recipe the stuffed chicken is served on a bed of spinach with a saffron sauce.

Chicken with Mushrooms and Tarragon

Serves: 4
Preparation time: 20 minutes
Cooking time: 45-50 minutes

INGREDIENTS

3 lb (1.5 kg) roasting chicken, cut into four portions
3 tbsp seasoned flour
1/4 cup (50 ml/2 fl oz) olive oil
2 tbsp (25 g/1 oz) butter
8 oz (225 g) wild or white, trimmed and sliced mushrooms
3 shallots, chopped
1/4 cup (50 ml/2 fl oz) brandy
2/3 cup (150 ml/1/4 pint) dry white wine
4 tomatoes, skinned, deseeded and chopped
1 tsp tomato paste
1 1/4 cups (300 ml/1/2 pint) chicken stock
salt and pepper

SERVE WITH:
rounded carrots
rounded rutabagas
scallions

GARNISH:
1 sprig tarragon

METHOD

1. Coat the chicken in seasoned flour.
2. Heat the oil and butter in a metal sauté pan and brown the chicken pieces for 20 minutes all round. Remove from the pan and keep warm.
3. Stir-fry the shallots and mushrooms for 2 minutes. Remove the surplus fat, pour in the brandy, flame it and immediately add the wine. Boil for 5 minutes. Stir in the chopped tomatoes, the tomato paste and stock. Reduce the sauce by boiling, uncovered, for 10 minutes.
4. Add the chicken pieces and reheat in the sauce with the sprig of tarragon. Cover with a lid and check after 10 minutes. Check seasoning and serve with the vegetables.

Breast of Chicken with Mango and Coconut

Serves: 4
Preparation time: 20 minutes, plus 15 minutes chilling
Cooking time: 20 minutes

INGREDIENTS

4 boneless chicken breast halves, skinned, with under fillet
1 fresh mango, peeled and chopped
1 egg
1 tbsp milk
2 tbsp seasoned flour
1/2 coconut, coarsely grated
oil, for deep frying

SAUCE:
juice and grated rind of 1 lemon
1/4 cup (50 ml/2 fl oz) dry white wine
1 tbsp sugar
1 1/4 cups (300 ml/1/2 pint) chicken stock
2/3 cup (150 ml/1/4 pint) heavy cream
salt and pepper

GARNISH:
1 large ripe mango cut into 8 slices

METHOD

1. Detach the under fillet from each breast half, then place the breasts and fillets between two sheets of plastic wrap and beat them gently with a meat mallet or rolling pin to flatten them evenly, like a scallop.
2. Place the breasts smooth side down and cut a line the length of the fillet, butterfly fashion, then slide the knife down each side, on its flat edge, making a pocket into the breast.
3. Fill the pockets with the chopped mango. Place the flattened fillet on top and roll up from the side like a cigar. Chill for 15 minutes.
4. Beat the egg in a small bowl and add the milk. Coat the chicken lightly with seasoned flour, then dip in the beaten egg and milk mixture and, finally, cover with the grated coconut.
5. Deep fry the chicken in oil at 325°F (170°C) for 8 minutes, until golden brown. Test the chicken to make sure that the meat juices run clear and are not still pink. Remove the meat from the hot oil and drain on paper towels.
6. For the sauce: boil the lemon rind and juice with the wine and sugar for 4 minutes until reduced by half. Add the stock and boil for 3 minutes to concentrate the liquid. Finally, add the cream and the seasoning and simmer for a further 3 minutes.
7. Pour a pool of the sauce on each of the plates. Cut each breast into six slices on the diagonal and place the slices in the shape of a fan in the center of each plate. Garnish with the mango slices.

CHEF'S TIPS:
This recipe was created by Christopher Oakes who runs his own restaurant, Oakes, just outside Stroud, Gloucestershire, in the west of England.

Serve with plain spinach or with a mixture of spinach and cream cheese.

Chicken with Pesto

Serves: 4
Preparation time: 15 minutes, plus 1 hour chilling
Cooking time: 15 minutes

INGREDIENTS

4 boneless chicken breast halves, skinned, with under fillets

STUFFING:
1/2 cup (15g/1/2oz) chopped fresh basil
1 tbsp chopped fresh parsley
2 tbsp toasted pine nuts
1/4 cup (25 g/1 oz) grated Parmesan or Pecorino cheese
3 garlic cloves, crushed
1 tbsp good olive oil
1/2 cup (100 g/4 oz) unsalted butter
salt and ground black pepper

COATING:
3 1/2 cups (200 g/7 oz) fresh, fine white breadcrumbs
1/4 cup (25 g/1 oz) finely grated Parmesan
1/4 cup (25 g/1 oz) finely chopped pine nuts
seasoned flour
1 egg, beaten
oil and butter, for frying

METHOD

1. For the stuffing: place all the ingredients, except the butter, in a food processor and process to a paste. Soften the butter slightly and add to the paste with the seasoning. Chill until firm.
2. Remove the tender fillets from the underside of the chicken breasts, place between two sheets of plastic wrap and beat with a rolling pin to flatten evenly.
3. Place the breasts smooth side down and cut a line down the middle, the same length as the fillets, then slide the knife down each side on its flat edge, as if you were filleting a fish, making a pocket in the breast.
4. Divide the butter mixture between the four chicken breast halves, filling each pocket. Place the beaten out fillets on top, then bring the edges of the breasts to the center, making a sausage shape. Chill well.
5. To make the coating: mix together the breadcrumbs, Parmesan or Pecorino cheese and pine nuts. Dip the breasts first into the seasoned flour, then into the egg and, finally, roll lightly in the crumb mixture.
6. Melt the butter and oil in a frying pan. Fry the chicken, turning once, for about 15 minutes over medium heat, until completely cooked. Serve immediately.

CHEF'S TIPS:
Different variations of this dish can be produced by changing the flavor of the butter by adding different herbs to it or by altering the coating – using chopped almonds or hazelnuts, for example. It is a good idea to make a large quantity of the flavored butter. It can then be molded into a sausage shape, kept in the freezer and cut into slices when required.

Serve with tagliatelle and a green salad.

Chicken with Asparagus and Wild Mushrooms

Serves: 4
Preparation time: 15 minutes
Cooking time: 20 minutes

INGREDIENTS

DUMPLINGS:
1/2 cup (100 g/4 oz) butter
2/3 cup (150 ml/1/4 pint) water
1 1/4 cups (150 g/5 oz) all-purpose flour
1 tbsp finely chopped cooked onion
1 tsp chopped tarragon
4 eggs
oil, for frying

3/4 cup (175 g/6 oz) butter
4 boneless chicken breast halves
1 tbsp finely chopped shallot or onion
2 tbsp white wine
2/3 cup (150 ml/1/4 pint) water
2 tsp heavy cream
8 oz (225 g) oyster or button mushrooms,
   trimmed and cooked in butter for 1 minute
1 tbsp chopped fresh tarragon
1 tsp lemon juice
salt
12 asparagus tips, lightly cooked

METHOD

1. Prepare the dumplings in advance. Melt the butter in the water and bring to a boil. Remove from the heat and beat in the flour, onion and tarragon. Continue beating with a wooden spoon until the mixture leaves the sides of the pan.
2. Allow the mixture to cool slightly, then beat in the eggs, one at a time, until the mixture forms a stiff and glossy paste. Place the mixture into a pastry bag with a 3/4-inch (2 cm) plain tip.
3. Pipe 1 1/2-inch (4 cm) dumplings over a pan of boiling water, cutting from the tip with a small knife, allowing the mixture to drop into the water. Alternatively, you could use a small spoon to shape the dumplings.
4. Simmer in batches for 2 minutes, remove with a perforated spoon and drain in a colander.
5. Melt 1/4 cup (50 g/2 oz) of the butter in a flameproof casserole and fry the chicken, skin side down, to seal. Add the shallots and wine, bring to a boil and add water.
6. Place in the oven at 350°F (180°C/Gas mark 4) for 15 minutes, until completely cooked. Remove the chicken and keep warm. Pour the juice through a strainer into a pan. Bring the liquid to a boil, add the cream and remaining butter in pieces. Stir in the mushrooms and tarragon with the lemon juice and the salt. Add the cooked asparagus and warm through.
7. Heat the oil and sauté the dumplings until well brown.
8. Pour the sauce over the chicken and garnish with the dumplings.

CHEF'S TIPS:

This is a special recipe from Paul Heathcote who owns the Longridge Restaurant, near Preston in Lancashire, England. Paul's cooking reflects a determination to acknowledge his roots and to celebrate the quality of local produce. Asparagus is one of the finest garnishes for tender, well-bred and well-fed, plump chicken.

Cantonese Chicken

Serves: 4
Preparation time: 12 minutes
Cooking time: 45 minutes

INGREDIENTS

3 lb (1.5 kg) oven-ready chicken
2 tbsp soy oil
4 tbsp sake or sherry
3 tbsp soy sauce or yeast extract
1 tbsp honey
1 1/2 tsp ground ginger
1 small onion, finely chopped
2/3 cup (150 ml/1/4 pint) chicken stock
2 tsp cornstarch
4 scallion curls, to garnish

METHOD

1. Prepare the chicken by cutting the breast and thigh portions into 2 x 3-inch (5 x 7.5 cm) pieces. Cut the wings into three portions and discard the end tips. Keep the drumsticks whole.
2. Heat the oil in a large frying pan, add the chicken and stir-fry for 10 minutes or until well browned. Drain off excess oil.
3. Combine the sake or sherry, soy sauce, honey, ginger and onion. Add to the chicken and stir well.
4. Take 2 tablespoons of the chicken stock and mix with the cornstarch. Add the remaining stock to the chicken, bring to a boil, cover and simmer for 30 minutes.
5. After 30 minutes, add the cornstarch paste and bring to a boil again, stirring. If the sauce is still very thin, boil rapidly to reduce down to a rich, golden sauce.
6. Place on a shallow platter and garnish with scallion curls.

CHEF'S TIPS:

If you are in a hurry to produce a meal, the cooking time for this dish could be reduced by removing the skin and bones from the chicken and cutting the flesh into strips – the discarded skin and bones could be used to produce a flavorsome stock.

This dish could be served with boiled seakale and scorzonera or spinach and fried salsify. Salsify and scorzonera are root vegetables, and both of them are best served peeled, blanched and fried in batter. They make an ideal garnish for fried chicken.

Chicken in Sweet and Sour Sauce

Serves: 4
Preparation time: 15 minutes
Cooking time: 25 minutes

INGREDIENTS

4 boneless chicken breast halves, skinned and diced
2 tbsp seasoned flour
2 tbsp oil
1 red bell pepper, deseeded and cut into cubes
1 medium onion, chopped
2/3 cup (150 ml/1/4 pint) chicken stock
8 apricots, halved
1 tsp tomato paste
1 tsp vinegar
2 tsp sugar
1 tsp ground ginger
1 small green chili pepper, deseeded and chopped
salt, to taste

METHOD

1. Dust the chicken with seasoned flour. Heat the oil in a shallow frying pan and stir-fry the chicken for 5 minutes. Add the bell pepper and onion and fry for 2 minutes.
2. Stir in the chicken stock, apricots and tomato paste and add the vinegar, sugar and seasoning, including the ginger and chili pepper. Simmer for 15 minutes. Season to taste.

CHEF'S TIPS:
It is now considered healthier to cook chicken without the skin, in order to reduce fat intake. This popular recipe is easy to prepare. The inclusion of apricots and bell peppers give the dish a unique flavor. Serve with Chinese noodles and strips of stir-fried parsnips and zucchini.

Chicken Curry

Serves: 4
Preparation time: 15 minutes
Cooking time: 35 minutes

INGREDIENTS

2 tbsp oil
1 medium onion, chopped
1 tbsp Madras curry powder
2 garlic cloves, crushed
4 chicken quarters, skinned
1 fresh mango, peeled and diced
2 1/2 cups (600 ml/1 pint) chicken stock
2 tsp cornstarch mixed with 3 tbsp water
3 tbsp water
salt, to taste

SERVE WITH:
saffron rice

GARNISH:
6 apricots, pitted and halved
2 bananas, sliced
8 pineapple cubes

METHOD

1. Heat the oil in a shallow pan and stir-fry the onion for 3 minutes. Sprinkle in the curry powder and cook for 30 seconds. Add the chicken, garlic and mango and brown for 3 minutes only.
2. Pour in the chicken stock and bring to a boil. Reduce the heat and simmer for 30 minutes. Thicken the sauce with the cornstarch and water. Season to taste with salt only.
3. Garnish the chicken with the apricots, bananas and pineapple cubes and serve with the saffron rice.

CHEF'S TIPS:
There are as many versions of curry as there are cooks. Some cooks sprinkle the 'magic powder' in after frying the chicken, others prefer to stew the chicken in a curry sauce. Whatever the method chosen, the fundamental way to ensure that the curry is a good one is to fry the spices lightly to bring out their flavor.

For the saffron rice, use 1 teaspoon of saffron for every 2 1/4 cups (450 g/1 lb) of rice. Infuse saffron threads first in a little boiling water before adding to the rice water.

Peppered Chicken with Garlic

Serves: 4
Preparation time: 12 minutes, plus at least 2 hours marinating
Cooking time: 35 minutes

INGREDIENTS

8 chicken thighs, skinned and scored
1 lemon, cut into wedges
1/4 cup (50 ml/2 fl oz) oil
1 tsp coarsely ground black pepper
2 garlic cloves, crushed
1/2 tsp dried basil
pinch of salt

GARNISH:
lemon wedges

METHOD

1. Squeeze 1 tablespoon juice from the lemon and reserve the remaining wedges for garnish.
2. Combine the lemon juice with the oil, garlic, pepper, basil and salt and pour over the chicken. Chill for 2 hours or overnight.
3. Cook the chicken under a hot broiler for 15-20 minutes or until tender, turning frequently and brushing with the remaining marinade throughout the cooking time.
4. Serve garnished with the lemon wedges.

CHEF'S TIPS:

This is one of the best-known Mediterranean chicken dishes and it is delicious served with a tomato, cucumber and lettuce salad with a vinaigrette dressing.

Lettuces used to be served braised with veal, pork or poultry. This is no longer fashionable, although there is no reason why lettuces, when they are good and cheap, should not be served in this way. As a salad ingredient lettuces are as popular as ever and, in my opinion, they should be eaten at every meal served as a course on their own, after the main dish.

Chicken Devils

Serves: 4
Preparation time: 15 minutes, plus
marinating overnight
Cooking time: 20-30 minutes

INGREDIENTS

2 tbsp (25 ml/1fl oz) vinegar
1/4 cup (50 ml/2 fl oz) oil
2 tbsp Worcestershire sauce
1 tbsp clear honey
2 tsp mustard
1/4 tsp chili powder or a few
    drops of Tabasco sauce
1 tsp dried thyme
salt and freshly ground black pepper
8 chicken portions

SERVE WITH:
mixed salad

METHOD

1. Combine the vinegar, oil, Worcestershire sauce, honey, mustard, chili powder or Tabasco sauce, thyme and seasoning in a shallow dish. Place the chicken in the dish, coat well, cover and leave to marinate in the fridge overnight.
2. Remove the chicken from the marinade. Place under a pre-heated medium broiler and cook for 20-30 minutes, basting regularly with the remaining marinade, until the chicken is cooked. Serve immediately with a mixed salad.

The following is a simpler version of the above recipe:

3 tbsp Worcestershire sauce
3 tbsp tomato paste
8 chicken drumsticks

1. Mix together the Worcestershire sauce and tomato paste. Toss the chicken drumsticks in the sauce and coat evenly. Arrange on a foil-lined broiler pan or cookie sheet. Heat the broiler or barbecue to moderately hot.
2. Broil or barbecue the drumsticks, turning occasionally, for about 15-20 minutes, until lightly browned and completely cooked.

CHEF'S TIPS:
The 'devil' part of the title comes from the very spicy chili marinade which the chicken is prepared and cooked in.

Chicken Peanut Pies

Serves: 12
Preparation time: 15 minutes
Cooking time: 25 minutes

INGREDIENTS

PIE DOUGH:
3/4 cup (175 g/6 oz) whole wheat flour
1/2 cup (50 g/2 oz) all-purpose flour
1/2 cup (100 ml/4 fl oz) water
1/4 cup (50 g/2 oz) butter or margarine
2 rounded tbsp smooth peanut butter

FILLING:
1 cup (100g/4oz) skinned and chopped cooked chicken
1 tsp ground cumin
2 scallions, chopped
1/2 tsp dried thyme
1 tbsp chopped fresh parsley
2 tsp lemon juice
2 tbsp natural low-fat yoghurt
salt and pepper
milk or beaten egg, to glaze

SERVE WITH:
salad

METHOD

1. Mix the flours together in a bowl. Place the water, butter and peanut butter in a small saucepan and heat gently until the butter has melted. Remove from heat and stir into the flours using a fork until a soft dough is formed.
2. Knead the pie dough lightly on a floured surface, then roll out two-thirds of the dough to line 12 muffin pans. Keep the remaining pie dough covered, to be used for making lids for the pies.
3. Combine all the filling ingredients in a bowl. Spoon into the muffin pans. Wet edges and cover with pie dough lids of the same diameter as the muffin pans.
4. Brush with the egg wash or milk. Bake at 400°F (200°C/Gas mark 6) for 20-25 minutes.
5. Serve with a salad.

CHEF'S TIPS:
Chicken pies are always popular. The chicken can be mixed with mushrooms, leeks, bacon or ham. Children will particularly appreciate these pies, made from a pastry to which peanut butter has been added.

Peanuts, which are also known as groundnuts, are not in fact nuts; they are an underground legume from which a very fine oil is also extracted. Groundnut, or arachide, oil is used extensively in France. Ground toasted peanuts can be mixed into sauces to produce a sauce rich in protein.

Supreme of Chicken Stuffed with Lobster

Serves: 2
Preparation time: 20 minutes, plus
2 hours chilling
Cooking time: 30 minutes

INGREDIENTS

2 boned chicken breasts, skinned, with under fillets
1 x 1 1/2-lb (675 g) cooked lobster
2 tbsp oil
2/3 cup (150 ml/1/4 pint) dry white wine
1 garlic clove
2 tsp tomato paste
4 tomatoes, skinned and deseeded
1 tsp tarragon
1 tsp basil
1 tsp cornstarch mixed with 2 tbsp water

STUFFING:
1 cup (225 g/8 oz) ground chicken breast
1 egg white
1/2 cup (100 ml/4 fl oz) heavy cream
salt and pepper
3 basil and tarragon leaves, chopped
pinch of chili powder
8 spinach leaves, blanched
oil and butter, for cooking
1 1/4 cups (300 ml/1/2 pint) chicken stock
basil and tarragon, to garnish

METHOD

1. Cut off the tail of the lobster and remove the claws and legs. Split the head. Cut off the eyes where the gravel bag is located and discard. Put the flesh from the tail, the green liver and the eggs, if the lobster is female, in a bowl and set aside. Crack the claws and remove the flesh.
2. Heat the 2 tablespoons of oil in a sauté pan and shallow fry the shells and legs only. Add the wine and boil for 10 minutes. Strain. Put this liquor into a small saucepan with the garlic, tomato paste, tomatoes, tarragon and basil. Boil until reduced to 3 tablespoons sauce. Cool.
3. For the stuffing: mix the ground chicken meat, the egg white, cream, chopped herbs and chili powder with 1 tablespoon of the lobster sauce to add color and flavor; keep the remaining the sauce. Add the diced lobster flesh, liver and eggs to the stuffing.
4. Flatten the chicken breast halves and flatten the under fillets separately. Wrap some of the stuffing in the spinach leaves and shape into two packages. Place each package in the center of the chicken scallops. Cover with the flattened under fillet and roll up the breast. Chill for 2 hours.
5. When ready to cook, brush the chicken with oil and broil for 6 minutes on each side. Brush with a little butter and bake for 10 minutes at 400°F (200°C/Gas mark 6).
6. Shape the remaining chicken and lobster stuffing into six oval shapes with two spoons dipped in hot water. Poach in chicken stock for 8 minutes, like dumplings, or quenelles.
7. For the sauce: reboil for 3 minutes and thicken with the cornstarch and water. Season to taste.
8. Cut each chicken package into five pieces, on the diagonal. Place the slices in the center of a pool of sauce with the quenelles, three per portion. Garnish with basil and tarragon.

CHEF'S TIPS:
This exciting dish was created by Irish chef Patrick O' Sullivan.

Chicken Stuffed with Crab

Serves: 4
Preparation time: 25 minutes, plus 40 minutes chilling
Cooking time: 30 minutes

INGREDIENTS

4 x 6-oz (175 g) chicken breast halves, with under fillet
1/2 cup (50 g/ 2oz) seasoned flour
1 egg, beaten
1 cup (50 g/2 oz) fresh breadcrumbs
2 tbsp (25 g/1 oz) sesame seeds
oil, for brushing and frying

STUFFING:
1 egg, beaten
2/3 cup (150 ml/1/4 pint) heavy cream
2 cups (50 g/2 oz) snipped chives
1 tsp chopped dill
1/4 cup (50 g/2 oz) chopped white crabmeat
salt and pepper

SAUCE:
2 tbsp (25 g/1 oz) mixed oil and butter
2 shallots, chopped
1 tbsp tarragon vinegar
2/3 cup (150 ml/1/4 pint) light cream
1 tsp Pernod or pinch star anise powder
2 tbsp (25 g/1 oz) butter
good pinch of paprika

GARNISH:
few strands saffron
2 tomatoes, peeled and halved
4 crab claws, cooked

METHOD

1. Remove the skin from each of the chicken breast halves. Peel away the under fillet from each. Brush the chicken with oil and place it between two sheets of plastic wrap. Gently flatten the breasts with a meat mallet or rolling pin to as thin as possible without tearing the flesh.
2. For the stuffing: grind the under fillets to a paste and place them in a bowl. Mix with the egg and beat for 30 seconds, adding the cream while mixing. Add the chives, dill and crabmeat. Season and chill for 20 minutes. Spread the crabmeat mixture equally over each piece of chicken breast. Roll up tightly into cigar shapes, coat in seasoned flour, dip in beaten egg and cover with a mixture of the breadcrumbs and sesame seeds. Wrap in foil and freeze for 20 minutes so that the chicken rolls keep their shape. Heat the oil in a pan and shallow fry the chicken breasts for 8 minutes. Keep warm.
3. To make the sauce: heat the oil and butter in a pan and shallow fry the shallots for 30 seconds, until translucent. Add the vinegar and reduce by half. Stir in the cream and boil for 8 minutes to reduce the sauce to a syrupy consistency and season. Add the Pernod or star anise, butter and paprika.
4. Pour a pool of the sauce onto each of the four serving plates and sprinkle with a few strands of saffron. Place a chicken breast on each plate. Cut each breast into three slices per portion. Place half a tomato and a crab claw beside each breast.

CHEF'S TIPS:
The crab stuffing complements the chicken extremely well. This dish is delicious, but quite rich, so serve with pilaf rice and a simple salad.

Boning and Stuffing Turkey

STEP-BY-STEP BONING AND STUFFING

Boning and stuffing a small turkey is like boning or stuffing a squab, chicken or duck. A bird prepared in this way is easier to carve and often much tastier. The stuffing will stretch the portions, making the meat go further and the dish cheaper. A skilled chef would take about 15 minutes to bone a turkey, a novice should allow a little longer.

1. Take a fresh turkey weighing 10 lb (4.5 kg). Cut along the length of the backbone to separate the carcass.
2. Remove the carcass by starting at the backbone and working around to the breast. Remove the leg and breastbone.
3. Lay the boned out turkey flat, breast down. Lift out the two under fillets and flatten with a meat pallet. Reserve to cover the stuffing.
4. Pack a first layer of prepared and seasoned stuffing into the carcass.
5. Cover the first layer with pre-soaked apricots (optional), then pack in second layer of stuffing.
6. Cover this second layer with the reserved under fillets.
7. Finally, add a third layer of stuffing.
8. Draw the bird together with running stitch and sew.
9. The prepared turkey is ready for cooking.

UNCOOKED TURKEY

Whole turkeys (fresh or frozen) can reach giant proportions, but for most of us a small bird of between 6-8 lb (3-4 kg) is suitable for most occasions and just right for family gatherings and picnics when value for money is often an important consideration.

Apart from whole birds, turkeys can also be bought as:
Portions: breasts, drumsticks, thighs (some already boned and stuffed), wings (either whole or tips only) and chops (similar to noisettes of lamb).
Turkey roasts: these are boned and rolled white and dark meat roasts, wrapped in pork fat and deep frozen, thawed and cooked as ordinary roasts.
Assorted packs: of ground and chunked meat, giblets and liver are also available. These are ideal for making stews, casseroles, soups and stocks or for pâtés and risottos.

COOKED TURKEY PRODUCTS

For cooks in a hurry, there is a choice of various cooked boneless turkey roll – some are already sliced, others may be cured or smoked. All will give plenty of lean meat with no wastage.

CONVENIENCE FOODS

There are a whole host of these turkey products – uncooked, ready-cooked or others requiring very little attention – nothing more than heating through or deep frying. Choose from turkey meat loaves and pâtés, burgers, crispy fries, fingers, croquettes and sausages.

STUFFING A TURKEY

If stuffing a turkey for roasting, allow about 1 lb (450 g) stuffing for the neck end of a bird weighing up to 14 lb (7 kg) and double the quantity for a larger bird

ROASTING A TURKEY

There are many theories about the best way to roast a turkey, but whichever way you choose make sure that the breast is covered with softened butter or margarine to keep it moist and tender during cooking. For extra flavor, lay slices of bacon on top of the softened butter or margarine.

Cover the bird with several layers of foil to prevent the flesh from drying out and toughening, but always remove the coverings for the last 30-40 minutes so that the bird can crispen and brown.

Wrap foil round the ends of the legs so that they don't burn during roasting. Dress them with turkey frills for serving at the table.

Stuffed Turkey with Chestnuts

Serves: 16 portions
Preparation time: 15 minutes
Cooking time: 1 1/2 hours

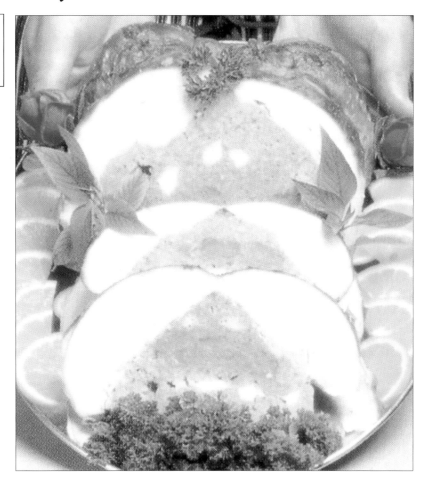

INGREDIENTS

10 lb (4.5 kg) turkey, boned
medium sherry (optional)

STUFFING:

2 lb (1 kg) ground pork
1 lb (450 g) ground bacon
generous 1 cup (225 g/8 oz) peeled cooked chestnuts
2 cups (50g/2oz) chopped fresh parsley
2 eggs, beaten
1/2 tsp black pepper
1/2 tsp mixed spice
3 tbsp rum or brandy
1 tsp salt
1 tsp dried thyme
1 3/8 cups (225 g/8 oz) pre-soaked apricots
   (or no-need-to-soak type)

METHOD

1. Combine all the stuffing ingredients, except the apricots, in a bowl to a compact mixture. (The apricots make a separate layer between the layers of stuffing).
2. Place the stuffed turkey on a trivet of bones (see page 196 for stuffing instructions). Pour a little melted butter over the turkey and season with salt and pepper.
3. Roast at 400°F (200°C/Gas mark 6) for the first 20 minutes. Reduce the heat to 350°F (180 C/Gas mark 4) for the following hour. Every 10 minutes baste the turkey with a ladleful of water, this will become your gravy base. You should finish with at least 2 1/2 cups (600 ml/1 pint) of gravy.
4. When the turkey is cooked, reduce this gravy by rapid boiling and season it. The gravy can be enriched with medium sherry, if liked.
5. Carve the turkey across into slices.

CHEF'S TIPS:
Serve with Brussels sprouts, roast potatoes and boiled baby carrots. The turkey can also be served cold with a mixed salad.

There are several fruits and nuts which can be added to the basic turkey stuffing – pitted prunes, apricots, apples, raisins, chestnuts, cashews, pistachios, almonds, pecans or macadamia nuts. Your selection will depend on personal preference.

Turkey Kiev

Serves: 4
Preparation time: 15 minutes, plus 30 minutes chilling
Cooking time: 12 minutes

INGREDIENTS

1/3 cup (75 g/3 oz) unsalted butter
1 tsp snipped chives
1 garlic clove, crushed
juice of 1 lemon
2 large turkey breast fillets
4 slices cooked ham
3 eggs, beaten
3 cups (175 g/6 oz) fresh white breadcrumbs,
    mixed with 2 tsp chicken seasoning, or
    1 tbsp chopped mixed herbs
oil, for deep frying

METHOD

1. Mix the butter with the chives, garlic and lemon juice.
2. Using a sharp knife, cut each turkey fillet in half widthwise and then slice through horizontally to make eight pieces. Pound with a rolling pin to form thin scallops.
3. Cut the ham into eight pieces, the same size as the scallops. Place on top of the scallops and spread with the garlic butter. Roll up tightly and chill in the fridge for 30 minutes or until the butter is firm.
4. Dip each turkey roll in the beaten egg and toss in the breadcrumbs seasoned with herbs. Coat again in the beaten egg and breadcrumbs to ensure that the turkey is completely covered.
5. Deep fry in hot oil for 5-6 minutes or until golden. Then bake at 400°F (200°C/Gas mark 6) for a further 6 minutes until cooked through. Drain on paper towels. Serve immediately.

CHEF'S TIPS:
Turkey stuffed with garlic and herb butter has been rather overdone in the past, and yet it still remains popular. Although the meat is deep fried, it is usually better to fry it for 6 minutes only and to bake it for a further 6 minutes; in this way the breadcrumbs do not become too hard or too brown.

Serve with sautéed potatoes and fresh vegetables or a salad.

Turkey Burgers Mexicana

Makes: 8
Preparation time: 20 minutes
Cooking time: 10 minutes

INGREDIENTS

1 1/2 lb (675 g) ground raw turkey meat
2/3 cup (150 g/5 oz) ground turkey liver
2 cups (100 g/4 oz) fresh breadcrumbs
1 small onion, chopped
1 small chili pepper, chopped
1/3 cup (50 g/2 oz) corn kernels
1 egg
seasoned flour
salt and pepper
a little oil

TOPPING:
1/2 cup (50 g/2 oz) grated Cheddar cheese
1 1/4 cups (150 g/5 oz) chopped scallions
2 large tomatoes, skinned, deseeded and chopped
1/4 cup (50 ml/2 fl oz) thick yoghurt

METHOD

1. In a bowl, combine the ground raw turkey and liver with the onion, breadcrumbs, egg, chili pepper, corn and seasoning. Divide into eight burgers and roll in seasoned flour. Dip in the oil and broil for 5 minutes on each side.
2. In another bowl, combine the ingredients for the topping, season to taste, and put a spoonful of the mixture on to each burger before serving.

CHEF'S TIPS:

Turkey is available in large boneless portions. In this recipe, breadcrumbs and corn kernels are added to the meat to make it go further and to give it more flavor. These turkey burgers are as good, if not better, than those prepared with beef or lamb. This is a perfect dish to serve to children.

Serve the burgers with an avocado salad with lemon dressing or with fried corn chips and hot baked beans.

Breast of Duck with Grapefruit

Serves: 4
Preparation time: 15 minutes
Cooking time: 20 minutes

INGREDIENTS

4 duck breast halves
a little cornstarch
2 tbsp oil
1/2 cup (100 ml/4 fl oz) sherry
2/3 cup (150 ml/1/4 pint) pink grapefruit juice
salt and freshly ground pepper
1 tbsp chopped fresh parsley

SERVE WITH:

1 pink grapefruit, peeled and segmented
broccoli
cauliflower
small potatoes

METHOD

1. Dust the duck breast halves with a little cornstarch on both sides. Heat the oil in a frying pan and gently fry the duck for 10 minutes, turning occasionally.
2. Remove the duck from the pan and keep warm. Add the sherry to the pan and bring to a boil.
3. Place 1 teaspoon of cornstarch in a small bowl, add a little grapefruit juice and mix until smooth.
4. Stir the cornstarch mix, the remaining grapefruit juice, seasoning and parsley into the pan and bring to a boil stirring constantly.
5. Slice the duck breasts diagonally and serve with the segments of grapefruit and vegetables.

CHEF'S TIPS:

Citrus fruits go well with duck. Although duck and orange is a more common combination, the sharper taste of grapefruit complements the naturally sweet flavor of the duck even better. A little vinegar or sugar can be added to the sauce to give it the tartness or sweetness you prefer.

Duck in Orange Sauce with Cherries

Serves: 4
Preparation time: 15 minutes
Cooking time: 1 1/2 hours

INGREDIENTS

5 lb (2.5 kg) duck
salt and pepper
pinch of cinnamon
1/2 cup (50 g/2 oz) seasoned flour
a little butter or oil

SAUCE:
2 lumps of sugar
juice of 2 oranges
1 tbsp wine vinegar
1 1/4 cups (300 ml/1/2 pint) brown demi glace sauce
    or thickened gravy
1 tsp tomato paste
4 mint leaves, chopped
1/2 cup (100 ml/4 fl oz) white port wine or sherry
1 tbsp Grand Marnier (or other orange liqueur)

GARNISH:
peeled segments of 2 oranges
12 pitted red cherries
1 tbsp snipped chives or mint leaves

METHOD

1. Season the duck inside and out with salt, pepper and cinnamon. Coat with a little butter or oil and dust with flour. Roast at 400 F (200°C/Gas mark 6) for 1 hour, then reduce the heat to 350°F (180°C/Gas mark 4) for a further 30 minutes. Baste the duck frequently with the fat and turn each time.
2. Remove the duck from the oven and drain the juice from the roasting pan for use in the sauce, also drain away the excess fat.
3. Put the roasting pan on top of the stove. Rub the sugar lumps with a little orange rind and place in the pan, moisten with vinegar and let caramelize. Add the brown sauce or thickened gravy, tomato paste, port, the juice of the oranges and the mint leaves. Boil for 10 minutes, then strain into a smaller saucepan. Add the Grand Marnier and season to taste. Using a zester, make strips of orange zest as thin as matches. Boil these in water for 10 minutes. Drain and add to the sauce. Reboil for 2 minutes.
4. Cut the duck into 4. Chop away the back bone and discard the ribs of the two breasts.
5. Place each duck portion on an oval plate coated with the sauce. Garnish with orange segments, pitted cherries and mint leaves or chives.

CHEF'S TIPS:
Duck in orange is a classic dish. The secret of the dish is to ensure that the caramelization is done perfectly – rub two lumps of sugar with orange rind and mixed with a tablespoon of wine vinegar before the brown sauce is added with the orange juice. To enhance the orange flavor add a few chopped mint leaves.

Serve the duck with a side plate of lettuce leaves and boiled small potatoes with chives.

Aromatic and Crispy Peking Duck

Serves: 4
Preparation time: 4-6 hours marinating
plus 5-6 hours cooling
Cooking time: 70 minutes

INGREDIENTS

4 lb (2 kg) duckling
2 tsp salt
1 tbsp Chinese five spice powder
3-4 scallions, chopped
3-4 slices ginger root (unpeeled), grated
5-6 tbsp dry sherry or sake

TO SERVE:
18-20 thin pancakes
1/2 cup (100 ml/4 fl oz) hoisin or plum sauce
1/2 cucumber, thinly shredded
4-5 scallions, thinly shredded
oil, for deep frying

CHINESE PANCAKES:
These can be made in advance, then stored in an air-tight
container until required.

2 cups (225 g/8 oz) all-purpose flour
pinch of salt
1/2 cup (100 ml/4 fl oz) water
a little sesame oil

METHOD

1. Remove the wings from the duck. Split it in half down the backbone (or use breast and leg quarter portions) and rub with salt on both sides.
2. Marinate in a deep dish with the spices, scallions, ginger and sherry for at least 4-6 hours, turning several times.
3. Braise the duck with the marinade for 1 hour, then remove from the cooking liquid and let cool for at least 5-6 hours. It is vital that you do this, since unless the duck is really cold and dry, the skin will not crispen.
4. Heat oil in a wok or deep fryer until smoking, place the duck pieces in the oil, skin side down, and fry for 6-8 minutes or until crisp and brown, turn once for the last 1 minute of cooking time. Remove the duck from the oil and drain.
5. To serve, scrape the meat from the bone. Place a little sauce, some strips of cucumber and scallion and some of the meat on each pancake and roll them up. Alternatively use crispy lettuce leaves instead of pancakes. Prepare as required and eat immediately.

CHINESE PANCAKES

1. Sift flour and salt into a bowl, add water and mix to form a dough. Knead lightly and divide into about 12 pieces.
2. Roll out into rounds, about 5-inch (12.5 cm) diameter. Lightly brush half of the rounds with oil on one side. Cover each one, matching the edges, with another un-oiled round and roll out gently.
3. Fry or cook on a griddle over a medium heat for 3-4 minutes, turning once, until firm but not brown.
4. Cool for a few minutes, then peel the pancakes apart.

CHEF'S TIPS:

This dish takes a very long time to prepare, and if you want the authentic taste there really are no short cuts, so start the day before with the marinade, and marinate the duck overnight. Crispy duck, however, is always popular, so serve it for a special dinner party and your guests are sure to appreciate your efforts.

Chinese pancakes can be bought from Asian food stores, or you can make your own – see recipe above.

Roast Duck

Serves: 5 – 1 lb (450 g) – dressed weight per person
Preparation time: 15 minutes
Cooking time: 1 1/2 hours

INGREDIENTS

5 lb (2.5 kg) duck

GRAVY:
fat from duck
juices from roasting pan
a few cooked bones and winglets (from above)
1 carrot, sliced
1 shallot, sliced
1 1/4 cups (300 ml/1/2 pint) water
1 tsp corn starch
2 tbsp water
salt and pepper
chili powder (optional)

GARNISH:
curly salad leaves
caramelized apple slices
apple purée

METHOD

1. Remove the back bone on both sides. Cut off the flap at the neck and discard as much fat as possible. Remove the collarbone and wishbone to make the carving easier. Before cooking, remove the winglets at the humerus joint (upper arm) and prick the bottom part with a carving fork.
2. Place the duck on a trivet of bones and winglets and cook for the first 15 minutes at 400°F (200°C/Gas mark 6), then reduce the heat to 350°F (180°C/Gas mark 4) for the remaining cooking time. Baste frequently. When cooked, drain the juice through a colander over a roasting pan.
3. Cut the breast by carving from the joint of the breast bone to the neck side. Remove the leg by lifting it out of its socket with a fork. Carve the breast into thin slices. Cut the leg in two, separating the thigh from the drumstick.
4. To make the gravy: remove as much fat as possible and in the roasting pan use the juices as a base for flavor. Add a few cooked bones and winglets, 1 shallot and 1 sliced carrot. Cook these ingredients in the roasting pan on top of the stove. Boil for 3-4 minutes to reduce the juice to a glaze. Add the water and boil for 10 minutes. Pour through a strainer. Collect the gravy in a saucepan. In a cup mix 1 teaspoon cornstarch and 2 tablespoons of water and add to a boiling sauce to thicken it. Season with salt, pepper and a little chili powder, if liked. Strain and keep hot.
5. Present slices of duck on a plate. Serve garnished with curly salad leaves, caramelized slices of apple, a sauce boat of gravy and apple purée.

CHEF'S TIPS:
Garden peas and roast potatoes are the ideal accompaniment for plain roast duck. An apple sauce and gravy can also be served with the duck, as can sage and onion stuffing.

Duck is undoubtedly a fatty bird and care must be taken in its preparation if the fat is not to overwhelm any other flavor. The surplus fat obtained from one duck can be as much as 2 1/2 cups (600 ml/1 pint). Although the fat lends a delicious flavor to sautéed potatoes, it is of very little use otherwise. Modern chefs prefer to cook wild duck breeds since they have the leanest and most flavored meat. However, a good free range farm duck can be delicious when carefully prepared. Cook it a little underdone. Allow longer cooking time for ducks with more fat – about 10 minutes extra.

Duck Leg with Shallots

Serves: 2
Preparation time: 15 minutes, plus marinating overnight
Cooking time: 30 minutes

INGREDIENTS

2 duck legs
2/3 cup (50 g/2 oz) salt
1 tsp mixed spices
1 tsp saltpeter (sodium nitrite)
1 tbsp oil

SAUCE:
1 1/4 cups (300 ml/1/2 pint) brown sauce (see page 29)
1 tsp tomato paste
juice of 1/2 orange
1 tsp Cointreau liqueur
salt and pepper

GARNISH:
2 tbsp oil
8 shallots, sliced
1 bunch of chives, snipped
a little heavy cream

METHOD

1. Mix the salt, saltpeter and spices together. Rub the duck legs with this mixture and let rest overnight. Wash the salt off with water. Brush the duck with oil and season with pepper. Roast at 350°F (180°C/Gas mark 4) for 30 minutes, basting the duck with its own fat and turning it over twice.
2. Boil the brown sauce with the orange juice and tomato paste. Add liqueur and season to taste.
3. Heat oil and stir fry the shallots over a low heat for 1 minute. Drain well.
4. Cut the legs into two pieces each and place on plates with some of the sauce. Surround with the shallots and chives. Pipe a thread of heavy cream on to the brown demi glace sauce and marble it with the point of a knife.

CHEF'S TIPS:
To get the full flavor of this dish it is important that the duck is allowed to marinate overnight in the brine. Pickling the duck in salt and saltpetre acts as a cure, and turns the flesh pink. The duck must then be cooked slowly in its own fat.

Breast of Goose in a Broth of Wild Mushrooms

Serves: 4
Preparation time: 1 1/2 hours, plus 1 hour marinating
Cooking time: 25 minutes

INGREDIENTS

1 goose breast half, boned and skinned
2/3 cup (150 ml/1/4 pint) medium sherry

STOCK:
goose bones and skin (from above)
1 onion, roughly chopped
1 carrot, roughly chopped
1 fennel bulb, roughly chopped
1 celery stick, roughly chopped
1 tsp yeast extract
salt and black pepper
2 tbsp goose fat or butter
8 oz (225 g) assorted wild mushrooms: chanterelles, morels,
    oyster, etc.
1 garlic clove, chopped

GARNISH:
1 bunch chervil or cilantro leaves, chopped

METHOD

1. Marinate the goose breast half in sherry for 1 hour.
2. Roast the goose bones and skin at 400°F (200°C/Gas mark 6) for 25 minutes. Put them into a stock pot with the vegetables, cover with water, and boil gently for 1 hour. Season to taste and add yeast extract for strength.
3. Poach the goose breast half for 20 minutes in the sherry and some of the stock. Then cut into slices.
4. Heat the butter or goose fat in a frying pan and stir-fry the mushrooms for 3 minutes. Add garlic and cook for a further 30 seconds. Pour some of the stock into soup bowls and arrange the goose on a bed of mushrooms. Sprinkle over chervil and cilantro to garnish.

CHEF'S TIPS:

This is a 'pot au feu' as my grandmother would have made it when an old farm goose was 'ready for the pot'.

Parsnips are a sweet and turnipy root vegetable that are best par-boiled and fried in butter. They make an excellent accompaniment for roast goose. Boiled chestnuts tossed in butter and mixed with brussel sprouts or lima beans, would also be an ideal accompaniment for this dish.

Serve with Brussels sprouts or fava beans with chestnuts.

Breast of Guinea Fowl en Ballotine

Serves: 2
Preparation time: 15 minutes
Cooking time: 1 hour

INGREDIENTS

2 guinea fowl breast halves
1/4 cup (50 g/2 oz) melted butter, for basting

STUFFING:
2/3 cup (150 g/5 oz) ground guinea fowl leg meat
2/3 cup (150 g/5 oz) ground pork
2 oz (50 g) chicken livers
1 egg
1 garlic clove, chopped
1 tbsp chopped fresh parsley
1 cup (50 g/2 oz) fresh breadcrumbs
salt and pepper

SAUCE:
1 fennel bulb, chopped
1 carrot, chopped
1 onion, chopped
1 tbsp yeast extract
2 tsp cornstarch mixed with 2 tbsp water
1/4 cup (50 ml/2 fl oz) Marsala wine

GARNISH:
12 small shallots
2 tbsp (25 g/1 oz) butter and oil for cooking

METHOD

1. Remove the skin and bones (reserve for making sauce) from the breasts, place between two sheets of plastic wrap and flatten with a meat mallet or rolling pin. Remember to also flatten the under fillet. Slit the breasts to form a pocket.
2. Combine all the ingredients for the stuffing in a bowl and mix them together. Fill each piece of breast with this mixture, cover with the under fillet, roll and tie with string.
3. Season with salt and pepper. Brush the guinea fowl with butter and roast at 400°F (200°C/Gas mark 6) for 30 minutes. Baste during the cooking with the butter and 3-4 tablespoons water, to keep the meat moist.
4. Boil the bones and the skin with the fennel, onion and carrot in 2 1/2 cups (600 ml/1 pint) water for 30 minutes. Strain and boil again to reduce the sauce to a quarter. Thicken the sauce with the cornstarch and water mixture. Add the yeast extract and the Marsala wine.
5. Heat butter and oil in a frying pan and stir-fry the shallots until golden. Add 1 cup (225 ml/8 fl oz) of the sauce and boil for 8 minutes until the shallots are tender. Carve breasts on the diagonal. Garnish with shallots and serve sauce separately.

CHEF'S TIPS:

The guinea fowl is a domesticated game bird and is related to the turkey, although it originated in Africa. A gamey flavor is much preferred by gourmets, so the bird should be hung for 24 hours in a cool, airy place before it is cooked. In all other respects, guinea fowl can be prepared and cooked like chicken.

Serve with pasta and braised celery.

Roast Squab

Serves: 2
Preparation time: 10 minutes
Cooking time: 45 minutes

INGREDIENTS

2 squabs, trussed and seasoned inside and out
2 bacon slices
2 tbsp oil

MARINADE:
2/3 cup (150 ml/1/4 pint) fresh cantaloupe juice and purée
3 tbsp soy sauce
1 tsp Cajun seasoning (with chili)

SAUCE:
1 tbsp oil
1 small shallot, chopped
2 tbsp soy sauce
1 tsp grated ginger
2/3 cup (150 ml/1/4 pint) stock
1 tsp cornstarch mixed with 3 tbsp cold water
salt and pepper

GARNISH:
4 slices of fresh cantaloupe melon, cut into wedges
a few chives

METHOD

1. Wrap the bacon slices around the squab breasts. Heat the oil in a sauté pan and brown the bird for 10 minutes. Transfer into a casserole and add the marinade ingredients. Cook at 400°F (200°C/ Gas mark 6) for 15-20 minutes. Remove the squabs from the oven when cooked. Take off the bacon slices and boil them with the remaining marinade until it is reduced by half.
2. To make the sauce: heat oil in a frying pan and stir-fry the shallots for 30 seconds. Add the soy sauce, ginger and stock and boil for 10 minutes. Pour in the reduced marinade from the squabs, check seasoning and thicken the sauce with the cornstarch and water mixture. Boil for 4 minutes to clear the starch.
3. Cut the birds in half and place on a dish, cover with the sauce and garnish with wedges of fresh melon and chives.

CHEF'S TIPS:
Squabs can be as tender and tasty as broiler chickens. Any other young bird – grouse, pheasant, guinea fowl or wild duck – may be used in this recipe.

Fresh, ripe cantaloupe or yellow-fleshed melons are recommended as garnish.

Quail with Asparagus

Serves: 4
Preparation time: 15 minutes
Cooking time: 40 minutes

INGREDIENTS

8 quails
2 cups (100 g/4 oz) chanterelle mushrooms (or other wild variety)
2 tbsp oil and butter

SAUCE:
2 tbsp oil
2 shallots, chopped
1 tbsp truffle peels (optional)
2 tarragon leaves, chopped
1 tsp yeast extract
2/3 cup (150 ml/1/4 pint) game stock or water
6 tbsp medium Madeira wine
1 tsp cornstarch mixed with 3 tbsp water
salt and pepper

FRENCH DRESSING:
3 tbsp walnut oil
1 tbsp lemon juice
1 tsp freshly chopped parsley
1 tsp Dijon mustard

GARNISH:
24 asparagus tips, boiled for 35 seconds only
2 whole fresh or canned truffles sliced thinly into four
    assortment of salad leaves: oak leaf, radicchio,
    lettuce, Belgian endive, etc.
4 yellow zucchini, sliced and blanched
2 tomatoes, skinned, deseeded and diced

METHOD

1. Remove the skin and breasts of the quails. Chop the bones and legs to provide flavor to a rich meaty sauce.
2. Heat oil in a pan and stir-fry shallots, mushroom stems (save the caps), truffle peels, bones and legs for 10 minutes. Add the tarragon, yeast extract and stock and boil for 15 minutes, finally add the wine. Thicken the sauce with the cornstarch and water mixture and boil for 4 minutes to clear the starch. Season to taste and strain the sauce.
3. Mix the ingredients for the French dressing in a bowl and prepare the salad garnish.
4. Heat the oil and butter in a pan and shallow fry the quail breasts for 5 minutes or so. Fry the caps of the chanterelles separately.
5. Pour a pool of sauce onto the plates. Place two slices of truffle on each plate as a base for the quail breasts. Arrange a nest of mixed salad leaves and mushrooms and place the sliced yellow zucchini, asparagus tips and diced tomatoes in the center.

CHEF'S TIPS:

There is very little meat on a quail and unless one wishes to eat half a dozen at a time, like Henry VIII, it is probably better to serve the meat in a delicate warm salad in the modern French style. Hot quail meat is well complemented by cold asparagus. Once again, any small game bird such as partridge, could be used instead of quail in this recipe.

Pheasant Sausage with Chestnut Purée

Serves: 4
Preparation time: 30 minutes plus, 1 hour soaking for sausage casing and chilling overnight for stuffed sausages
Cooking time: 30 minutes

INGREDIENTS

36-inch (90 cm) length sausage casing
a little flour
2 eggs, beaten
brown breadcrumbs
butter for frying

STUFFING:
1/2 cup (25 g/1 oz) fresh white breadcrumbs
1 small shallot, chopped and cooked for1 minute in oil
1/2tsp grated nutmeg
3 tbsp hot milk
1 cup (225 g/8 oz) raw pheasant breast, skinned and diced
1/2 cup (100 g/4 oz) butter
1 egg
1 tbsp whiskey
1 1/4 cups (300 ml/1/2 pint) heavy cream
salt and white pepper

GARNISH:
generous 1 cup (225 g/8 oz) chestnut purée (fresh or canned)
1/2 cup (100 g/4 oz) potato paste (mashed with a
    little butter and 1 crushed clove garlic)
1/3 cup (75 ml/3 fl oz) heavy cream
1 tbsp butter
basil leaves, to season
sage leaves, to garnish

GAME SAUCE:
2 tbsp oil, 2 legs, raw bones and skin of pheasant, 1 small onion, quartered, 2 cups (100 g/4 oz wild mushrooms, cleaned and sliced, 3 sage leaves, 1/2 cup (100 ml/4 fl oz) beer, 1 tsp tomato paste, 1 tsp yeast extract, 1/2 tsp mixed spice, 1 tsp cornstarch mixed with 2 tbsp water

METHOD

1. Soak the sausage casing in water for 1 hour.
2. Combine all the ingredients for the stuffing in a food processor. Process the mixture to a fine purée. Leave to chill.
3. Meanwhile, prepare the game sauce. Heat the oil in a pan and brown the pheasant skin, bones and legs for 12 minutes to develop a gamey flavor. Add the onion, mushrooms and sage and after 5 minutes of frying, transfer into a saucepan with 2 1/2 cups (600 ml/1 pint) water, the beer, tomato paste, yeast extract and mixed spice. Boil for 1 hour. Strain and thicken with cornstarch mixture. Boil again for 5 minutes to clear the starch. Season to taste.
4. Tie one end of the casing with a knot. Fit a pastry bag with a plain tip, fill with the stuffing mixture and pipe into the casing until full, then tie loose end with a knot. Poach the sausage in 2 1/2 quarts (2 liters/3 1/2 pints) of water at simmering point for 20-25 minutes. Remove carefully and cool the sausage. Twist every eight inches (20 cm), then let rest overnight.
5. Cut into four sausages, coat with the flour and dip in the beaten egg, then roll in the breadcrumbs.
6. Heat a little butter and cook the sausages until golden for 3 minutes.
7. Combine the hot potato and chestnut purées. Mix with butter and cream and season to taste.
8. Place a spoonful of the purée, neatly shaped with a spatula on four plates. Top with one sausage and pour game sauce around. Garnish with fresh sage leaves.

CHEF'S TIPS:
Both animal or synthetic sausage casings are available for the stuffing of any kind of forcemeat or even fish. The flesh of the breast without the skin is finely ground and made to a purée, like mousse, with the addition of eggs and heavy cream. We then use a pastry bag to fill sausage casing. When made very light, the mixture is the same texture as quenelles. If preferred, the sausage casings can be omitted and the stuffing shaped into burgers and fried.

Stuffed Leg of Chicken on Stir-Fried Vegetables

Serves: 6
Preparation time: 30 minutes
Cooking time: 30 minutes

INGREDIENTS

6 chicken legs, boned

STUFFING:
1 lb (450 g) mushrooms
1 medium onion
2 tbsp (25 g/1 oz) butter
2 garlic cloves, crushed
1/2 cup (15 g/1/2 oz) chopped fresh basil
8 oz (225 g) fresh spinach, washed
1 boneless chicken breast, half
1 egg, beaten
salt and black pepper

VEGETABLES:
1 medium bulb of celery root
2 carrots
2 tbsp olive oil
8 oz (225 g) bacon
1 small cabbage

METHOD

1. To bone the chicken legs, place skin side down on a board and using a sharp knife, cut through the meat to expose the thigh bone. Working down towards the drumstick, scrape the meat away from the bone until you reach the middle joint. Cut carefully around the joint to release the meat, taking care not to cut the skin. Scrape the meat away from the drumstick bone, and when you reach the end knuckle, grasp the bones firmly and pull inside out to release the bone. Discard the bones and turn the leg meat skin side out, ready for stuffing.
2. For the stuffing: grind the mushrooms, or finely chop them in a food processor. Place in a pan and cook, stirring, until all the free liquid has evaporated. Let cool.
3. Cook the onion in butter with the garlic and basil, until softened. Let cool.
4. Place the spinach in a pan with just enough water to cover the leaves. Cook for 1 minute or until wilted. Drain well and cool.
5. Grind, or finely chop in a food processor, the chicken breast and spinach. Mix with the mushrooms, onion, egg, salt and pepper. Spoon the stuffing into the boned chicken legs and secure with wooden toothpicks. Chill.
6. For the vegetables: peel the celery root and cut into 1/2-inch (1 cm) cubes, peel and slice the carrots into thin strips and chop cabbage into 1-inch (2.5 cm) squares. Heat the oil and cook the celery root and carrots gently until just soft. Chop the bacon and fry until golden, then add the cabbage and other vegetables.
7. Fry the chicken until golden, then place in a baking pan and bake at 425°F (220°C/Gas mark 7) for 25-30 minutes, until the juices run clear, not pink.
8. Spoon the warm vegetables onto serving plates. Remove the toothpicks from the chicken legs and slice each into four and arrange on top of the vegetables. Serve with a rich gravy made from the cooking juices.

CHEF'S TIPS:

This dish was created by television chef Gary Rhodes who runs the famous Greenhouse Restaurant in London. Mr Rhodes insists that British food and British chefs are the best. His own success is due to his consistently high standard of cooking and his artistic style of presentation, as well as to his fundamental belief that, above all else, food must taste good. Allow yourself time to bone the chicken legs.

If you do not have any wooden toothpicks, wrap the stuffed legs tightly in buttered foil. The chicken will brown and hold together perfectly.

ALL ABOUT GAME

Introduction

In my grandparents' country village most households bred rabbits and goats for the table and hare and deer meat was widely available. I remember at the age of fourteen learning how to kill, truss, dress and cook a rabbit for Sunday lunch. This was my introduction to animal anatomy and the art of butchery.

The hunting and consumption of game are still a matter of survival in many countries of the world and bison (buffaloes), bears, boars, deer and goats still roam wild in many places.

In this chapter of the book I have grouped together the animals that are most commonly considered as "fair game" for food. For butchery purposes bison (buffalo) can be treated like beef and most beef recipes can be applied equally well to bison (buffalo) meat. Deer and goats have the same bone structure as sheep, and wild boars have the same conformation as pigs but are more gamey with a strong-smelling characteristic which is the reason why boar meat must be marinated in wine like venison. The meat of all these animals can be treated similarly.

In recent years meat from deer and bison (buffaloes) have become increasingly fashionable in Australia and, as a result, these animals are becoming big business and are being bred in controlled conditions to improve the quality of the meat. Goat production has also increased. Goat milk, cheese and yoghurt have all become very popular and the meat, which from a young animal can be as tender as lamb, is also in demand. Wild boars are still hunted for meats, which is much appreciated by gourmets.

RABBIT

In France, we have as many recipes for rabbit as we do for chicken. These include: Lapin Bordelaise, in red wine; Lapin Normande, with apples and Calvados; Lapin á la moûtarde, with mustard; Lapin Flamande, with dried prunes. There are also many patés, pies, terrines and other entrées that are made using rabbit meat.

Tame rabbits are best eaten between two and three months old. Wild rabbits have a better flavor and tend to grow bigger. In most French cookery books you will find recipes using rabbit in the poultry section. I feel, however, that it is more appropriate to classify them as game, as you would hare, and that is why you will find rabbit in this section of the book.

Rabbits and hares differ in size and in the characteristics of the flesh. Hare meat is reddish, like venison, but rabbit flesh is whiter than chicken meat.

- An old hare should be cooked slowly to reduce the toughness of the flesh.
- Wild rabbit is smaller than tame rabbit and the flesh is whiter and more juicy than that of a hare.
- Tame rabbit is bred for the table or for its skin. The flesh of a young animal is firm and white.

Test of the tenderness of a rabbit. The under-jaw will break easily when pressed hard between the fingers and thumb.

Hanging. Hang for a few days to develop the gamey flavor of the hare or rabbit. It should be hung by the forelegs, to retain the blood. The older the hare is, the longer it should be hung.

Wild rabbits sometimes have flesh flavored with the wild thyme on which they feed.

THE CUTS OF A HARE OR RABBIT

Saddle: This is the name given to the whole body portion of a hare or rabbit, after the legs have been removed. Before using as a saddle, cut off the portion containing the lungs, heart, etc., and then trim the sides, cutting all the ribs very short. With the point of a filleting knife, remove all the skin and sinews from the back and underside. The saddle is always larded with thin strips of fat.

Fillet: This is the whole fillet, when it has been removed from both sides of the saddle, cleared of skin and sinews, cut lengthwise into two or three slices and afterwards flattened, trimmed and prepared either with egg and breadcrumbs or flour.

Paupiettes: Thin fillets, beaten well, trimmed and stuffed accordingly, then rolled up into paupiettes.

Legs: Legs of young animals should be used for sautés and casseroles; those of old animals for jugged hare, stuffings and mousses, etc.

Forelegs: When large, these are cut from the body to be used for sautés and pies, etc. When small, they are not cut off individually, but used as part of the ribs on the underside, in the same way as the forequarter of mutton is cut.

Front ribs: Generally used for stocks or stews.

DEER SOLD AS VENISON

Wild deer have been hunted throughout Europe and the Middle East from earliest times until the present day. From the Middle Ages onwards, great country houses often had deer parks, and many still do. Today, most venison comes from farmed deer. Deer farming has greatly increased in recent years to meet the steadily growing demand for this healthy meat. Farmed red deer grow to about 115 lb (50 kg) on average, wild deer tend to be smaller.

Deer are naturally gregarious animals. In the wild, deer live in large herds and when farmed they are kept in open fields, surrounded by high fences, in which they can graze in peace. Deer farmers provide shelter for their animals and supplement their diet with hay and root vegetables, but deer cannot be 'factory farmed' as some other animals can.

Farm-bred venison has all the attributes of wild venison, being high in flavor and low in fat but, at the same time, it is also very tender and meets rigorous hygienic standards. Farm-bred venison is available all year round where as wild deer can only be killed in season.

The best meat is considered to be that from a buck or stag between 18 months and 2 years old. The meat is close grained, dark in color and very lean. The meat does not have the marbling of fat present in beef. Venison from an 18 month old buck will have a fat content of 6 per cent, meat from an older animal may have slightly more fat, but what fat there is, is largely unsaturated. Venison is therefore a very useful meat for those requiring a low-cholesterol or low-fat diet. The flavor of the meat is determined by the length of time it is hung. Traditionally, venison from wild deer was hung for a long time in order to tenderize it and this was responsible for its gamey flavor.

Venison has the lowest fat content of any farmed red meat. For this reason all venison joints should be wrapped in pork fat or bacon in order to prevent the meat from becoming too dry.

Quality. The flesh is best in a two-year-old animal, when the fat is clear, bright and thick.

Hanging. When freshly killed, venison should be dusted all over with an equal mixture of flour and ground black pepper. It should be hung for 2-3 weeks, until the meat is tender and has developed the gamey flavor. It should be kept in a larder that is cool and draughty.

BUTCHERY PREPARATION

Farmed venison should be treated like sheep from the butchery point of view. Generally cut into hindquarters; also into leg, saddle, rib chops and medallions.

METHODS OF PREPARATION

1. The haunch is a large joint which can be braised or roasted. Marinate first in wine and herbs, although this is not essential if the deer is young and tender.
2. The leg is prepared as leg of mutton; the skin and sinews are removed and it is then larded finely, and marinated with spices, oil, vinegar, white wine, salt and pepper for about 24 hours.
3. The saddle is prepared as usual, trimmed neatly, the sinews removed from the surface and larded as finely as possible; then marinated or used as it is.

COOKING WITH VENISON

Cuts from the loin, leg or best end ribs are most suitable for broiling. Whole joints can be boned and stuffed with ground pork to make the meat go further. Venison is marinated to improve the flavor of the meat and to preserve it. You must ensure that the meat and marinade are refrigerated.

Most lean venison meat, i.e. from the legs and shoulders, can be cut into cubes and stewed like Beef Bourguignon. But remember that venison will cook in half the time that it takes to cook the beef.

Like lamb, venison is usually served with fruit jellies, e.g. red or blackcurrant, crab apple, blueberry, raspberry or cranberry jelly. Plums or cherries make good garnishes for venison.

Venison can be combined with pork sausage meat to make pâtés and terrines that are ideal for the cold table.

Venison may be kept deep frozen for at least 12 months. Cutlets, chops and steaks should be packed individually in plastic wrap and over-wrapped. Ground meat can be packed in polythene bags. Cooked venison can be packed for freezing in the same way.

GOAT

I have chosen to include goat in the game section rather than anywhere else in the book in order to keep it distinct from the meats commonly available from butchers and supermarkets.

Goats are reared primarily for the quality of their milk. Goat milk is more digestible than cow's milk and it contains higher amounts of niacin and thiamine. It is also used to produce very fine cheeses and yoghurt.

Only young goat meat is worth roasting or broiling. The meat from older animals can be used in curries or stews.

Goat meat is popular with gourmets and it is rapidly becoming as acceptable as lamb.

BREEDS OF GOAT
Today's domesticated goats are descendants of the Pasang (Capra aeragus), which probably originated in the Middle East, the earliest recorded being from Persia. Wild goats like the Ibex, Markhor, Tahir and Rocky Mountain are all perfectly edible, but have a very strong gamey flavor.

Modern breeds of goat are classified into four main groups: the prick-eared Swiss goat; the long, drooping eared Nubian; the dwarf or Guinea goat and the Angora goat, which is bred for its wool.

The Swiss breeds known as Saanens and Toggenburgs are found all over France, Germany, Switzerland and Scandinavia. These goats are kept for the good quality of their milk and meat.

BISON (BUFFALO)

Bison (buffalo) meat has been eaten in Africa and Asia for centuries and it is now appearing on menus in the United States, Canada and Australia. It can be cooked and served like beef but I have decided to include bison (buffalo) in the Game chapter of this book for the simple reason that it is still a wild cattle in many parts of the world.

Zebu cattle are found extensively on most of the continents of the world. They are characterized by a prominent hump above the shoulders, pendulous skin under the throat, on the dewlap, navel and the sheath of the males. The rump is drooping, the head is long and narrow and the ears are long and drooping. The horns differ widely according to sex and strain; the color also varies from shades of grey to black. The size and form of the cattle are influenced by the climate, soil and feed that is available. In India the cattle are used for work and milk production only.

Bison (buffaloes) were originally introduced into Australia from Indonesia in 1800 – there are now 30,000 domesticated bison (buffalo) living in disease-free areas of the country. A substantial bison (buffalo) meat export industry has developed with Europe since the meat from the Australian breeds is leaner than meat from the European animals.

Wild bison (buffaloes) are among the most dangerous of the big game animals, although, when they are domesticated, they can become quite docile. In the United States, bison (buffalo) meat has been a staple part of the diet of the Native Americans for many years. They continue to eat the meat today in cured, smoked and dehydrated forms.

Rabbit Scallops Savoy Style

Serves: 4
Preparation time: 30 minutes, plus 1 hour to bleach the meat
Cooking time: 15 minutes

INGREDIENTS

1 x 3 lb (1.5 kg) rabbit on the bone
    (to yield approximately 1 lb (450 g)
    of lean meat)
1 garlic clove, chopped
1 tbsp heavy cream
1/2 cup (50 g/2 oz) fresh white breadcrumbs
salt and white pepper, to taste
3 tbsp seasoned flour
2 tbsp oil, to fry

SAUCE:
1 small shallot, chopped
4 tbsp dry or medium sherry
4 tbsp stock (made from the rabbit bones)
1 tbsp yeast extract
4 tbsp heavy cream
salt and pepper

SERVE WITH:
1/2 lb (225 g) flat noodles
1/4 cup (50 g/2 oz) butter
1/2 cup (50 g/2 oz) red bell pepper, deseeded and cut into thin strips
salt and black pepper
2 tbsp grated Cheddar cheese

GARNISH:
1 bunch watercress
4 thin lemon slices

METHOD

1. Soak the boned flesh of rabbit in salted water for 1 hour to bleach the meat white. Drain well and ground it twice to obtain a very fine grain, not too coarse in texture.
2. In a bowl mix the ground rabbit meat with the garlic, cream breadcrumbs and seasoning. Divide into four balls and flatten them to four thin scallops. Rub in the seasoned flour and shake the surplus off.
3. Heat the oil in a pan and shallow fry the scallops for 2 minutes on each side. Remove from the heat and keep warm.
4. To make the sauce: stir-fry the chopped shallot, in the same pan, until translucent, for 4 minutes on a low heat and add the sherry, stock and yeast extract. Boil for 4 minutes and stir in the cream. Boil for 1 minute. Season to taste and strain.
5. Boil the noodles for 10 minutes. In the meantime, heat the butter in a clean shallow pan and stir-fry the red bell pepper for 2 minutes. Add the hot strained noodles. Season to taste and sprinkle with the grated Cheddar cheese.
6. Pour a little pool of the sauce on each plate and position one scallop in the center. Serve with the noodles and garnish with the watercress and a slice of lemon.

CHEF'S TIPS:

Imported rabbits from Australia were used in all types of recipes in Britain during the Second World War. The most popular and simplest dish was to ground the lean meat of the rabbit and to shape it into burgers, thinned down with a wood mallet to thin scallops and shallow fried in butter to order. Sometimes they were coated with nuts and breadcrumbs and served with a delicious fresh herb tomato sauce.

This is my version of this recipe, which was served at the Savoy hotel, London at the time while I was working during a vacation from my wartime service in the Royal Navy, where I was conscripted as a Petty Officer chef to the Admiralty in London.

Rabbit Fricassée

Serves: 4
Preparation time: 20 minutes
Cooking time: 1 hour

INGREDIENTS

3 tbsp mixed oil and butter
1 tame rabbit, cut into 8-10 pieces
3 tbsp seasoned flour
1 small glass of brandy
1 1/4 cups (300 ml/1/2 pint) dry white wine
1 1/4 cups (300 ml/1/2 pint) stock or water
1 bouquet garni
2 garlic cloves, crushed
1/2 cup (100 ml/4 fl oz) heavy cream
3 lean slices of bacon, rindless and diced
12 small mushrooms
12 small onions
pinch of ground mace
4 small carrots, sliced
salt and pepper

GARNISH:
1 tbsp chopped fresh parsley and thyme

METHOD

1. Heat 2 tablespoons of the oil and butter in a large saucepan and brown the rabbit on all sides. Remove the rabbit from the pan and keep warm. Sprinkle the seasoned flour into the frying pan to absorb the fat. Add the brandy, wine, stock or water, bouquet garni and garlic. Stew gently for 1 hour. Add the cream when the rabbit is cooked. Season to taste.
2. In another pan, heat the remaining oil and butter and fry the bacon, mushrooms and onions until golden for 4 minutes. Drain well and add to the stew for the final 12 minutes. Season to taste with a good pinch of mace. Boil the carrots for 5 minutes and add to the stew. Sprinkle with chopped parsley and thyme, and check seasoning.

CHEF'S TIPS:
This delicious dish should persuade those people who are reluctant to eat rabbit to try this nutritious meat.

Serve with boiled potatoes or shell-shaped pasta.

Jugged Boneless Hare with Mushrooms and Cherries

Serves: 4
Preparation time: 30 minutes
Cooking time: 1 hour

INGREDIENTS

2 tbsp oil
1 lb (450 g) hare meat, neatly diced
1 medium onion, chopped
1 fennel bulb, chopped
1 1/4 cups (300 ml/1/2 pint) dark red wine
1 1/4 cups (300 ml/1/2 pint) game stock or
    water and a bouillon cube
1 tsp tomato paste
4 leaves of lovage
4 tbsp (25 g/1 oz) brown roux*
salt and pepper
pinch of ground mace and cinnamon
4 mushrooms, caps and diced stalks

GARNISH:
8 small onions
8 cherries, pitted (fresh or canned)
4 leaves of lovage
4 strands of chives with buds on

METHOD

1. Heat the oil in a shallow pan and fry the meat for 10 minutes until brown. Add the onion and fennel and stir-fry for another 4 minutes. Discard the surplus oil and add the wine, stock or water, tomato paste and lovage leaves. Simmer for 1 hour.
2. Strain the liquid into another pan and mix in the roux to thicken the sauce. Boil for 4 minutes. Strain, discarding the flavorings, and reheat the hare meat in the sauce.
3. Add the seasoning, spices, mushroom caps and diced stalks. Boil the small onions separately for 4 minutes only.
4. Serve the meat casserole on plates with a garnish of cherries and the small onions. Garnish the side of the plate with lovage leaves and the strands of chives.

CHEF'S TIPS:
Lovage and celery give the sauce in this recipe its distinctive flavor. Raw lovage leaves are an edible salad item.

*The roux is made by mixing 1 tablespoon of fat or butter with the same quantity of flour. Cook for 2 minutes until lightly brown. Alternatively, use cornstarch or arrowroot to thicken sauces. For this method, use 2 teaspoons of cornstarch or arrowroot per 2 cups (450 ml /3/4 pint) of boiling sauce.

Goat Curry with Lemon Aspen Rice

Serves: 4
Preparation time: 20 minutes
Cooking time: 50 minutes

INGREDIENTS

2 lb (1 kg) stewing goat, cut into small strips
2 tbsp oil
1 green chili pepper, chopped with seeds
2 garlic cloves, chopped
1 small piece of fresh ginger root,
    peeled and chopped
1 tsp coriander seed, ground
1 tsp cumin seed, ground
a good pinch turmeric
1 large onion, chopped
2 basil leaves, chopped
1/2 cup (50 g/2 oz) macadamia nuts,
    finely chopped
6 lemon myrtle or lemon balm leaves, chopped
2 1/2 cups (600 ml/1 pint) light stock
1 1/4 cups (300 ml/1/2 pint) coconut milk

SERVE WITH:
generous 1 cup (225 g/8 oz) long grain rice
2 1/2 cups (600 ml/1 pint) light stock
1 tsp lemon aspen or lemon grass
finely chopped lemon grass leaves, to garnish

METHOD

1. Heat 1 tablespoon of the oil in a wok and brown the meat for 10 minutes. Pound together the chili pepper, garlic and ginger and then fry in the remaining oil, with the dry spices, for 5 minutes.
2. Process the onion, herbs and nuts in a food processor. Add to the fried meat. Simmer for 10 minutes, then add the stock, coconut milk and a little salt. Cook in a lidded casserole dish on the stove top for about 40 minutes, or until tender.
3. Meanwhile, cook the rice. Boil stock and add the rice and choppped lemon aspen or lemon grass and cook for 15-17 minutes. Let stand for a further 15 minutes and season with salt. Serve the curry garnished with the chopped lemon grass leaves. The rice may be served separately.

CHEF'S TIPS:

If you have the time, curries made with fresh spices taste better than those made with commercially prepared powdered mixtures. Spices, like perfumes, lose their fragrance very quickly once they have been exposed to the air. A pestle and mortar are invaluable tools for grinding fresh spices.

There are many recipes for curry and numerous varieties of rice with which to serve it. Remember that it is the mixture of spices, garlic and onions that gives each curry its particular flavor. It is possible to use a mixture of spices that will make a curry acceptable even for Western children who are, perhaps, unused to spicy food. Red chili peppers are more peppery than the green ones and the use of chili seeds will make the dish even hotter.

Fresh fruits make attractive garnishes to serve with curry – pineapple, mangoes, papaws for instance – not only look good, but are refreshing and cooling to eat. Lemon aspen is a herb used for flavoring the rice. Lemon grass could also be used.

Goat Noisettes with Hazelnuts

Serves: 4
Preparation time: 12 minutes, plus 2 hours marinating
Cooking time: 20 minutes

INGREDIENTS

8 x 3-oz (75 g) noisettes of young goat
2 tbsp oil, for broiling

MARINADE:
1 1/2 tbsp (15 g/1/2 oz) freshly grated ginger root
1 tbsp (15 g/1/2 oz) sugar
1/2 cup (100 ml/4 fl oz) soy sauce
1 scallion, chopped
juice of 1 orange

SAUCE:
1 tbsp oil
1 small onion, chopped
1 tsp curry powder
1 tsp lemon grass, chopped
scant 1 cup (200 ml/7 fl oz) coconut water or
    plain water
1 1/4 cups (300 ml/1/2 pint) meat stock
1 tsp redcurrant jelly
salt and black pepper

GARNISH:
basil leaves
2 scallions, sliced
1 red bell pepper, diced
12 hazelnuts, toasted and chopped

METHOD

1. Combine all the ingredients for the marinade in a large shallow dish and soak the noisettes for 2 hours. Remove the meat from the marinade and pat dry. Reserve the marinade. Brush the noisettes with oil and broil for 12 minutes.
2. To make the sauce: heat the oil in a frying pan and fry the onion for 2 minutes, then add the curry powder. Cook for 30 seconds, then mix in all the ingredients and the reserved marinade and boil for 20 minutes. Season to taste. Strain the sauce.
3. Pour a pool of the sauce onto each plate and place two noisettes per portion in the center of the sauce. Garnish with diced bell peppers, scallions and basil leaves. Sprinkle chopped nuts over the meat.

CHEF'S TIPS:

Young goat meat has the same delicate texture as spring lamb. This recipe combines goat tenderloin with an unusual nutty sauce with an Asian flavor. The tenderloin is tied into neat noisettes.

Corsican Goat Rib Chops

Serves: 4
Preparation time: 15 minutes
Cooking time: 20 minutes

INGREDIENTS

2 rib roasts of goat meat, (allow 2-3
   rib chops per portion) skin removed,
   trimmed and seasoned
oil, for frying
4 garlic cloves, cut into slivers
1 1/4 cups (300 ml/1/2 pint) well-reduced meat gravy or brown
   sauce (see page 29)

MARINADE:
1/4 cup (50 ml/2 fl oz) olive oil
juice of 1 lemon

SERVE WITH:
4 zucchini, sliced
4 slices of goat cheese

GARNISH:
2 red and 2 yellow bell peppers, halved and
   deseeded
a little oil

METHOD

1. Combine the oil and lemon for the marinade in a bowl. Insert the slivers of garlic into the meat by making a few slits. Brush the meat with the marinade and seal the meat in a roasting pan over high heat on top of the stove for 5 minutes. Transfer the roasts to a hot oven at 400°F (200°C/Gas mark 6) for 20 minutes. Cut the cooked meat by slicing between the ribs.
2. Brush the shiny side of the bell peppers with oil and broil until the skin begins to blister. Remove from the heat and peel away the skin. Blanch the zucchini for 3 minutes only.
3. Pour a pool of gravy or sauce onto the plates with the goat rib chops. Cut the bell peppers into triangles and sandwich with goat cheese. Serve as a garnish with the zucchini.

CHEF'S TIPS:

Goat dishes are very popular in Corsica where the meat is plentiful. The best rib roast of goat meat can be roasted like lamb, and like lamb should be served slightly underdone and pink. Goat is delicious served with redcurrant jelly or Cumberland sauce to accompany it.

Here, a garnish of broiled bell peppers, zucchini and goat cheese harmonizes well with the meat.

Goat Loin Calabria

Serves: 4
Preparation time: 15 minutes, plus 2 hours marinating
Cooking time: 20 minutes

INGREDIENTS

2-lb (1 kg) goat loin roast, trimmed
2 tbsp oil

MARINADE:
3 tbsp clear honey
1 tbsp ginger syrup
1/2 tsp lightly crushed mustard seeds
1/2 tsp lightly crushed fennel seeds or anise
    seeds
1/2 tsp lightly crushed coriander seeds
1 1/4 cups (300 ml/1/2 pint) red Italian wine

SAUCE:
1 1/4 cups (300 ml/1/2 pint) meat stock

GARNISH:
2 tbsp olive oil
4 cherry tomatoes, skinned
4 small mushrooms, peeled
8 scallion bulbs
a few black olives
4 sage or basil leaves

METHOD

1. Mix together all the marinade ingredients in a bowl. Marinate the meat for 2 hours, turning it over twice.
2. Remove the meat from the marinade and pat dry. Heat the oil in a roasting pan on top of the stove and brown it on all sides.
    Transfer the meat into a hot oven at 400°F (200°C/Gas mark 6) for 20 minutes. Goat meat should be juicy, but not too pink. Rest the meat, but keep it warm while you prepare the sauce.
3. To make the sauce; boil the marinade for 5 minutes. Add the stock and reduce it by half, season to taste. Pour in the meat juice.
4. Heat the oil and toss the garnish ingredients for 2 minutes.
5. Slice the loin and place 3 slices on each plate with the sauce. Garnish with the vegetables.

CHEF'S TIPS:

Calabria is the region of Italy near the 'heel'. A profusion of herbs and spices grow wild in the area and there are a number of ancient herbal remedies designed to 'soothe' the fiery temperament for which the Italians from this part of Italy are famed.

Haunch of Venison with Potato and Nut Purée

Serves: 8-10
Preparation time: 30 minutes, plus 2 hours soaking in salt solution and marinating overnight
Cooking time: 2 hours

INGREDIENTS

SALT SOLUTION:
4 1/2 cups (1 liter/1 3/4 pints) water
1 1/3 cups (100 g/4 oz) salt
2 tbsp vinegar

MARINADE:
4 tbsp olive oil
1 1/4 cups (300 ml/1/2 pint) red table wine
1 medium onion, sliced
8 black peppercorns, crushed
1 tsp mustard seeds

MEAT:
4 lb (2 kg) haunch of venison, boned and tied with string
1/2 tsp of each of the following spices ground together:
    cumin, coriander seeds, cardamom, clove and ginger salt
6 slices of bacon

SAUCE:
1 tbsp oil
2 tbsp (25 g/1 oz) butter
1 onion, finely chopped
4 tbsp (25 g/1 oz) flour
1 tbsp sugar
16-20 dried prunes, soaked in a cup of wine or hot tea
1 tbsp gin
juice of 1/2 lemon
salt and pepper
cornstarch (optional)

SERVE WITH:
2 cups (225 g/8 oz) ground pecan nuts, mixed
    with 2 cups (450 g/1 lb) mashed potato
1 egg
1/4 cup (50 g/2 oz) butter
mint leaves, to garnish

METHOD

1. Make up the salt solution and soak the meat for 2 hours to remove traces of blood. Rinse, drain and pat dry.
2. Mix the marinade ingredients together in a large bowl or large earthenware container. Place the meat in this mixture, turning it occasionally, and leave in the fridge overnight.
3. Remove the meat from the marinade and pat dry. Rub the haunch with the spices and a little salt. Wrap the roast with the bacon slices and place it in a shallow roasting pan.
4. Roast the meat in a hot oven at 400°F (200°C/Gas mark 6). Baste the roast with the strained marinade every 20 minutes. After 40 minutes reduce the heat to 350°F (180°C/Gas mark 4). A haunch of venison of this size will take a total of 2 hours to cook through.
5. To make the sauce: heat the oil and butter and gently stir-fry the onion. Sprinkle over the flour and cook for 30 seconds. Stir in the marinade liquid (there should be 1 1/4 cups (300 ml/1/2 pint). Add sugar, salt and pepper. Boil for 10 minutes. Season and strain into another saucepan. Pour in the dried prunes and the wine, in which they have been soaking, and the gin. Simmer for 10 minutes. Finally, add the lemon juice. The sauce can be thickened with a little cornstarch if desired.
6. Prepare the pecan nut and potato purée and press through a strainer to form a smooth purée. Beat in the egg and butter – it should have the consistency of whipped cream. Season to taste. Pipe scrolls or rosettes onto an oiled cookie sheet and bake for 10 minutes at 400°F (200°C/Gas mark 6).
7. Slice venison and arrange on plates. Serve with prune sauce and a piped baked scroll of nut and potato purée. Garnish with the mint leaves.

CHEF'S TIPS:
Ground pecan nuts mixed with mashed potato and enriched with eggs and cream and dried prunes are ideal accompaniments for this venison roast.

Young farm deer meat can be made less reddish by bleaching it in a strong salt solution before being soaked in the wine marinade and cooking. Distilled vinegar is stronger than other vinegars.

Braised Venison Casserole Balsamic

Serves: 8-10
Preparation time: 20 minutes, plus 4 hours marinating
Cooking time: 60 minutes

INGREDIENTS
2 1/2 lb (1.15 kg) lean venison meat,
    cut into cubes

MARINADE:
3 scallions, chopped
3 tbsp (25 g/1 oz) grated fresh ginger root
1/2 cup (100 ml/4 fl oz) sake or sherry
2 1/2 cups (600 ml/1 pint) water
salt and pepper
1/4 cup (50 ml/2 fl oz) Balsamic vinegar

SAUCE:
2 tbsp oil
2 shallots, chopped
1 garlic clove, chopped
4 1/2 cups (1 liter/1 3/4 pint) stock or water
1 small chili pepper, chopped
1/2 bell pepper, cooked to a purée*
scant 1/4 cup (50g/2oz) tomato paste

METHOD
1. Combine all the ingredients for the marinade in a bowl. Place the meat in the bowl and marinate for 4 hours. Remove the meat, drain and pat dry. Keep the remaining marinade liquid for making the sauce.
2. Heat the oil in a flameproof casserole on top of the stove and cook the meat for 5 minutes until brown on all sides. Add the shallots and garlic and cook for 10 seconds. Pour in the stock, reserved marinade, tomato paste, bell pepper purée, chili pepper and season to taste. Transfer the casserole to the oven and cook for 1 hour at 350°F (180°C/Gas mark 4).

CHEF'S TIPS:

This dish has an Asian flavor, the sauce being similar to a sweet-and-sour sauce. If you use the more tender meat from the loin, this dish, cooked for just 1 hour, produces really succulent meat.

Serve the casserole with a selection of seasonal vegetables which have been cooked separately, such as baby carrots, mushrooms, fennel, green beans and baby squash.

*To produce a bell pepper purée, first split and deseed the bell pepper. Broil until the skins blister, then peel off the skin. Chop and cook in oil until soft, then mix to a puree in a blender.

Braised Stuffed Venison with Blueberry Sauce

Serves: 8
Preparation time: 30 minutes, plus marinating overnight
Cooking time: 1 1/2 hours

INGREDIENTS

2 lb (1 kg) boneless shoulder of venison

MARINADE:
1 1/4 cups (300 ml/1/2 pint) red wine
6 juniper berries
1 onion, sliced
1 carrot, sliced
1 garlic clove, chopped
2 tsp vinegar
1 tsp Chinese five spice powder

STUFFING:
1 tbsp oil
1 medium onion, chopped
1 cup (225g/8 oz) pork sausage meat
1 egg
1/2 cup (50 g/2 oz) ginger cookies, in crumbs

1 cup (50 g/2 oz) chopped wild mushrooms
salt and black pepper
3 tbsp rum, brandy or gin
1 tbsp chopped fresh parsley

SAUCE:
3 tbsp oil
1 1/4 cups (300 ml/1/2 pint) game stock (made using bones)
1 tsp tomato paste
1 tbsp cornstarch mixed with 3 tbsp water

GARNISH:
8 tartlet shells, baked blind
2 cups (225 g/8 oz) fresh blueberries
1/4 cup (50 g/2 oz) redcurrant jelly, warmed

METHOD

1. Combine the ingredients for the marinade in a large container and soak the meat overnight, covered with a lid, and stored in a fridge. Remove the meat from the liquid and pat dry. Keep the marinade liquid for the sauce.
2. Mix all the stuffing ingredients into a paste and fill the center of the meat. Roll the meat up and tie with string.
3. Heat the oil in a flameproof casserole and brown the venison all over for 15 minutes. Add the reserved marinade, stock and tomato paste and braise at 350°F (180°C/Gas mark 4) for 1 1/2 hours, covered with a lid.
4. Remove the joint from the liquid, add 1 cup (100 g/4 oz) of the fresh blueberries to the sauce and bring to a boil. Thicken the sauce with the cornstarch and water, boil for a further 10 minutes. Process in a blender and season to taste.
5. Fill the tartlet shells with the remaining blueberries and bake for 15 minutes at 350°F (180°C/Gas mark 4).
6. Slice the meat and arrange on plates with a tartlet each. Pour a pool of sauce around. Use fresh uncooked blueberries to top up the tartlets and brush warmed redcurrant jelly over the raw berries to improve their appearance.

CHEF'S TIPS:

All braised venison meat will taste better if it is allowed to marinate for at least 24 hours. The marinade liquid can be used as stock to make a very tasty sauce.

In this recipe, berries are used in the sauce and also as a filling for a tartlet garnish to decorate the dish. Braised celery and green beans can be served separately as accompaniments for the venison.

Venison Rib Chops with Split Peas

Serves: 4
Preparation time: 15 minutes
Cooking time: 8 minutes

INGREDIENTS

8 fresh venison rib chops, trimmed
2 tbsp olive oil

SAUCE:
breast trimmings (from above)
1 onion, finely chopped
6 juniper berries
1 1/4 cups (300 ml/1/2 pint) red wine
1 1/4 cups (300 ml/1/2 pint) brown sauce
  (see page 29)

GARNISH:
1 cup (225 g/8 oz) yellow split peas,
  cooked to a purée*
1/4 cup (50 g/2 oz) butter
salt and pepper
1 bunch watercress

METHOD

1. First make the sauce: boil the breast trimmings with the onion, juniper berries and red wine. When it is reduced, strain and return to the pan, with brown sauce. Check seasoning.
2. Heat the oil in a frying pan and shallow fry the chops for 4 minutes on each side. They will taste better if slightly underdone.
3. Mix the peas with the butter and season to taste with the salt and pepper.
4. Place two chops on each plate, coat with the sauce and garnish with the watercress and split pea purée.

CHEF'S TIPS:
Fresh venison rib chops from farmed animals do not need to be marinated. When you prepare the rib chops, reserve the breast trimmings for flavoring the sauce.

*To purée the split peas, first boil for 15-20 minutes then drain, add a little butter and mash them.

Venison Rib Chops with Sour Cherries

Serves: 4
Preparation time: 15 minutes, plus
marinating overnight
Cooking time: 40 minutes

INGREDIENTS

8 venison rib chops, trimmed
8 heart-shaped fried bread croutons, to garnish
oil, to fry

MARINADE:
1 1/4 cups (300 ml/1/2 pint) red wine
1 large onion, sliced
1 carrot, sliced
1 sprig of thyme
1 garlic clove, chopped

SAUCE:
2 tbsp oil
1 1/4 cups (300 ml/1/2 pint) game stock (made
   with the venison bones)
1 tsp tomato paste
1 tsp yeast extract
2 tsp cornstarch mixed with 3 tbsp water
salt and black pepper
1/4 tsp ground cinnamon
1 lb (450 g) sour cherries, pitted

METHOD

1. Place the rib chops in an earthenware bowl and cover with the red wine, onion, carrot, thyme and garlic. Let soak overnight in the fridge.
2. Remove the chops from the marinade and pat dry. Drain the vegetables and prepare a sauce using the marinade liquid.
3. Heat half the oil in a pan and stir-fry the onion and carrot from the marinade for 5 minutes until lightly brown. Add the marinade, stock, chopped garlic from the marinade, tomato paste and yeast extract. Boil for 30 minutes then strain into another saucepan. Mix the cornstarch and water in a cup and stir into the boiling sauce. Season to taste. Add the cinnamon and cherries and simmer for a further 10 minutes.
4. Heat the oil and shallow fry the chops for 3 minutes on each side.
5. Place the chops on a serving dish, cover with the sauce and garnish with the heart-shaped croutons, fried separately in olive oil.

CHEF'S TIPS:
Venison is marinated to improve the flavor of the meat and to tenderize it. You must ensure that the meat and the marinade are refrigerated.

Loin of Venison Jelly Roll Kelly

Serves: 4
Preparation time: 30 minutes, plus 20 minutes resting time
Cooking time: 30 minutes

INGREDIENTS

1 lb (450 g) venison sirloin, trimmed
2 tbsp oil
8 oz (225 g) puff pastry (see page 29)
4 prepared pancakes (see page 51)
1 egg yolk, beaten with 1 tbsp water
1 1/4 cups (150 g/5 oz) each carrot, leek, green
    and yellow zucchini and cabbage, all cut
    into long strips
oil and butter, for cooking

STUFFING:
1/2 cup (100 g/4 oz) butter
2 cups (100 g/4 oz) mushrooms, sliced
1 small onion, finely chopped
1 garlic clove, chopped
1 cup (25 g/1 oz) fresh thyme
4 cups (225 g/8 oz) soft white breadcrumbs
salt and freshly milled pepper

SAUCE:
1 1/4 cups (300 ml/1/2 pint) red wine
1 1/4 cups (300 ml/1/2 pint) game stock, reduced
    to a glaze
small piece fresh ginger root, finely chopped
2 tbsp honey
1 cup (100 g/4 oz) blackberries

GARNISH:
1 1/4 cups (150 g/5 oz) wild mushrooms
4 large potatoes, cut into parisienne
    balls (scoop with a melon baller)

METHOD

1. Trim the venison, removing all the sinews. Heat oil in a frying pan until very hot and seal the meat. Set aside to cool.
2. To make the stuffing: sauté the mushrooms, onion, garlic and thyme in the butter in a pan. Add the breadcrumbs and allow to cool. Season to taste with the salt and pepper.
3. Roll out the puff paste and assemble as for Beef Wellington (see page 29). Spread stuffing on the venison and roll up. Wrap first in pancakes, then in paste. Rest for 20 minutes before baking. Brush with egg wash and bake in a moderate oven 350°F (180°C/Gas mark 4) for 30 minutes. It should be cooked rare.
4. While the meat is cooking, prepare the sauce: boil the red wine to reduce by half. Add the stock, ginger and honey. Purée half the blackberries and add them to the sauce. Boil again to reduce slightly. Then remove pan from the heat and add the rest of the blackberries.
5. Prepare and blanch the 'spaghetti' of vegetables. Pan fry the wild mushrooms and sauté or deep fry the Parisienne potatoes. Toss the 'spaghetti' of vegetables in butter, arrange in the center of each plate with two overlapping slices of venison per person. Pour on the sauce. Garnish with the mushrooms and potatoes. Serve hot.

CHEF'S TIPS:
To save time, use ready-prepared puff paste.

Be careful not to overcook the venison.

Fillet of Spring Field Venison Limerick Style

Serves: 4
Preparation time: 1 hour
Cooking time: 45 minutes

INGREDIENTS

4 x 6-oz (175 g) venison fillet steaks, trimmed
2 tbsp oil
12-16 large spinach leaves, thoroughly washed

FILLING:
1/2 cup (100 g/4 oz) lean ground pork
2 tbsp soft white breadcrumbs
1 egg
3 tbsp heavy cream
1 tbsp Irish Whiskey
salt and pepper

GAME SAUCE:
2 tbsp oil
1 onion and 1 carrot, diced
1 fennel bulb, diced
1 slice of bacon, diced
1 cup (50 g/2 oz) mushroom trimmings
1 tbsp flour

1 tbsp tomato paste
1 tbsp yeast extract
1 1/4 cups (300 ml/1/2 pint) red wine
1 1/4 cups (300 ml/1/2 pint) strong game stock
pinch of cinnamon
2 tbsp blackcurrant juice or syrup
1 tbsp red wine vinegar
1 1/4 cups (150 g/5 oz) blueberries

MILLEFEUILLE GATEAU:
a little wholewheat flour
8 oz (225 g) puff pastry
2 tbsp oil and butter
1 small onion, chopped
2 1/2 cups (150 g/5 oz) chopped mixed wild mushrooms
pinch dried thyme
1 garlic clove, chopped
1 tbsp fresh white breadcrumbs
1 egg
4 tbsp heavy cream
4 small white mushrooms, cooked in butter

METHOD

1. Brush the venison steaks with oil and season. Broil for 5-6 minutes and cool completely.
2. Combine the ground pork, breadcrumbs, egg, cream, Irish Whiskey and seasoning in a bowl. Mix to a smooth paste and spread over the steaks to cover them all around, top and sides.
3. Blanch the spinach leaves for 10 seconds and re-fresh in iced water. Drain and pat dry on a cloth. Wrap each steak with spinach leaves, allowing three leaves per steak. The steaks are to be steamed for 6 minutes only when ready to serve with sauce and garnish.
4. To make the game sauce: heat the oil and stir-fry the vegetables, bacon and mushroom trimmings for 8 minutes. Stir in the flour, tomato paste and yeast extract to form a paste and dilute it with the red wine and stock. Boil for 20 minutes. Strain it and season to taste. Add cinnamon, blackcurrant syrup or juice, vinegar and blueberries. Simmer for 5 minutes.
5. For the Mushroom Millefeuille: dust a pastry board with a little whole wheat flour and roll paste to a 1/4-inch (5 mm) thickness. Cut in three 6-inch (15 cm) diameter rounds. Prick the rounds all over with a fork. Place the pastry rounds on a well oiled cookie sheet and bake at 400°F (200°C/Gas mark 6) for 15 minutes. Let rounds cool completely.
6. Prepare the duxelle filling: heat oil and butter and stir-fry the onion and mushrooms for 5 minutes. Add thyme and garlic, then breadcrumbs, egg and cream. Season to taste.
7. Fry the white mushrooms in butter for 4 minutes.
8. Spread the mushroom filling over two paste rounds only. Sandwich them and place the plain one on top. Cut in four portions. Coat the top with a little reduced sauce.
9. Now steam the wrapped steaks for 6 minutes. Carve each steak in 3 slices laterally. Arrange on serving plates with one slice of mushroom gâteau. Garnish top with one fried mushroom. Serve sauce separately.

CHEF'S TIPS:
The stock for the game sauce needs to be made in advance with the trimmings of game and bones. To garnish this dish, make a millefeuille of mushrooms by sandwiching a duxelle of mushrooms between three layers of baked puff pastry. Cut into portions to serve. A pastry cornucopia, filled with mixed vegetables, also makes an attractive accompaniment.

Bison Steaks with Goat's Cheese and Pumpkin Sauce

Serves: 4
Preparation time: 15 minutes
Cooking time: 30 minutes

INGREDIENTS

4 x 6-oz (175 g) bison fillet steaks,
   2-inches (5 cm) thick
oil, for cooking the steaks
2 oz (50 g) cylinder fresh goat's cheese,
   cut into four slices
salt and pepper

SAUCE:
1/4 cup (50 g/2 oz) butter and oil
1 red onion, thinly sliced
1 lb (450 g) peeled pumpkin pulp
   cut into 1-inch (2.5 cm) pieces
1 garlic clove, chopped
1 1/4 cups (300 ml/1/2 pint) stock
1 small sprig of thyme
1 tbsp clear honey
2/3 cup (150 ml/1/4 pint) white port wine
1/3 cup (75 ml/3 fl oz) heavy cream
salt and black pepper

GARNISH:
pieces of peeled pumpkin

METHOD

1. Heat the butter and oil in a saucepan and stir-fry the onion for 6 minutes, without browning. Add the pumpkin, garlic, stock, thyme, honey and wine. Boil for 18 minutes until the vegetables are tender. Pour into a food processor and process to a thin purée. Reheat the sauce and stir in the cream. Season to taste with the salt and pepper.
2. Brush the steaks with oil, season and broil or pan fry for 6 minutes on each side. Put a slice of goat's cheese on the top of each steak and broil until the cheese turns lightly brown and begins to bubble. Blanch the pumpkin for garnish, for 10 minutes in boiling water.
3. To serve, pour a pool of sauce onto each plate and place the steak in the center. Garnish with pieces of pumpkin.

CHEF'S TIPS:
The usual garnish for bison meat is turned butter squash or pumpkin, both make an interesting change from carrots and turnips

Roast Fillet of Bison Florentina

Serves: 4
Preparation time: 15 minutes
Cooking time: 10 minutes

INGREDIENTS

1 1/4 lb (550 g) bison fillet in one piece, trimmed
2 tbsp oil
salt and pepper

LEEK PUREE:
2 tbsp (25 g/1 oz) butter
2 leeks, white part only, cut into thin
    julienne strips
1/3 cup (75 ml/3 fl oz) reduced stock
2/3 cup (150 ml/1/4 pint) heavy cream
5 basil leaves, chopped

POTATO AND SPINACH CAKE:
1 lb (450 g) potatoes, peeled, sliced and fried
1 lb (450 g) fresh spinach, thoroughly washed
1/4 cup (50 g/2 oz) butter
1 clove of garlic, chopped

METHOD

1. Season the fillet. Heat oil in a frying pan and cook the meat to seal it for 5 minutes, until brown all round. Transfer the meat to a roasting tray and cook for 10 minutes at 400°F (200°C/Gas mark 6). Remove from the oven and let rest for 5 minutes. Cut into thin slices.
2. To make the leek purée: heat the butter and stir-fry the leeks. Add the stock and the meat juices. Boil for 3 minutes then stir in the cream and chopped basil. Season to taste.
3. Cook washed spinach without water for 4 minutes. Drain and squeeze out any surplus moisture. Add the butter and garlic and reheat.
4. Overlap fried sliced potatoes into small cakes and sandwich them with cooked spinach, as shown in photograph.
5. Place slices of bison on each plate with a pool of the leek purée. Serve with the potato and spinach cake.

CHEF'S TIPS:
There is probably no meat as tender as that from lightly roasted tenderloin of bison. If liked, insert slivers of garlic into the meat for a stronger flavor.

Bison Steaks with Kumquat Chutney

Serves: 4
Preparation time: 15 minutes, plus 2 days for chutney
Cooking time: 12 minutes

INGREDIENTS

4 x 6-oz (175 g) bison fillet steaks
2 tbsp oil

CHUTNEY:
1 lb (450 g) kumquats
1 tbsp baking soda
generous 1 cup (225 g/8 oz) sugar
2/3 cup (150 ml/1/4 pint) vinegar
1 tsp mixed spice
1 tsp grated ginger root
1 small green chili pepper, sliced
pinch of salt

GARNISH:
4 patty pan squash
4 large carrots, peeled
1 large potato, peeled

SAUCE:
1 1/4 cups (300ml/1/2 pint) red wine brown sauce

METHOD

1. To make the chutney: wash the kumquats in warm water. Put them in a large bowl and sprinkle them with the baking soda to soften the skin. Pour 2 1/2 cups (600ml/1pint) of boiling water over the kumquats and let soak for 2 hours, until the liquid is cold. Drain and rinse thoroughly. Prick every kumquat with a fork to allow the syrup to penetrate. Boil them in fresh water for 15 minutes. Remove from the water and put the kumquats in a small saucepan with the sugar, vinegar, spice, ginger and chili pepper and boil for a further 15 minutes. Let soak in this syrup for 2 days before use.
2. Season the steaks and brush with oil. Broil for 10-15 minutes.
3. Cut the carrots and potatoes into thin wafers. Fry them and drain them well. Boil the patty pan squash for 7 minutes, with a pinch of sugar and salt.
4. Cut each steak into three slices. Place the slices in a pool of the red wine brown sauce and garnish with the carrots, potatoes and boiled baby squash. Serve with the kumquat chutney.

CHEF'S TIPS:

In this dish the kumquats are made into a chutney and served as a garnish for the meat. The chutney needs to be prepared at least two days in advance. The patty pan squash, used for garnish, are a variety of small round squash. They can be easily grown in the garden.

Bison Steaks with Asian Spices

Serves: 4
Preparation time: 15 minutes, plus 1 hour marinating time or overnight
Cooking time: 10-16 minutes

INGREDIENTS

4 x 6-oz (175 g) bison fillet steaks, trimmed

MARINADE:
2 oz (50 g) liquorice root
1 cinnamon stick
peel of 1 tangerine
6 peppercorns, crushed
1 1/4 cups (300 ml/1/2 pint) water
1/3 cup (50 g/2 oz) sugar
1 star anise
1/4 cup (50 ml/2 fl oz) soy sauce

SAUCE:
1 tsp sugar
black pepper
1/4 cup (50 ml/2 fl oz) red wine vinegar
1 tbsp tomato paste
1 tbsp brandy
1/4 cup (50 ml/2 fl oz) port wine
1/2 cup (100 ml/4 fl oz) concentrated stock
1 tbsp butter

VEGETABLE ROLL:
2 tbsp (25 g/1 oz) butter
2 shallots, chopped
1 cup (100 g/4 oz) diced celery root
4 mushrooms, chopped
1/4 cup (50 ml/2 fl oz) concentrated stock
1/4 cup (50 ml/2 fl oz) light cream
1/2 cup (150 g/5 oz) chestnut purée
2 tbsp (25 g/1 oz) candied orange peel
1 garlic clove, chopped

METHOD

1. To make the marinade: combine all the marinade ingredients in a saucepan and bring to a boil. Continue to boil until reduced by one-third then let cool. When cold, mix in a food processor and marinate the steaks for 1 hour.
2. Remove the steaks from the marinade and broil or cook over a barbecue.
3. To make the sauce: put the sugar and black pepper into a saucepan and cook until the sugar starts to caramelize. Add the red wine vinegar, tomato paste and brandy, then boil to reduce. Add the port and reduce the sauce further, then add the stock and continue to reduce to a glaze. Stir in the butter.
4. For the vegetable roll: put the butter in a frying pan and sauté the shallots until clear. Add the celery root and mushrooms and cook for 1 minute. Pour in the stock and cream, boil to reduce the sauce and let cool. Put the mixture in a bowl with the chestnut purée, candied orange peel and garlic. Roll in greased foil and chill. When the meat is ready, slice the vegetable roll and place a slice on top of each buffalo steak. Return the steaks to a hot oven or barbecue for 2 minutes. Pour the sauce over the steaks and serve.

CHEF'S TIPS:

The liquorice marinade may give this dish the appearance of having been cooked in Coca-Cola, but the root and star anise do give this bison meat a certain 'je ne sais quoi'. It is certainly a dish worth trying. If you prefer you can use venison steak instead of the bison meat.

Serve this dish with cooked chard leaves, sautéed mushrooms and small boiled leeks.

Bison Spanish Steak

Serves: 2-3
Preparation time: 15 minutes
Cooking time: 12 minutes

INGREDIENTS

6 x 3-oz (75 g) bison tournedos steaks
2 tbsp oil

TAPENADE:
4 dried figs, minced
1 tbsp tomato paste
scant 1 cup (150 g/5 oz) pitted and finely chopped
    black olives
4 anchovy fillets, desalted (soaked
    in milk) and chopped
1 garlic clove, chopped
1 tbsp pickled capers
6 basil leaves, chopped
1 tbsp olive oil

SAUCE:
1 1/4 cups (300 ml/1/2 pint) red Spanish wine
1 1/4 cups (300 ml/1/2 pint) strong stock
1 small chili pepper, sliced
2 tomatoes, skinned, deseeded and chopped
salt to taste

GARNISH:
2 tomatoes, skinned and diced
red chili pepper, sliced
fresh cilantro leaves
onion rings, crisply fried

METHOD

1. Brush the steaks with oil, season and broil according to requirement – rare (5 minutes), medium (10 minutes) or well-done (15 minutes).
2. Mix all the ingredients for the tapenade to a firm purée in a processor.
3. Boil all the sauce ingredients to reduce the liquid by half. Season and strain.
4. Place two or three small tournedos on each plate with some of the sauce. Serve with two oval-shaped spoonfuls of tapenade and garnish with the tomatoes, chili pepper, cilantro leaves and onion rings.

CHEF'S TIPS:

This recipe is really a variation of Beef Tapenade: the steaks are served with a purée of black olives, anchovy fillets and capers. Use the thin end of the fillet tenderloin to produce small round tournedos, no larger than 2 inches (5cm) in diameter.

Garnish the dish with crisply fried onion rings.

Bison Salsa Agridolce

Serves: 4
Preparation time: 25 minutes, plus 2 hours marinating
Cooking time: 1 hour approximately

INGREDIENTS

2 lb (1 kg) bison tenderloin, skinned, trimmed
    and tied with a string
2 tbsp oil, for frying

MARINADE:
2/3 cup (150 ml/1/4 pint) olive oil
2/3 cup (150 ml/1/4 pint) port wine
salt and pepper

SAUCE:
2 tbsp Balsamic vinegar
2 shallots, sliced
2 1/2 cups (600 ml/1 pint) strong meat stock
1/3 cup (50 g/2 oz) golden raisins
1/2 cup (50 g/2 oz) pine nuts
2 tbsp clear honey
8 mint leaves
1 tsp cornstarch mixed with 2 tbsp water

MOSTARDO CHUTNEY:
1/3 cup (50 g/2 oz) candied or dried figs
1/3 cup (50 g/2 oz) candied ginger
1/3 cup (50 g/2 oz) candied peel
1 1/4 cups (300 ml/1/2 pint) reduced stock
1 tbsp clear honey
1 tbsp ginger syrup
1 tsp Dijon mustard
1/2 tsp cornstarch mixed with 1 tbsp water
mint leaves, to garnish

SERVE WITH:
Potato cakes (see page 105)

METHOD

1. Combine all the marinade ingredients in a large container. Soak the meat steaks for 2 hours, turning them over twice. Drain the meat and pat dry.
2. Heat the oil in a frying pan and sear the meat for 8 minutes until brown. Transfer the tenderloin to a roasting pan and cook at 400°F (200°C/Gas mark 6) for 12-15 minutes for rare, or 20-25 minutes for well-done. Remove the meat from the oven and drain off any excess fat. Let rest for 15 minutes, allowing the meat juices to flow a little.
3. Remove the meat to another dish and boil the meat juices in the roasting pan. Deglaze with Balsamic vinegar and boil until almost evaporated. Add the shallots, meat stock, golden raisins, pine nuts and honey and boil for 20 minutes. Add the mint leaves and seasoning and simmer for a further 5 minutes. Thicken, if necessary, with the mixed cornstarch and water.
4. Boil the chutney ingredients for 10 minutes. Add the mustard last. The chutney, like the sauce, can be thickened with a little cornstarch.
5. Cut the meat into thin slices and arrange three slices per portion on each plate. Serve with the golden raisin sauce and a spoonful of chutney. Garnish with the mint leaves. Serve with the potato cakes.

ALL ABOUT BUFFETS

Introduction

There are so many dishes that are suitable to serve as part of a buffet, since any cooked meat can be eaten cold, that the choice is almost limitless. When preparing a buffet do not forget the many delicatessen specialities of the 'charcuterie trade'; you have available to you the whole range of cooked or smoked meats and poultry, as well as many ready-prepared pies and terrines.

The appearance of a buffet table is always vitally important. Use a selection of garnishes, salads and sauces to make the meal as attractive as possible and do not forget the many mayonnaises, dressings, aspics, dips, mousses and crudités that can be served to enhance the main dishes.

Cold roast beef, ham, pork, turkey and chicken can all be served for a buffet-style party. Carving in front of guests can be unnecessarily laborious, so simply present the already sliced meat on large platters.

Terrines, pâtés, pies and other pastry dishes should be cut into portions. Mousses and dips should, whenever possible, be made and served in individual molds. To ensure that the food looks fresh, leave the final touches, including glazing and garnishing, until a few hours before the buffet is to be eaten.

Every item should have its own distinct taste – the flavor, color and texture should not be disguised. Even aspic jelly should have the same flavor as a rich consommé. Remember that as far as a buffet is concerned the fresher the food looks the better it will please your guests. Many different sauces can be produced quickly and easily from a mayonnaise base. You can add ingredients such as tomato catsup, mixed fresh herbs, cream, yoghurt, fruit purée or spices.

This chapter aims to present only a small selection of the kind of dishes that you can make to produce a simple buffet. Remember that it is not the expensive items like foie gras, caviar or smoked luxuries that will impress your guests, but rather the wholesomeness of the entire selection of dishes and the way in which the foods complement each other. Keep it simple. Make it look appetizing, attractive, fresh and tasty and it will be a success.

PREPARATION OF TERRINES AND GALANTINES

A *terrine* is an earthenware or metal dish fitted with a lid, like a casserole, and generally oval or oblong in shape. It is used chiefly for cooking pies or making French pâtés that take their name from the dish in which they are cooked.

A *galantine* is a coarser pâté with cubes or strips of meat embedded in the forcemeat. These coarse pâtés are often garnished with pistachios, truffles, peppers or peppercorns. The forcemeat is wrapped in a band of lard, cabbage or spinach leaves.

A *ballotine* is, as the word suggests, a parcel of meat wrapped in a cloth and poached in stock, like a pudding. The basis of the parcel is often a boned and stuffed bird. When cooked, the meat is glazed with aspic and sliced like a meat loaf.

HOW TO TURN OUT A MOLD

Let a mold stand for at least 1 hour in a cool place. When ready, dip the mold into hot water for 3 seconds, then carefully wipe the sides of the mold and turn it quickly onto a prepared dish, the bottom of which can be lined with a thin layer of set aspic jelly. Place the garnish around the unmolded mousse.

GARNISHING

Use some thinly sliced cooked vegetables or hard-cooked eggs to garnish the mousse. Before beginning, place the cut vegetables, etc. on a small plate with melted aspic jelly. The plate should stand over a pan or basin of hot water to keep the jelly liquid. Pick up the cuttings with the point of a small knife and garnish as required.

Boned Chicken with Italian Stuffing

Serves: 12
Preparation time: 1 hour, plus chilling overnight
Cooking time: 1 1/2 hours

INGREDIENTS

5 lb (2.25 kg) chicken, boned (see page 169)

FORCEMEAT:
1 cup (225 g/8 oz) pork sausage meat
1 small onion, chopped
3 garlic cloves, chopped
1/2 cup (50 g/2 oz) grated Parmesan cheese
1 egg
1 cup (50 g/2 oz) washed, dried and chopped field mushrooms
1 cup (50 g/2 oz) soft brown breadcrumbs
3 basil leaves, chopped
1 tbsp chopped parsley
1/2 cup (50 g/2 oz) chopped pine nuts
2 tomatoes, skinned, deseeded and chopped
thick slice of red bell pepper, diced
1 tsp salt
good pinch each of black pepper, nutmeg and celery salt
1 1/4 cups (300 ml/1/2 pint) aspic jelly, to coat (see page 20)

METHOD

1. Bone the chicken.
2. Combine all the ingredients for the forcemeat in a large mixing bowl. Place the forcemeat inside the boned chicken. Wrap and sew the bird with strings. Wrap in cheesecloth and poach in a large pan on top of the stove for 1 1/2 hours, simmering gently. Let cool and chill overnight.
3. Unwrap the chicken and coat with the aspic jelly. Cut in thick slices.

CHEF'S TIPS:

This Continental stuffing has a robust garlicky taste. A tomato salad would be an ideal accompaniment for this excellent summer dish.

Garnish with salad leaves.

Spicy Peanut and Pork Terrine

Serves: 8
Preparation time: 25 minutes
Cooking time: 1-1 hour 45 minutes

INGREDIENTS

16 slices of bacon, derinded
1 tbsp oil
1 medium onion, chopped
2 garlic cloves, chopped
1/2 green bell pepper, cored, deseeded and chopped
1/2 red bell pepper, cored, deseeded and chopped
1 tsp chili powder
1 1/2 lb (675 g) ground pork
1 egg, beaten
1 tbsp chopped fresh cilantro
3/4 cup (75 g/3 oz) chopped roasted peanuts

GARNISH:
slices of bell peppers
finely chopped roasted peanuts

METHOD

1. Stretch each slice of bacon slightly using the back of a knife. Use the slices to line the bottom and sides of a lightly greased 2 lb (1 kg) loaf pan, reserving enough bacon to cover the top of the loaf.
2. Heat the oil in a frying pan and add the onion, garlic, bell peppers and chili powder and fry together until softened, then let cool slightly.
3. Mix together the pork, egg and cilantro in a bowl. Stir in the onions and bell peppers and spoon half the resulting mixture into the lined loaf pan.
4. Sprinkle in a layer of peanuts and then top with the remaining half of the pork mixture. Smooth over the surface, fold over the bacon and cover with the remaining slices to completely enclose the filling.
5. Place the loaf pan in a hot oven at 400°F (200°C/Gas mark 6) and cook for 1-1 1/4 hours or until cooked and set. Cover with a sheet of foil if the bacon is becoming too brown.
6. Turn the terrine out onto a serving plate and garnish with the slices of bell peppers and chopped peanuts. Serve in slices.

CHEF'S TIPS:

There are hundreds of different varieties of nuts, yet in most recipe books you will find the same types used time and again – almonds, chestnuts, hazelnuts, pistachios, pine nuts and walnuts. Delicious though these nuts are, why not be more adventurous in your selection. In the recipes in this book you will find that I have introduced a few more varieties – such as pecans, macadamia, candle nuts, coconuts and cashews.

Peanuts, called cacahouettes or arachides in French, come from a vegetable plant exploited mainly for its oil. The peanuts themselves have become popular as a snack, but their rich protein content should not be overlooked. They make an excellent addition to terrines and dips, improving both the flavor and texture.

Perfect Chicken Liver Pâté

Serves: 8
Preparation time: 30 minutes, plus 30 minutes marinating and chilling overnight
Cooking time: 30-45 minutes (individual), 1 1/2 hours (whole terrine)

INGREDIENTS

1 lb (450 g) prepared chicken livers
1 1/4 cups (300 ml/1/2 pint) cold milk
1 tsp salt
1 small pinch saltpeter*
1 egg, beaten
1 1/4 cups (300 ml/1/2 pint) heavy cream
1/4 cup (50 g/2 oz) sweet butter
1 tbsp brandy
1 pinch white pepper
1 pinch grated nutmeg
1 tsp celery salt

GARNISH:
lettucc leaves
shredded lettuce
sprigs of parsley
diced apple

SERVE WITH:
toast or brióche

METHOD

1. Oil an oblong earthenware terrine, capacity 4 1/2 cups (1 liter/1 3/4 pints), or use eight individual ramekin dishes each with a capacity of 1/2 cup (100 ml/4 fl oz).
2. Remove the gall bags from the livers without bursting them. Clean the livers and soak them in milk containing the salt and saltpeter. Let marinate for 30 minutes. Rinse the liver in a colander, under the tap, and pat dry.
3. Place the livers, egg, cream, butter, brandy, seasoning and spices in a blender and process to obtain a thin purée. Pass the mixture through a fine strainer.
4. Pour the mixture into the terrine or the individual dishes. Cover the container(s) with foil and place in a deep roasting pan half-filled with water. Cook at 325°F (170°C/Gas mark 3) for 30-45 minutes, if individual molds are used or 1 1/2 hours if the pâté is being cooked in a single terrine. Remove the container(s) from the oven and the pan and let cool. Chill overnight.
5. Turn the individual pâtés out onto the lettuce leaves. Slice the oblong pâté, by dipping a knife into hot water, and garnish with the shredded lettuce leaves, parsley and diced apple. Serve with toast or brióche.

CHEF'S TIPS:

A similar pâté can be made using calves' or lambs' livers, but ensure that the skin and sinews are removed from the livers before grinding. For an even better flavor, diced, fresh truffles can be mixed with the raw mixture.

In my opinion, it is possible to produce an excellent pâté from chicken livers, just as good as any pâté made with the ubiquitous 'foie gras' from force-fed geese. To make the pâté pink, simply soak the liver in a pickling salt mixture for at least 30 minutes before it is needed. The liver could also be marinated in milk to improve the flavor and color. This pâté is extremely rich and, therefore, each portion need be no more than 2 oz (50 g). Chill overnight before serving.

*The saltpeter (sodium nitrate) can be bought from the butchers or at the drug store.

Chicken and Ham Terrine

Serves: 8
Preparation time: 1 hour, plus chilling overnight
Cooking time: 1 1/2 hours

INGREDIENTS

FORCEMEAT:
1 cup (225 g/8 oz) ground raw chicken
1 egg, beaten
1/3 cup (75 ml/3 fl oz) heavy cream
1/4 cup (50 ml/2 fl oz) brandy or gin
1 tsp salt
pinch of ground pepper
pinch of grated nutmeg

4 chicken livers, cleaned
1 pinch saltpeter
1/4 cup (50 ml/2 fl oz) milk
4 slices of bacon, derinded
thin slices of bacon, to line the mold
1 lb (450 g) cooked ham
1/2 cup (50 g/2 oz) peeled pistachio nuts
2 oz (50 g) canned truffles, cut into small cubes
1 1/4 cups (200 ml/1/2 pint) aspic jelly (see page 18)

GARNISH:
truffles
pistachios

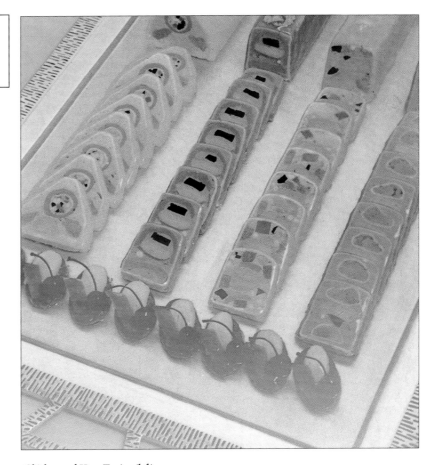

Chicken and Ham Terrine (left)

METHOD

1. To make the forcemeat: combine the ground chicken with the egg and cream in a bowl. Add the brandy or gin and seasoning.
2. Soak the cleaned chicken livers in milk and saltpeter for 30 minutes. Rinse the liver and pat dry with a clean cloth. Wrap each liver in the bacon slices.
3. Line a triangular mold with the thin slices of bacon.
4. Cut the ham into four thin slices and into four big cylindrical strips, 1-inch (2.5 cm) in diameter.
5. Place a layer of the chicken forcemeat on the bottom of the mold and the wrapped livers in the center. Place a strip of ham around the edges and cover with more forcemeat.
6. In a bowl, mix together about 2/3 cup (150 g/5 oz) of the remaining chicken forcemeat with the pistachios and truffles. Place this mixture on top of the ham slices and roll them up. Put these rolls in the middle of the mold and cover with the remaining chicken forcemeat.
7. Place the mold in a deep roasting pan half-filled with water and cook at 350°F (180°C/Gas mark 4) for 1 1/2 hours. Let cool and chill overnight.
8. Unmold, drain off the fat, and coat with the aspic jelly. Garnish the top with truffles and pistachios and cut into thick slices to serve.

CHEF'S TIPS:
You require a triangular mold with a capacity of 4 1/2 cups (1 liter /1 3/4 pints). Line the sides of the mold with thin slices of bacon. Keep several thin slices of this bacon ready to wrap around the pieces of chicken.

Ox Tongue and Liver Terrine

Serves: 8
Preparation time: 1 hour
Cooking time: 1 1/2 hours, plus chilling overnight

INGREDIENTS

FORCEMEAT:
1 cup (225 g/8 oz) sausage meat
1/4 cup (50 g/2 oz) ground pigs' liver
2 tbsp whiskey
1 egg, beaten
1 tsp salt
good pinch of ground nutmeg, pepper and mixed spice
2 oz (50 g) truffles
1/2 cup (50 g/2 oz) skinned pistachio nuts

5oz (150 g) lambs' liver
1 cup (225 ml/8 fl oz) milk
pinch of saltpeter
4 slices of bacon, derinded
8 oz (225 g) cooked, pickled ox tongue, cut into four strips
thin slices of bacon, to line tin
1 1/4 cups (300 ml/1/2 pint) aspic jelly (see page 18)

GARNISH:
pineapple pieces

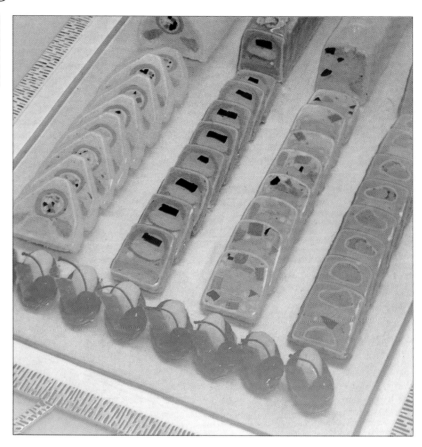

Ox Tongue and Liver Terrine (second left)

METHOD

1. To make the forcemeat: combine the sausage meat with the pigs' liver, whiskey, egg, seasoning, truffles and pistachio nuts in a bowl.
2. Soak the pieces of lambs' liver in cold milk to which a pinch of saltpeter has been added, for 1 hour. Remove the liver from the milk and rinse. Cut into four strips and wrap the liver in the bacon slices.
3. Line a 2 lb (1 kg) loaf pan with the thin bacon slices. Build up the content of the terrine in layers: place a layer of forcemeat in the bottom of the dish, cover with the wrapped liver and strips of ox tongue and top with the remaining forcemeat. Cover the terrine with a lid and place in a deep roasting pan, half-filled with water.
4. Bake at 350°F (180°C/Gas mark 4) for 1 1/2 hours. Let cool and chill overnight.
5. Unmold the terrine onto a board, coat with the aspic and garnish with small pieces of pineapple. When ready to serve, cut into eight slices.

CHEF'S TIPS:

To freeze any of the terrines in this chapter follow this recipe to the end of step five, cut the terrine into slices, interweave each slice with greaseproof paper to allow easy removal, then overwrap in plastic wrap. Seal, label and freeze for up to one month.

To serve from the freezer, remove from the wrappings and thaw at room temperature for about 3 hours, then serve.

Veal and Bacon Terrine

Serves: 8
Preparation time: 40 minutes, plus chilling overnight
Cooking time: 1 1/2 hours

INGREDIENTS

FORCEMEAT:
1 cup (225 g/8 oz) ground lean veal
1 egg
2/3 cup (150 ml/1/4 pint) heavy cream
1 tsp salt
good pinch of grated nutmeg, celery salt and mixed spice
1 tbsp gin
1/2 cup (50 g/2 oz) skinned pistachio nuts
2 oz (50 g) truffles, cut into small cubes

4 slices of bacon, derinded
8 oz (225 g) calves' liver, cut into four strips
thin bacon slices, to line terrine
1 1/4 cups (300 ml/1/2 pint) aspic jelly (see page 18)

GARNISH:
lemon slices

METHOD

1. To make the forcemeat: combine the ground veal with the egg, cream, seasoning and gin and mix in the pistachio nuts and truffles.
2. Wrap the liver in the bacon.
3. Line a 4 1/2 cup (1 liter/1 3/4 pint) terrine with the thin slices of bacon.
4. Put a layer of the veal forcemeat in the bottom of the mold. Place the wrapped liver in the center and top with the remaining forcemeat to fill the terrine. Cover with a lid and cook for 1 1/2 hours at 350°F (180°C/Gas mark 4). Remove from the oven and let cool. Chill overnight.
5. Unmold the terrine onto a board. Coat with aspic and garnish with lemon slices. Cut into 16 slices when ready to serve.

CHEF'S TIPS:
Line an oblong terrine, capacity 4 1/2 cups (1 liter/1 3/4 pints) with thin bacon slices.

Liver and Pork Terrine

Serves: 8
Preparation time: 1 hour, plus chilling overnight
Cooking time: 1 1/2 hours

INGREDIENTS

8 oz (225 g) calves' liver, with skin removed
1 cup (225 ml/8 fl oz) milk
pinch of saltpeter (sodium nitrate)
salt and pepper
3 slices of ham
1 tbsp rum
2 oz (50 g) canned truffles
thin strips of bacon, to line terrine
aspic jelly (optional) (see page 18)

FORCEMEAT:
1 cup (225 g/8 oz) pork sausage meat
1/4 cup (50 g/2 oz) ground pigs' liver
1 egg
1/4 cup (50 g/2 oz) skinned pistachio nuts
1 tsp salt
pinch each of pepper, nutmeg and mixed spices

GARNISH:
berries

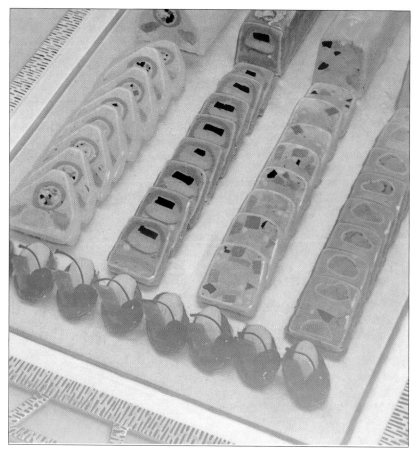

Liver and Pork Terrine (right)

METHOD

1. Soak the calves' liver in the milk with a pinch of saltpeter (sodium nitrate) for 1 hour. Rinse the liver in cold water and pat dry. Season the liver with salt and pepper and cut into three strips. Wrap the strips in the slices of ham. Sprinkle all over with the rum.
2. To make the forcemeat: combine the sausage meat, ground pigs' liver, egg and pistachio nuts in a bowl. Season with the pepper and spices.
3. Cut the truffles into strips.
4. Line an oblong terrine with a capacity of 4 1/2 cups (1 liter/1 3/4pint) with the thin strips of bacon, then fill as follows. Place a layer of forcemeat on the bottom and top it with the liver wrapped in ham. Cover with another layer of forcemeat with truffle strips to fill the terrine. Cover with a lid and place the terrine in a deep roasting pan, half-filled with water. Cook at 350°F (180°C/Gas mark 4) for 1 1/2 hours. Remove from the oven and let cool. Chill overnight.
5. Turn the terrine out onto a board, coat with the aspic jelly, if liked, and garnish with the berries or other fruits. Cut into slices, to serve.

CHEF'S TIPS:
The reason for soaking the liver in milk and saltpeter (sodium nitrate) is to remove all traces of blood, and thus lighten the color of the terrine.

Country Potato and Pork Loaf

Serves: 8
Preparation time: 20 minutes
Cooking time: 1-1 1/2 hours

INGREDIENTS

1/4 cup (50 g/2 oz) butter
1 tbsp oil
2 medium onions, chopped
1 celery stick, chopped
1 cup (225 g/8 oz) lean ground pork
4 eggs, beaten
1 cup (225 g/8 oz) mashed potatoes
2 tbsp chopped fresh parsley
1 tsp chopped tarragon
salt and black pepper
6 bacon slices, derinded and scalded

GARNISH:
lemon slices
cubes of cucumber

SERVE WITH:
French dressing

METHOD

1. Heat the butter and oil in a frying pan and stir-fry the onions and celery for 1 minute, without browning.
2. Mix the onion and celery together with the ground pork, beaten eggs, mashed potatoes, herbs and seasoning.
3. Line the base and sides of a 2 lb (1 kg) loaf pan with the bacon slices, reserving some for the top. Fill with the meat and potato mixture and cover with the remaining bacon. Place greased foil over the top of the loaf. Set the loaf pan in a roasting pan, half-filled with water and bake in a moderate oven at 350°F (180°C/Gas mark 4) for 1-1 1/2 hours. Let cool.
4. Turn the loaf out onto a serving dish and garnish with the lemon slices and cubes of cucumber. Serve the loaf with a French salad dressing.

CHEF'S TIPS:

Potatoes are added to pies and terrines not solely to economize on the amount of meat needed, but also because they enhance the flavor and the texture of the dishes. In this recipe the potatoes complement the flavor of the bacon. The bacon is first scalded in boiling water for 10 minutes to desalt it. Drain and dry before using.

Tarragon: this typically French herb has a sweet and spicy odor with fresh green, slightly balsamic undertones. Tarragon is used in tomato and pasta dishes, in fish soups and in poultry, lamb and beef casseroles. It is a favorite flavoring to complement duckling or goose.

Chicken and Bacon Pie with Blackcurrants

Serves: 8
Preparation time: 15-20 minutes
Cooking time: 1 hour

INGREDIENTS

SAVORY PIE DOUGH:
This recipe will make 1 lb (450 g) savory pastry. To make half the amount simply halve all the quantities.

2 1/2 cups (275 g/10 oz) all-purpose flour
scant 3/4 cup (190 g/6 1/2 oz) butter
pinch of salt
pinch of mustard
1 egg

FILLING:
1 cup (225 g/8 oz) ground lean pork
1/4 cup 50 g/2 oz) diced bacon
1 cup (225 g/8 oz) diced cooked chicken
1 egg
1 tsp salt
1/2 tsp each black pepper and cinnamon

GARNISH:
2 cups (225 g/8 oz) blackcurrants or cranberries
1/4 cup (50 g/2 oz) sugar

METHOD

1. To make the pie dough: cut the butter into the flour. Add the salt, mustard and egg. Mix to form a dough.
2. Oil a 2 lb (1 kg) deep pie mold or loaf pan and line with the pie dough to a thickness of 1/4-inch (5 mm), retaining some pie dough to make a pie lid.
3. Combine all the filling ingredients in a bowl and mix well together; spoon the mixture into the lined mold or pan. Brush the edges of the pie dough with water and cover with the pie dough lid. Seal firmly. Bake for an hour at 375°F (190°C/Gas mark 5). Let cool.
4. Cook the blackcurrants or cranberries and sugar for 1 minute only until sugar dissolves and the fruits soften. Do not cook for any longer as the fruits will begin to lose its shape. Top the cooked pie with the blackcurrants or cranberries. Alternatively, leave the fruit raw and glaze them with aspic jelly (see page 18) or with a little hot redcurrant jelly.

CHEF'S TIPS:
Pies made with a good savory pastry are always welcome and are an excellent stand-by for unexpected guests. The pies will freeze well and can be stored for up to three months.

Serve with a green salad and onion rings tossed in vinaigrette.

Gala Bacon, Pork and Chicken Pie with Bell Peppers

Serves: 4
Preparation time: 30 minutes, plus 4 hours cooling and chilling
Cooking time: 30 minutes (individual),

INGREDIENTS

2 lb (900g) savory pie dough (see page 246)

FILLING:
1 lb (450 g) pork tenderloin, trimmed, but with a little
    fat left on
2/3 cup (150 ml/1/4 pint) stock, for basting

FORCEMEAT:
1 cup (225 g/8 oz) minced raw skinless chicken breasts
1 egg
1/4 tsp black pepper
1/4 tsp mixed spice
1 tsp salt
8 oz (225 g) diced bacon
1/4 cup (50 g/2 oz) diced red bell pepper
1/4 cup (50 g/2 oz) diced green bell pepper
1/4 cup (50g/ 2oz) cooked sweet corn kernels

egg wash, for glazing
1 1/4 cups (300 ml/1/2 pint) strong aspic jelly (see page 18)

METHOD

1. Grease the bottom and the sides of the pan or mold. Roll the pie dough out onto a floured pastry board to a thickness of 1/4-inch (5 mm). Cut strips of pie dough to line the mold reserving some pie dough for the top.
2. Roast the pork tenderloin at 400°F (200°C/Gas mark 6) for 20 minutes only. This lets the flavor develop. From time to time, baste the meat with some stock to keep it moist. Let cool completely in the liquid.
3. To make the forcemeat: combine the chicken with the egg and seasoning in a bowl. Mix in the diced bacon, bell peppers and sweet corn.
4. Put a layer of the forcemeat mixture at the bottom of the pie. Place the well-seasoned pork on top and pack it around and on top with the remaining forcemeat. Brush the edges of the brim of the pie dough with water and cover with a pie dough lid. Crimp the edges tightly. Using pastry cutters, cut out leaf shapes and use these to make a pattern on top of the pie. Make two holes in the pie dough, one at either end, and insert a small funnel, made of hardboard, into the pie to let the steam escape during baking. Brush the top of the pie with the egg wash.
5. Bake in a hot oven at 400°F (200°C/Gas mark 6) for 1 1/2 hours. After one hour, cover the top of the pie with a piece of greased foil to prevent the pastry from browning too much. Let cool for at least 2 hours.
6. When cold, make two small holes in the pastry and pour in some semi-set aspic. This aspic will fill the gap left when the meat shrinks during cooking. Chill the pie for a further 2 hours. When cold, cut into slices to serve.

CHEF'S TIPS:
This chef's pie can form the center of your buffet as it is a meal in itself.

You will need a 4 lb (2 kg) loaf pan or other pie mold, preferably fitted with hinges on the side for easier removal of the pie once it is baked. Do not pour in the jelly into the pie before it is completely cold. Always start with plenty of pie dough rather than risk running short. Any excess can always be used for some individual tartlets.

Italian Lamb and Spinach Pie

Serves: 10
Preparation time: 30 minutes, plus 2 hours cooling
Cooking time: 40-50 minutes

INGREDIENTS

PIE DOUGH:
5 1/2 cups (625 g/1 lb 6 oz) all-purpose flour
1 tsp salt
1/2 cup (100 g/4 oz) sweet butter
2 tbsp (25 ml/1 fl oz) oil

FILLING:
1 1/2 lb (675 g) leg of lean lamb, cut into fine strips
1/4 cup (50 ml/2 fl oz) olive oil
1/2 cup (100 g/4 oz) diced bacon
1/2 tsp chili powder
2 garlic cloves, crushed
1 1/2 lb (675 g) spinach, blanched and well drained
2 tbsp chopped parsley
4 eggs, beaten
1 cup (100 g/4 oz) grated Parmesan cheese
1/2 tsp ground nutmeg
salt and pepper

1/4 cup (50 ml/2 fl oz) melted butter

METHOD

1. For the pie dough: sift together the flour and the salt into a large bowl. Cut in the butter. The mixture should have a grainy texture. Add the oil and knead well, adding a little lukewarm water to achieve a smooth dough. Set aside.
2. For the filling: sauté the lamb in hot oil for about 5 minutes. Add the bacon, chili and garlic and sauté for a further 2 minutes.
3. Remove from the heat and add the spinach, parsley, eggs, cheese and nutmeg. Stir well. Season to taste, then set aside to cool.
4. Roll out two-thirds of the pie dough into a thin sheet. Repeat with the remaining third.
5. Brush a large pie pan or springform cake pan with the melted butter and line it with the larger sheet of pie dough.
6. Spoon the filling into the pie, dampen the edges of the pie dough, cover with the remaining sheet, pinching the edges to seal well.
7. Prick the center of the dough with a fork and brush with melted butter. Bake at 400°F (200°C/Gas mark 6) for 40-50 minutes. Serve cold, cut into thick slices.

CHEF'S TIPS:
In this dish the lamb and bacon complement each other very well and the flavor of the spinach is enhanced by the addition of the nutmeg.

Bacon and Cress Salad

Serves: 2
Preparation time: 10 minutes
Cooking time: 8 minutes

INGREDIENTS

1 tbsp olive oil
4 slices of bacon, derinded and cut into small squares
2 bunches of watercress
1 bunch of corn salad leaves
2 oranges, segments only
freshly ground black pepper

METHOD

1. Heat the oil in a frying pan, and toss the bacon pieces for a few minutes until crisp. Arrange the watercress and lettuce leaves on serving plates with the segments of orange. Season with black pepper. (There is no need to add dressing to this salad, since it is flavored so well by the juice from the orange segments and the fat from the bacon.)
2. Pour over the hot bacon and the oil.

CHEF'S TIPS:
This is the most basic of all warm salads, first featured in the late eighties when *nouvelle cuisine* started to become popular.

Bacon Salad with Banana and Pineapple

Serves: 4
Preparation time: 12 minutes
Cooking time: 20 minutes

INGREDIENTS

1/2 head iceberg lettuce, shredded
3/4 cup (175 g/6 oz) broiled and chopped lean bacon
2 slices of fresh peeled pineapple, cut into chunks
2/3 cup (150 g/5 oz) scrubbed, cubed and boiled potatoes
1 medium banana, peeled and sliced

DRESSING:
1/3 cup (75 ml/3 fl oz) mayonnaise
1/3 cup (75 ml/3 fl oz) plain yoghurt
1 tbsp fresh pineapple juice
1 tbsp apple purée
1 tbsp snipped fresh chives

METHOD

1. Place the lettuce leaves on a large serving plate.
2. Combine the dressing ingredients in a bowl and season to taste. Pour half the dressing into a jug to serve separately, pour the rest into a large mixing bowl. Stir in all the other ingredients: bacon, fruits and potatoes. Toss well and arrange on top of the shredded lettuce leaves.

CHEF'S TIPS:
The term 'composite salad' is applied to any salad combining meat or poultry with vegetables or fruits, usually bound in mayonnaise or yoghurt dressing.

Black Pudding and Bacon Salad

Serves: 2
Preparation time: 12 minutes
Cooking time: 8 minutes

INGREDIENTS

2 eggs
2 tbsp red wine vinegar
2 handfuls of mixed salad leaves: corn salad, dandelion,
    lettuce, cress, oak leaves, radicchio, etc.
2 tbsp oil
4 slices of lean bacon, cut into strips
5 oz (150 g) black pudding, cut into strips
1 1/2 cups (75 g/3 oz) sliced white mushrooms

DRESSING:
2 tbsp olive oil
1 tbsp vinegar
1 tbsp chopped fresh parsley
juice of 1/2 lemon
1 garlic clove, chopped
1 tsp mustard
salt and black pepper

METHOD

1. Poach the eggs in 2 1/2 cups (600 ml/1 pint) of boiling water with the vinegar. Make sure to wrap the white as it sets around the yolk to reform in perfect ovoid shape. Remove with a perforated spoon after 3 minutes. Keep warm in hot salted water.
2. Wash the salad leaves and drain well. Combine the salad dressing ingredients in a bowl and toss the salad leaves. Season with salt and black pepper.
3. Heat the oil in a pan and toss the bacon strips until crisp for 4 minutes. Drain well. In the same oil, fry the black pudding for 1 minute only. Remove, and fry the mushrooms for 1 minute only.
4. Build up a nest of the salad leaves in the center of each plate. Arrange the bacon strips, black pudding and mushrooms around the salad. Place a hot poached egg on top of each salad.

CHEF'S TIPS:

What the French created as *salade tiède* is a development of a bacon dressing, which has been used in France since the Roman occupation. In my youth, we often picked the dandelion leaves for such a salad. It was tossed in a garlic vinaigrette without oil. Diced bacon and crôutons were fried in pork fat and added to the green leaves by way of complementing it. This gave rise in the early eighties to the popularity of this salad, which became a favorite appetizer or even main course, with the addition of mushrooms, and other meat such as black pudding, as illustrated in this recipe.

WEIGHT AND MEASURE CONVERSIONS

Weight Metric	Weight Imperial		Volume Metric	Volume Imperial	US Cup		Temp C°	Temp F°	Gas Mark
15 g	1/2 oz		50 ml	2 fl oz	1/4		110	225	1/4
20 g	3/4 oz		75 ml	2 1/2	1/3		130	250	1/2
25 g	1 oz			fl oz	3/8		140	275	1
40 g	1 1/2 oz		100 ml	4 fl oz	1/2		150	300	2
50 g	2 oz		150 ml	5 fl oz	5/8		170	325	3
75 g	3 oz		200 ml	6 fl oz	3/4		180	350	4
100 g	4 oz			7 fl oz	7/8		190	375	5
150 g	5 oz		225 ml	8 fl oz	1		200	400	6
175 g	6 oz		275 ml	9 fl oz	1 1/8		220	425	7
200 g	7 oz		300 ml	10 fl oz	1 1/4		230	450	8
225 g	8 oz			11 fl oz	1 3/8		240	475	9
250 g	9 oz			12 fl oz	1 1/2				
275 g	10 oz		400 ml	14 fl oz	1 3/4				
300 g	11 oz			16 fl oz	2				
350 g	12 oz		1/2 liter	20 fl oz	2 1/2				
375 g	13 oz			(1 pint)					
400 g	14 oz		750 ml	1 1/4	3				
425 g	15 oz			pints					
450 g	16 oz		900 ml	1 1/2	-				
				pints					
1 kg	2 lb		1 liter	1 3/4	-				
1.5 kg	3-3 1/2 lb			pints					
2 kg	4 lb								
2.5 kg	5 lb								
3 kg	6 lb								
3.5 kg	7 lb								
4 kg	8 lb								

Quantities are given in metric, Imperial and US cup *avoir dupois* measures. Rarely do exact conversions from imperial/US measures to metric measures give convenient working quantities, therefore, metric measures have been rounded off to a more handy unit – 1 ounce equals 25 grams (28.5 grams is the exact conversion of 1 ounce).

REMEMBER: Follow only one set of quantitiess for any single recipe. Metric/Imperial/US measures are not interchangeable. Also note that standard cup measures cannot be given for weights of ingredients – it depends on the ingredient – i.e. 8 oz of rice (uncooked) equals 1 cup and 4 oz of flour also equals 1 cup.

WEIGHT AND MEASURE CONVERSIONS

Spoons Metric	Spoons Imperial	Linear Measure Metric	Linear Measure Imperial	Bar Measures	Bar Measures
1.25 ml	1/4 tsp	3 mm	1/8 in	Dash	4-6 drops
2.5 ml	1/2 tsp	5 mm	1/4 in	Teaspoon	1/6 fl oz
5 ml	1 tsp	1 cm	1/2 in	Tablespoon	1/2 fl oz
15 ml	1 tbsp	2.5 cm	1 in	Pony/liquer	1 fl oz
30 ml	2 tbsp	4 cm	1 1/2 in	glass	
	(1 fl oz)	5 cm	2 in	Jigger	1 1/2 fl oz
3 tsps	1 tbsp	6.5 cm	2 1/2 in	Wine glass	4 fl oz
2 tbsp	1 fl oz	7.5 cm	3 in	Cup	8 fl oz
16 tbsp (US)	1 cup (US)	10 cm	4 in		
		12.5 cm	5 in		
		15 cm	6 in		
		18 cm	7 in		
		20 cm	8 in		
		23 cm	9 in		
		25 cm	10 in		
		30 cm	12 in (1 ft)		
		35 cm	14 in		
		38 cm	15 in		
		45 cm	18 in		
		60 cm	24 in		
		92 cm	36 in		

in